IMAGES
of America

ROSEVILLE

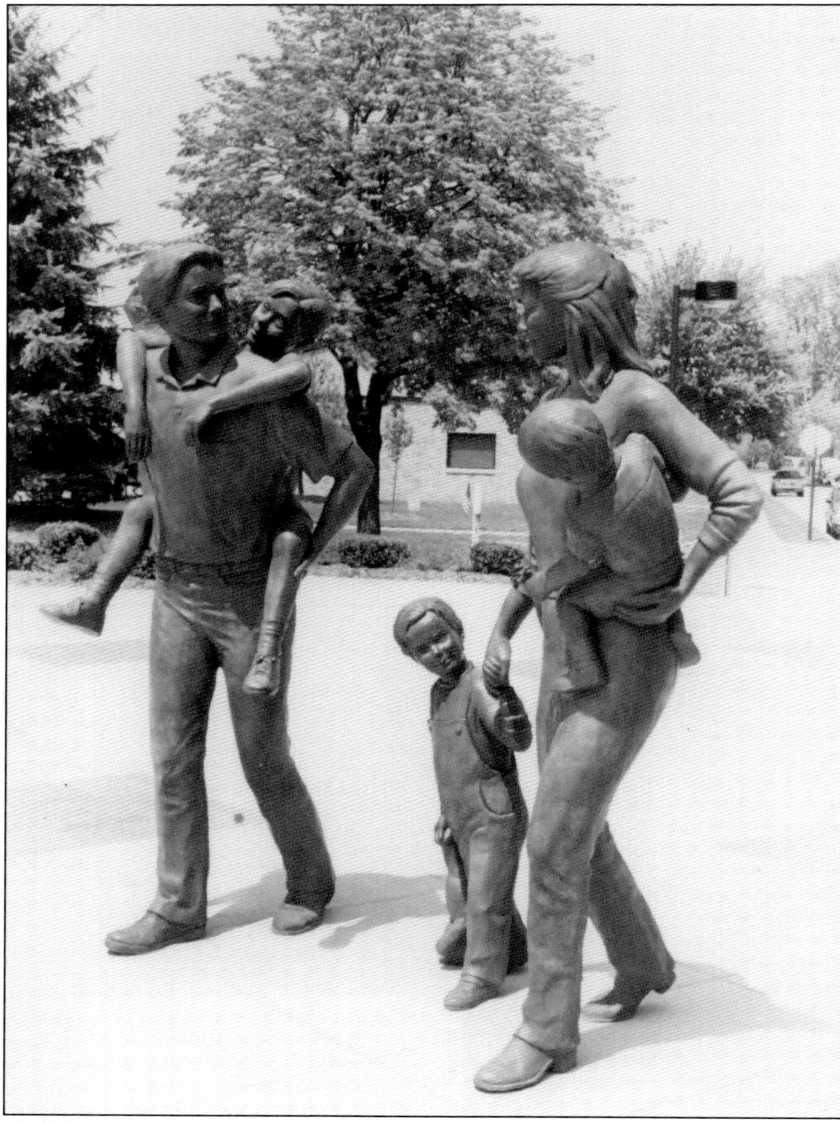

The *Rosebuds* bronze sculpture by Janet B. Trimpe was installed on the Roseville civic plaza in 2001. The *Rosebuds* title refers to the children who, like rosebuds with proper caring, will blossom into valued members of the community. The *Rosebuds* name and imagery of a mother and father and three children approaching the Roseville Library and municipal offices also depict and reflect Roseville as a family community. (Courtesy of the Roseville Public Library.)

On the Cover: The original Roseville Theatre opened in 1927 and closed in 1996. Attorney J. Russell LaBarge Sr. opened an office in the building in 1938. The Roseville Department Store was also located there. Bob's Barber Shop, where the confectionery store is on the right, is still owned and operated by Bob Quaine, who has cut hair at that location for 63 years. The Roseville Theatre building is now owned by the Reverend Ross Collette, pastor of Deeper Life Ministries. The "V" for Victory at the top of the building glowed red, white, and blue in its day. (Courtesy of the Roseville Public Library.)

IMAGES
of America

ROSEVILLE

John and Terry Minnis

ARCADIA
PUBLISHING

ISBN 978-1-4671-1456-1

Published by Arcadia Publishing
Charleston, South Carolina

Printed in the United States of America

Library of Congress Control Number: 2015946840

For all general information, please contact Arcadia Publishing:
Telephone 843-853-2070
Fax 843-853-0044
E-mail sales@arcadiapublishing.com
For customer service and orders:
Toll-Free 1-888-313-2665

Visit us on the Internet at www.arcadiapublishing.com

This book is dedicated to Richard McRill, who made a loving, happy home for his family in Roseville, Michigan.

CONTENTS

Acknowledgments

We would like to thank all the people who took time out of their busy lives to help us compile the material for this book on Roseville, Michigan.

Special thanks goes to the Roseville Public Library staff, particularly director Jacalynn Harvey and archivist/librarian William Holleran. We are also grateful to the Roseville Historical and Genealogical Society Board: Pres. Pat Chownyk, Vice Pres. Jane May, recording secretary Gail Elliott, treasurer Janice Carter, directors Ann Spybrook, John Schober, and Ken Schramm, and membership chairperson Barbara Kushner. Thanks to Elizabeth Clemens at Wayne State University's Walter P. Reuther Library, who came up with at least one photograph not found elsewhere.

We want to give a tip of the hat to our friends on the Facebook page "I Grew Up in Roseville" and Terry Koss, whose photograph of the Susie Q restaurant was essential, and to fellow Arcadia Publishing author Harry Skrdla, whose photographs and knowledge of the Gratiot Drive-In were invaluable. We would also like to thank Joan Duchene, Madeline Gaffigan, Diana Brincat, Doreen Tavernier-Evans Baughn, and Karen Clancy-Williams, as well as Joseph Bartalino, Dwain Lusk, Dorothy McRill, William Spengler, and Marilyn Choma Waldmeir.

With the City of Roseville, we wish to acknowledge Mayor Pro Tem Jan Haggerty for the many photographs of her late husband, Leonard Haggerty, a Roseville legend; city clerk Richard Steenland; director of economic development Jason Friedmann; purchasing assistant Paul Van Damme; city administrator Scott Adkins; administrative assistant Virginia Green; and, especially, city treasurer Mickey Switalski, who wrote the introduction to this book. Sometimes help came from unexpected sources, such as Brian Goff at the famous Bronner's Christmas Wonderland in Frankenmuth, Michigan.

We would be remiss if we failed to acknowledge the many business and commercial photograph contributors to this book, including Martyna Nowak at National Coney Island and Shannon Gottschalk, marketing manager at Macomb Mall.

Lastly, we would like to thank our Arcadia Publishing editor, Jesse Darland, who strived to keep us on track and provided much useful help and advice.

Unless otherwise specified, all photographs are courtesy of the Roseville Public Library.

INTRODUCTION

Roseville incorporated as a city in 1958, but the region has had an even longer history.

Gertrude Stein once opined, "A rose is a rose is a rose," but the denizens of Roseville staged a couple of colorful battles over the name of the community. The eventual winner was Denison Rose, a hero from the War of 1812. The fledgling farming community merited its first postmaster in 1836, when tavern-keeper William Rose was appointed by Andrew Jackson's irascible postmaster, Amos Kendall. The post office became known as the Roseville Post Office in honor of his father, Denison. Eventually, that name stuck to the community.

Before that, Irish settlers had engineered the change of the name from Orange Township to Erin Township, exchanging the English king of the Glorious Revolution, William of Orange, for the Gaelic word for Ireland. Later, when a wooden-plank toll road was constructed between Detroit and Mount Clemens, the community, including what is now Eastpointe, was simply referred to as "Halfway," perhaps shorthand for "the middle of nowhere." Photographs in this book attest to the rudimentary nature of the settlement of Halfway at that time, though by the turn of the 20th century it boasted a tollhouse, general store, repair shop, and hotel for travelers. That plank road eventually became Gratiot Avenue (M-3), with a key junction at Utica Road, the heart of modern Roseville's downtown. Utica Junction was yet another contender for the community's name. In the end, Roseville prevailed. The tollgate sign giving the rates of toll now hangs in the city library.

Clearly, religion was important to the early settlers, and they established several churches that still stand as landmarks in the city. The oldest, St. Mark Lutheran Church, founded in 1853, was later built in the idyllic triangle formed by East Park and West Park Streets and 11 Mile Road. Erin Presbyterian Church followed in 1860, east of the intersection of Gratiot Avenue and Common Road, and Sacred Heart Catholic Church appeared a year later at Utica Junction. As a mother church, Sacred Heart gave birth to Roseville parishes St. Athanasius, Holy Innocents, St. Angela, and St. Donald, along with some 18 other parishes carved from its territory. The church eventually hosted a primary, secondary, junior high, and finally a high school, which closed in 1971. Since demolished, parochial school land was repurposed for an expansion of the church cemetery.

In 1895, the Rapid Railway Company established the interurban, an electric streetcar service, connecting Detroit to Mount Clemens and eventually Port Huron. The interurban's first carbarn and powerhouse were in Roseville, north of 11 Mile Road, with the tracks running adjacent to the Fort Gratiot Plank Road. Streetcars operated for 35 years until the popularity of automobiles and the collapse of the economy caused their demise in 1930.

As one mode of transport faded away, another was rising. Michigan's first commercial airport, Packard Field, opened at Gratiot Avenue and Frazho Road in 1919 on a portion of the Templeton farm. It drew its name from Packard Motor Car Company, which built an early fighter plane near the end of World War I. The field was later known as Hartung Airport, hosting air shows, training, and aircraft development. The complex played a significant role in the development of aviation in Macomb County.

Aviation innovation gave way to commercial innovation when Michigan's first shopping center replaced the airport. The Eastgate Shopping Center, with its block-towered Federal Department Store, was constructed on the site in 1954. Although Federal and its tower were destroyed by a fire in 1978, Eastgate Shopping Center remains open today.

The seat of government for the city has endured several permutations. In 1886, the Erin Township Hall was built at the corner of Gratiot Avenue and 11 Mile Road. At one time, this building was the town hall for the present cities of Eastpointe, Roseville, St. Clair Shores, and part of Fraser. Roseville incorporated as a village in 1926, with John Asmus elected as its first president. When the Roseville Municipal Building was constructed in 1929 at the corner of Gratiot and Meier Road, both the village and township offices were moved into it. The present municipal complex, at Gratiot just south of Common Road, was constructed in 1974.

In the aftermath of World War II, with the GI Bill offering easy financing, Roseville experienced a population explosion. It peaked at just over 60,000 in the census of 1970 and has hovered around 50,000 since the new millennium. The new city elected its first mayor, Arthur Waterman, in 1958 and developed rapidly in the 1950s and 1960s. The development of the interstate freeway had a big impact on Roseville. I-94 forms half of its eastern border, while I-696 bisected the city at 11 Mile Road. It was now easy for residents and visitors to travel quickly in almost any direction. Parallel to the commercial thoroughfare of Gratiot Avenue, Groesbeck Avenue (M-97), with its many tool shops, factories, and industrial parks, became an important manufacturing strip.

As Roseville grew as a commercial center, it attracted new styles of suburban life. The Art Deco green Roseville Theatre built in 1927 at Utica Junction was joined by the Gratiot Drive-In with its waterfall, playground, and massive screen, operating from 1948 to 1984 despite young patrons hiding in the car trunk or scaling the back fence to avoid admission fees. Eastgate Shopping Center with its iconic nuclear sign, Korvette's at 12 Mile Road (now known as Roseville Towne Center), and Macomb Mall, an early regional shopping center, brought shoppers from as far away as Canada to Roseville.

The expanding car culture brought about cruising Gratiot Avenue and fast-food establishments like Top Hat with its red and white ceramic tile, A&W with its carhops, Susie Q with its stainless-steel rotating cone, McDonald's, and Burger King to the strip, along with summer evenings of teenage hijinks. Early innovators like the Detroit Italian Bakery and Terry's Submarines spawned many imitators in the pizza and sandwich sector.

Presidential visits to Roseville included John F. Kennedy's campaign speech at Eastgate in 1960 and a visit by Bill Clinton to the Roseville Recreation Center in 1999. Kennedy had autographed a wooden school desk during his visit, which hung in the school administration building until leaders pulled it down so Clinton could add his signature. The battered desktop with the famous autographs hangs proudly on the Wall of Honor at the Roseville Community School Administration Building on Church Street.

This book details in photographs and captions Roseville's origins as a farming community, industrial and commercial center, transportation hub, and cultural touchstone. These images reveal the foundations of Roseville today and point to its future tomorrow.

—Mickey Switalski
Roseville City Treasurer

One

Planks to Rails to Community

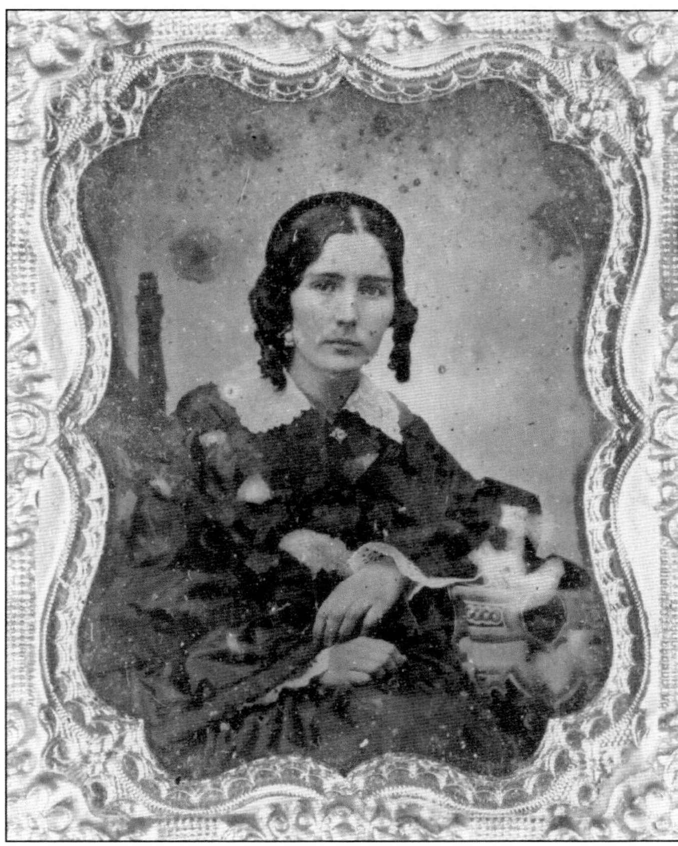

This is believed to be Mary Rose, the daughter of Denison Rose, for whom the city is named. Denison was a hero of the War of 1812 and father of William Rose, Roseville's first postmaster. Mary Rose married John William Wylde in Roseville on October 3, 1842. She died on April 16, 1909, and is buried in Clinton Grove Cemetery in Mount Clemens.

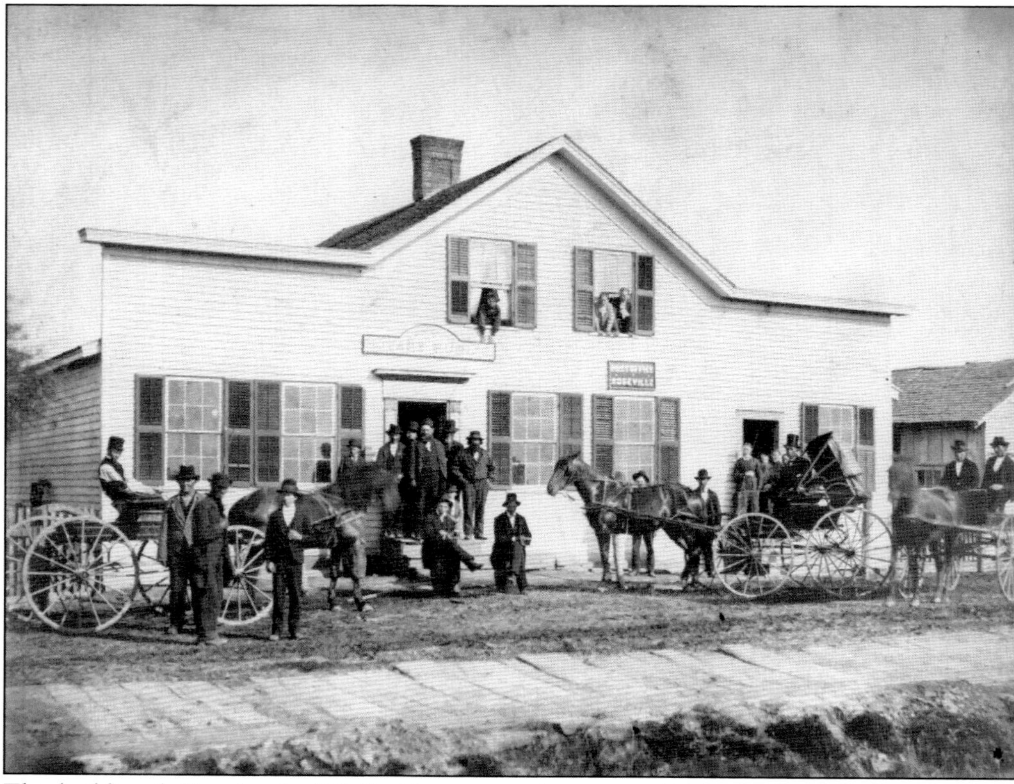

This building, believed to be 10 Mile House near what is now 10 Mile Road and Gratiot Avenue, was one of the turnpike's hotels in 1880. The building also served as the Roseville Post Office and housed a notary public. Gustavus Schuchard, a German farmer, moved to the Roseville area in 1852 and was named postmaster on April 18, 1866. He and his wife, Madeline, were the parents of nine children.

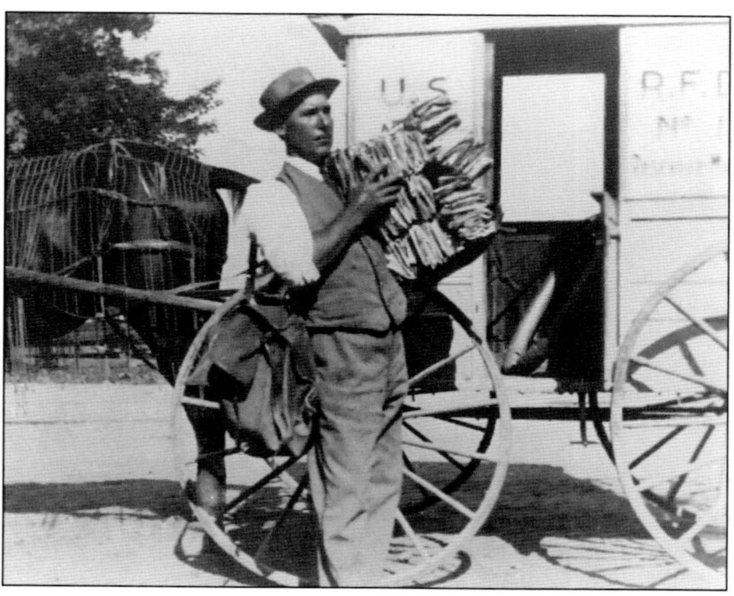

Robert Kern, with his horse-drawn mail wagon, served as the first postman for the communities of Roseville, East Detroit (now Eastpointe), St. Clair Shores, and part of Warren. Kern later learned the electrical trade, working as an electrician on the interurban railway. When the village of Halfway reincorporated as the city of East Detroit in January 1929, Kern was elected as the city's first mayor, serving from 1929 to 1931.

The Erin Township Hall, featuring Victorian and Hawaiian accents, was built in 1886 at the corner of Gratiot Avenue and Town Hall Road (later 11 Mile Road). The Italianate clapboard structure served as the town hall for current-day cities of Eastpointe (formerly East Detroit), Roseville, St. Clair Shores, and part of Fraser.

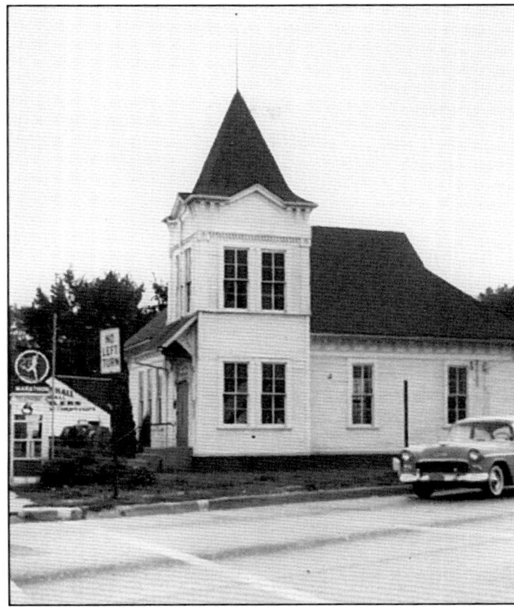

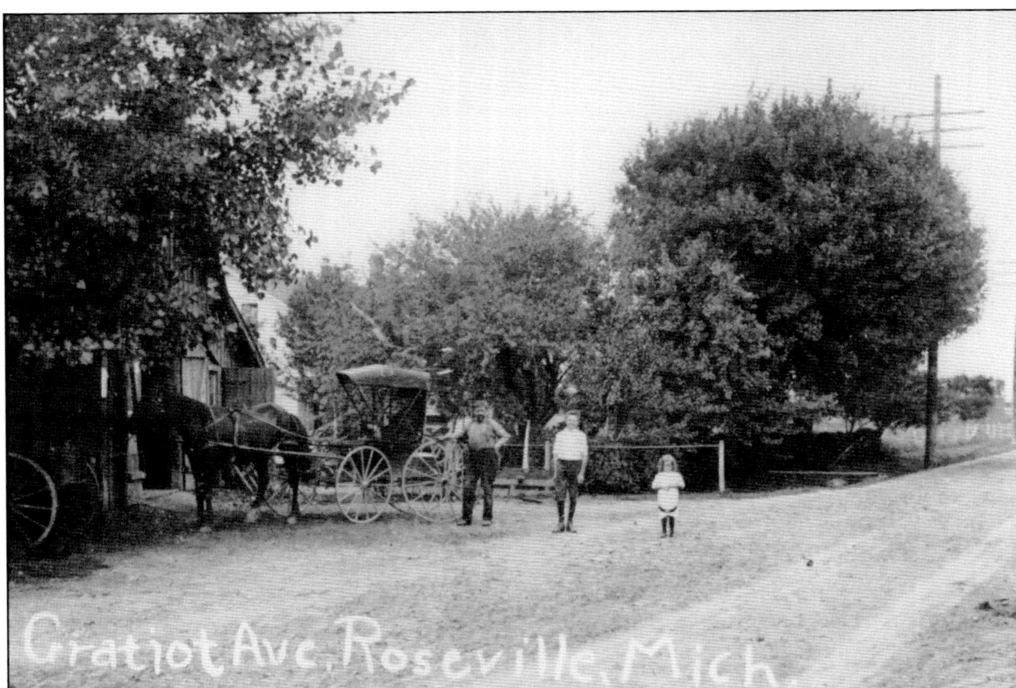

The wagon tracks pictured here around the turn of the 20th century made up what was the Gratiot Turnpike, which would one day become an interurban electric-car route and, later, a major boulevard and thoroughfare. The horse-drawn carriage harkens back to a pre-automobile age, while the utility poles indicate electric streetcars and telephones cannot be far behind. In 1905, the Peninsular Electrical Light Company was granted the franchise to provide electricity to the farms along the turnpike. In 1915, Detroit Edison (now DTE Energy) became the permanent electric provider and is still to this day. Telephone service quickly followed.

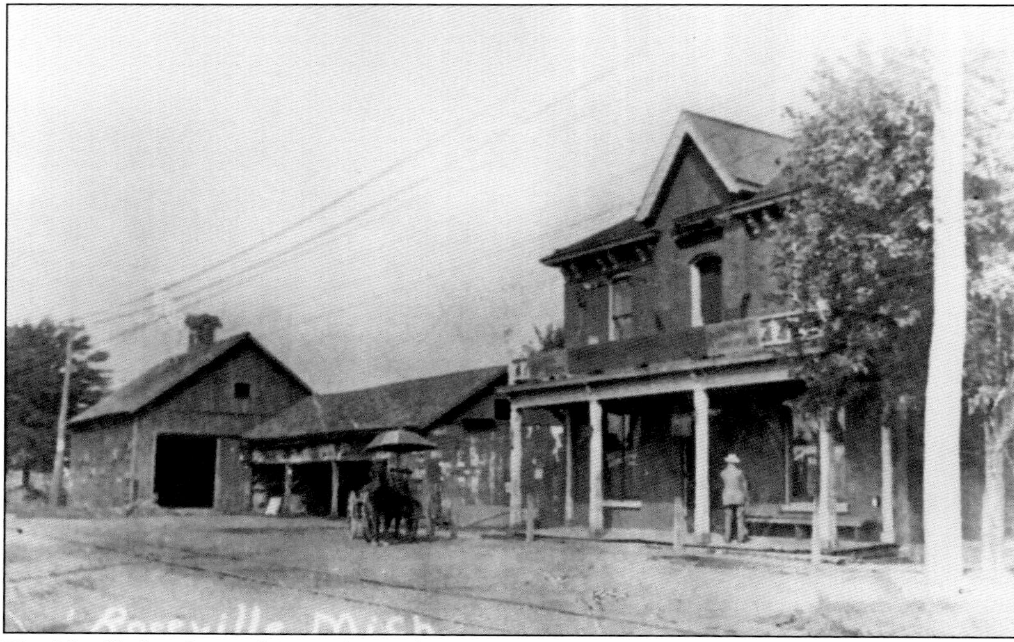

The Haselhuhn General Store, located on Gratiot Avenue and Bloss Road (now Frazho), served as a saloon and one of the first lending libraries in the area. On September 28, 1909, Otto C. Haselhuhn was appointed postmaster, and a post office was opened on the site. The interurban tracks can be seen in the front of the store.

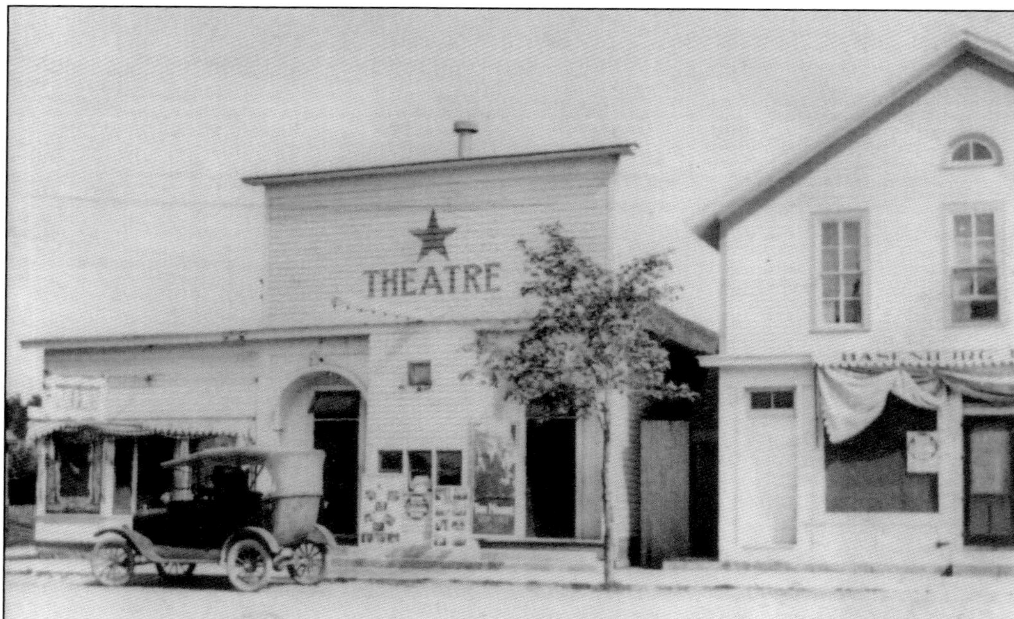

The Haselhuhn Building on Gratiot Avenue, at 11 Mile Road, served as the first theater in Roseville. Apps Hardware and Apps Electric later occupied the buildings at 26850 and 26852 Gratiot Avenue. Some may remember the Apps slogan from 1921, "Apps is apt to have it." In 1983, a White Castle restaurant replaced the historic building and is still serving sliders to this day.

In 2007, the City of Roseville obtained new streetlight banners from Bronner's, the famous Christmas store in Frankenmuth, Michigan. Among the banners chosen was this one depicting historic Utica Junction, where the Gratiot and Erin-Shelby (Utica) Plank Roads met. The banners are still in use, as the city plans a major renovation of the area to restore and maintain its historical character. (Courtesy of Bronner's Christmas Decorations.)

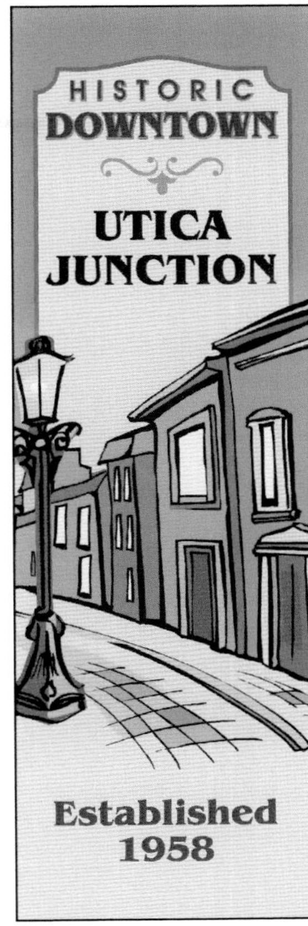

The Van Howe General Store and Inn, seen here in the early 1900s, stood at the intersection of Gratiot Avenue and Utica Road in Roseville. The building that had been owned by the Morans became the property of David Van Howe and his bride in 1901. David Van Howe later became vice president of Roseville's first bank when it opened in 1923, on the same corner the general store had occupied for many years.

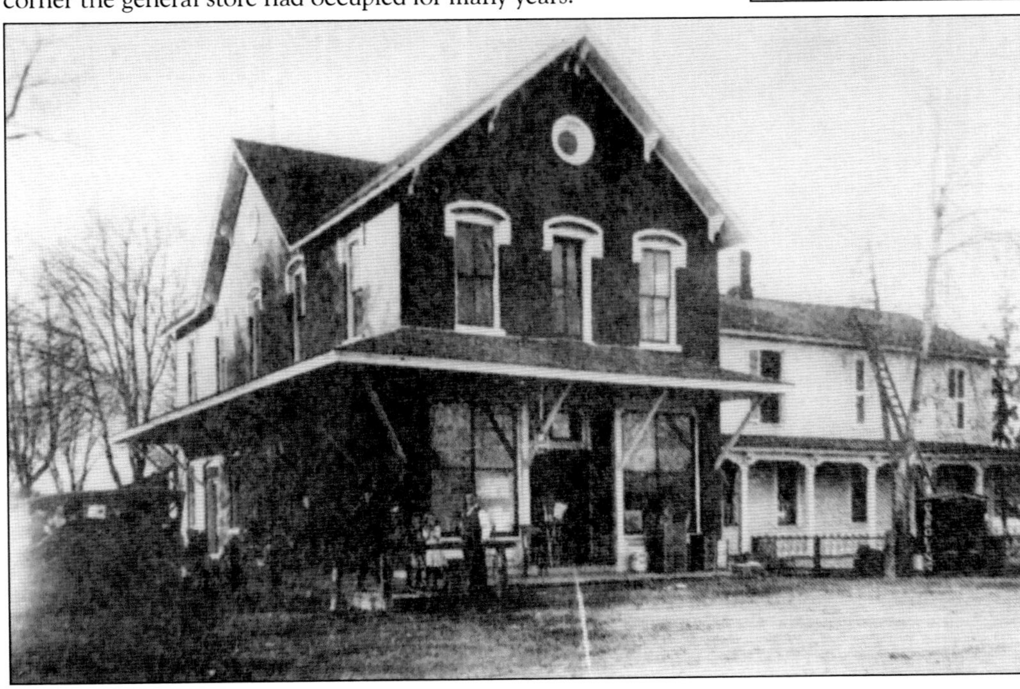

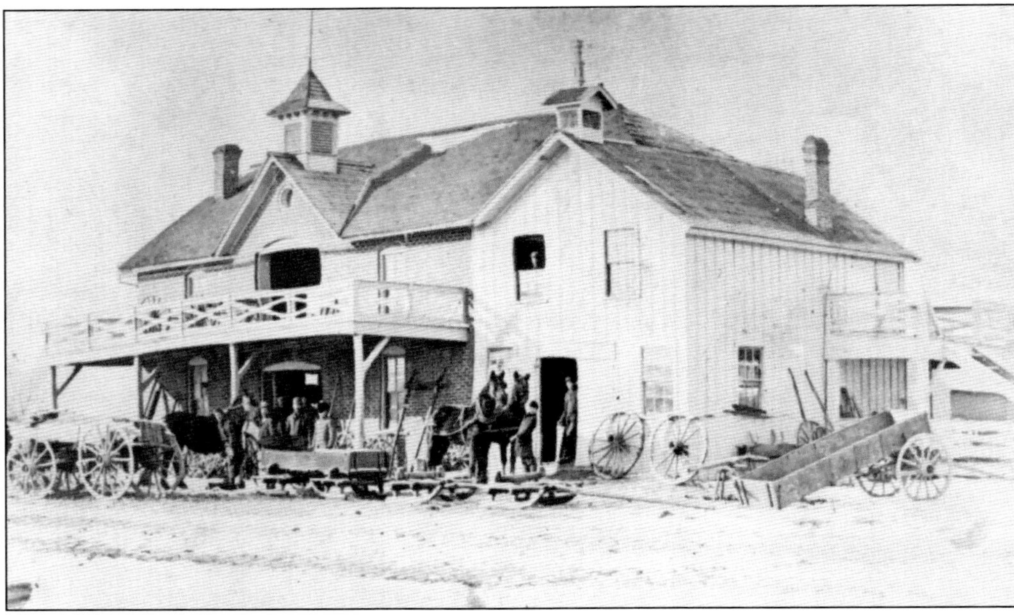

The Dedenbach and March Carriage Shop operated at the corner of Gratiot Avenue and Utica Road in an area where Walter Lauer had earlier opened a block of stores. Joseph Dedenbach was the proprietor of the wagon factory, and John March worked as a blacksmith. By 1910, Dedenbach had taken a job as a laborer with the Detroit United Railway.

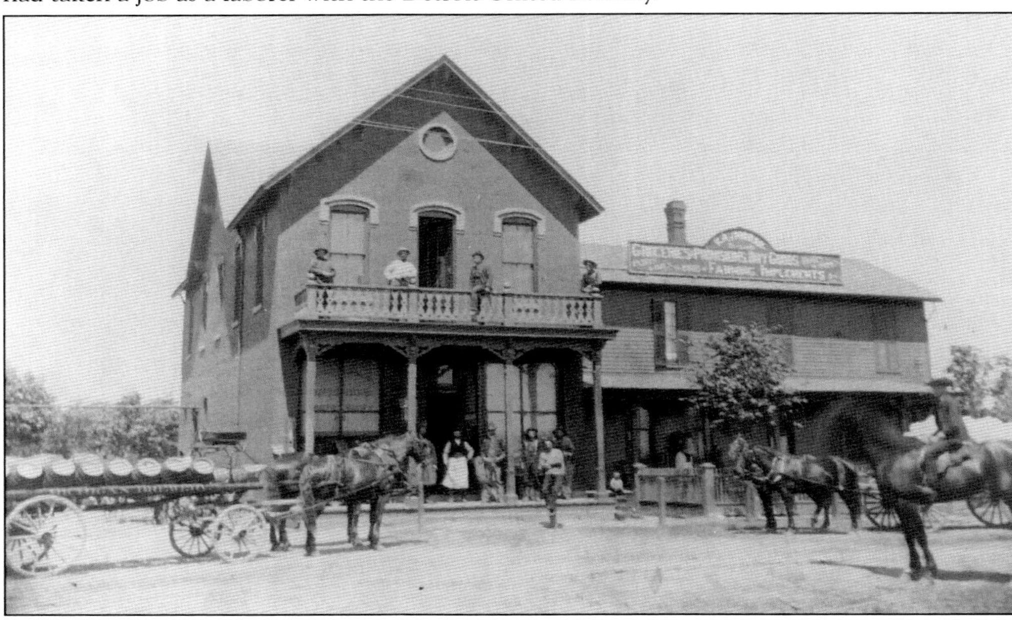

The brick structure seen here was built in 1875 by Henry Wiegand. A portion of the frame building was constructed in 1836 and known both as the Junction House and the Martin Hotel, named after original owner John Martin. The wooden structure was removed from the early inn and moved by the Moran family from its original site across the road, while the rest of the inn was demolished. The Moran name can still be seen in the sign advertising groceries, provisions, and dry goods, as well as farming implements.

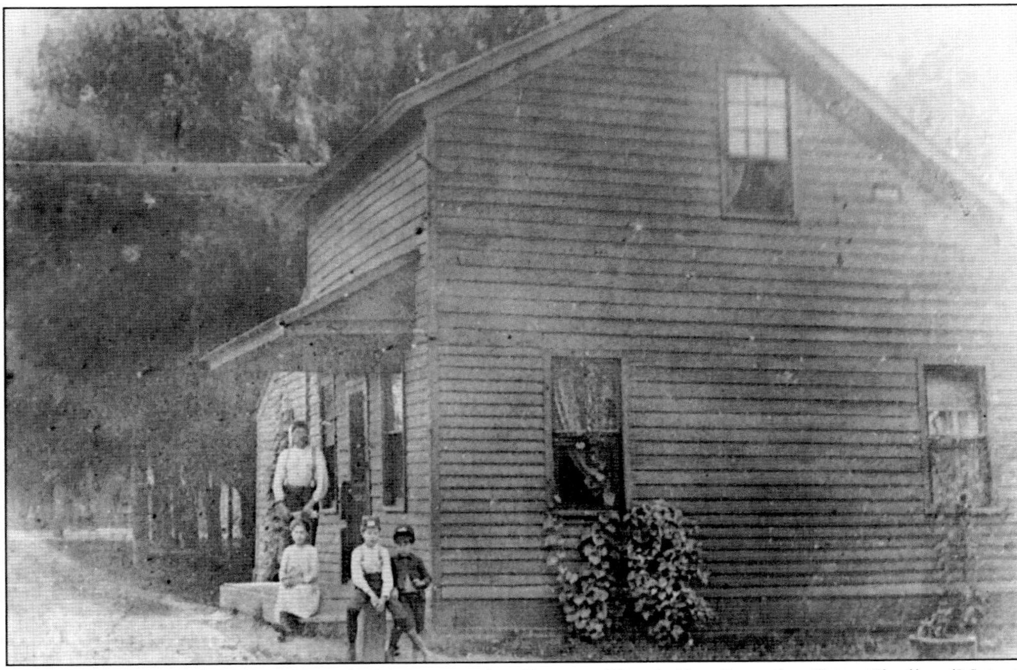

The tollhouse and gate pictured above, on the Gratiot Plank Road at the Erin-Shelby (Utica) Plank Road, or "The Junction," were the last on the toll road between Detroit and Mount Clemens on the way to Port Huron (Fort Gratiot). The tollhouse was operated by John and Joseph Dedenbach. The Gratiot Turnpike route was surveyed in 1827, and the swampy land was cleared. Three-inch planks were laid across felled tree trunks to form the road. In 1846, the State of Michigan authorized a privately operated toll road, the Gratiot Turnpike. Since most wagons were loaded going to Detroit, southbound traffic had the right-of-way on the one-lane plank road, forcing northbound traffic to detour. Below, Norman (left) and Marl Dedenbach, grandsons of John Dedenbach, hold an original tollgate sign.

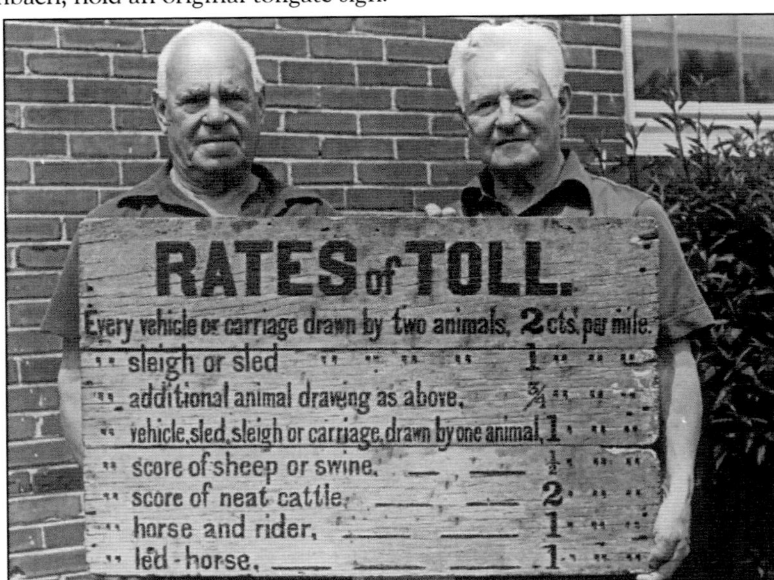

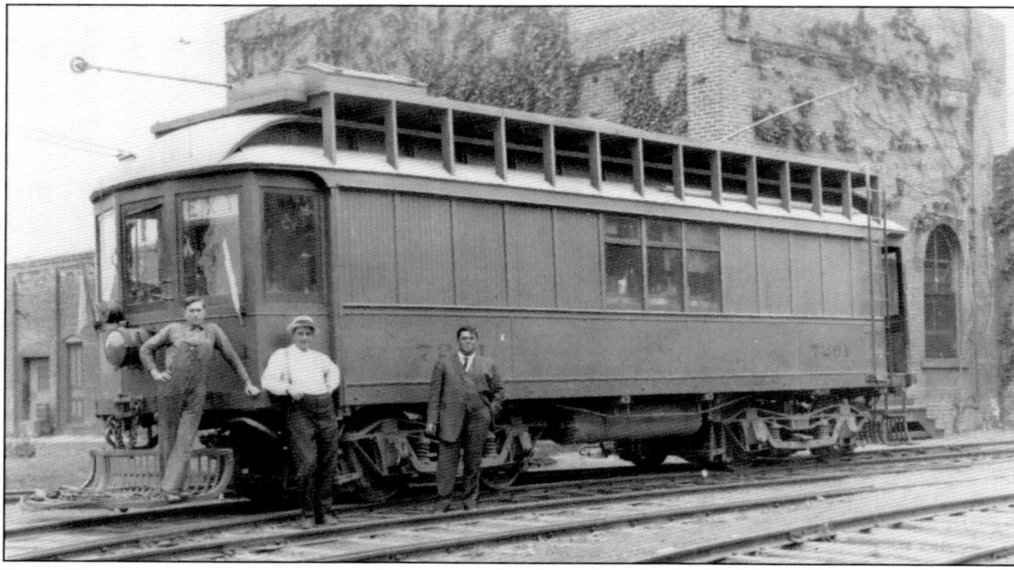

Roseville was an important interurban stopping point on the Detroit United Railway between Detroit and Port Huron. As the halfway point between Detroit and Mount Clemens, a carbarn and power station, seen above around 1900 behind the car and workmen, were located in Roseville on Gratiot Avenue just south of Sycamore Street. In 1903, a fire destroyed much of the carbarn. An AT&T facility is located at the site today. The unidentified men pictured below around 1900 pose alongside a typical interurban car. The term "interurban" was coined by Charles L. Henry, a state senator in Indiana. In 1905, the US Census Bureau defined an interurban as "a street railway having more than half its trackage outside municipal limits." In 1930, interurban service to Port Huron was discontinued; however, the City of Detroit's Department of Street Railways continued streetcar service to Mount Clemens for two more years, until September 10, 1932.

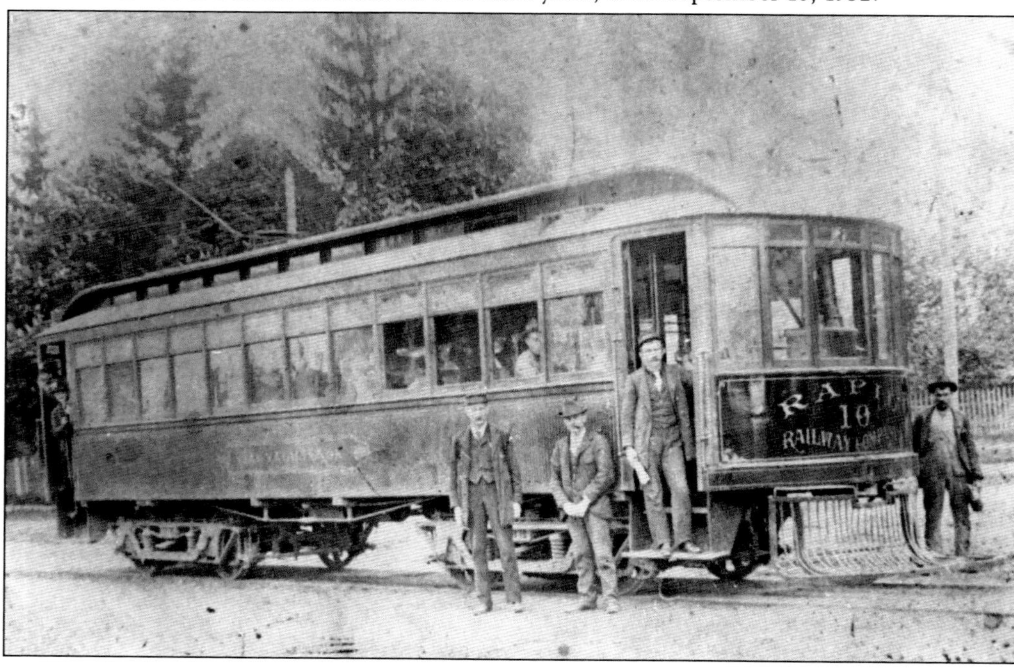

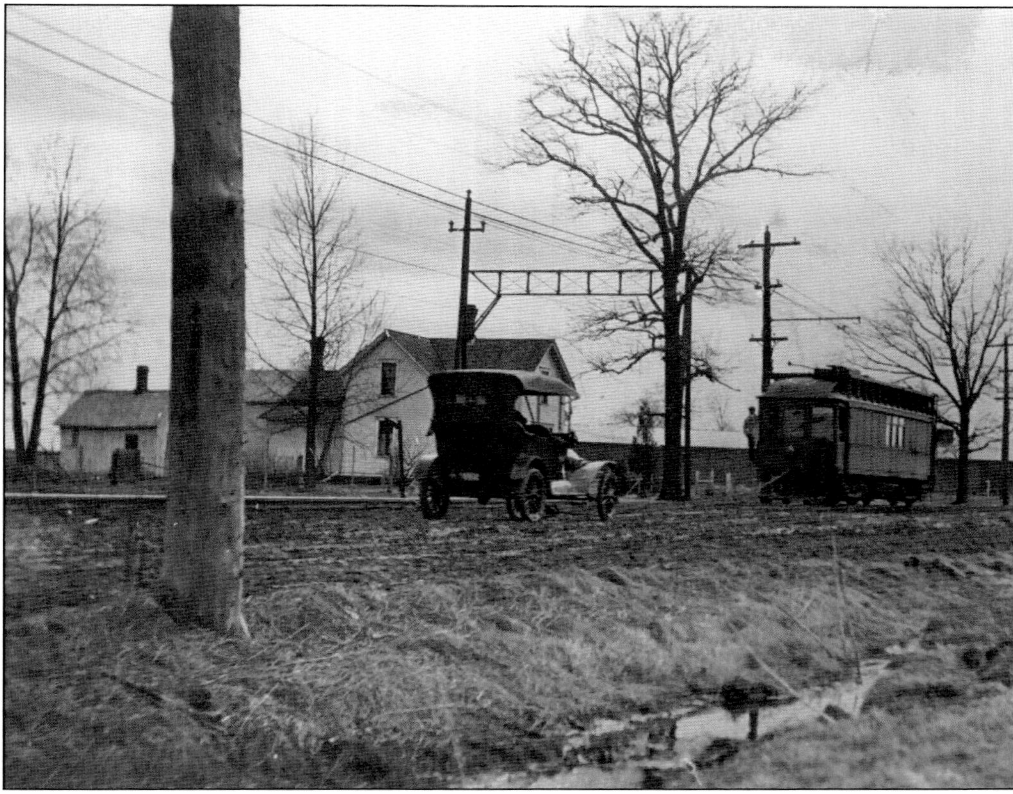

The coming of the automobile may have made folks more independent, but they were susceptible to getting stuck in the mud—particularly on Gratiot Avenue at Roseville Boulevard in April 1916. Above, an interurban gives a motorist in a 1915–1916 Model T a tow. Bill Harris, a member of the *Model T Forum*, identifies the bigger, more expensive car below as a 1914 Cadillac, indicated by the oval rear window. Between 1908 and 1927, some 15 million Model T "Tin Lizzies" were built by the Ford Motor Company. The 1914 Cadillac featured an electric starter, which in 1912 had earned Cadillac the coveted Dewar Trophy awarded by the Royal Automobile Club of England for the advancement of the automobile industry. Cadillac was the only carmaker to have earned the trophy twice, the first time in 1908 for interchangeable parts.

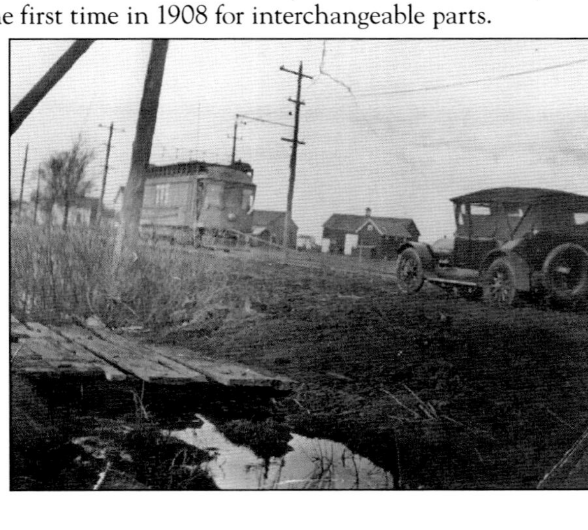

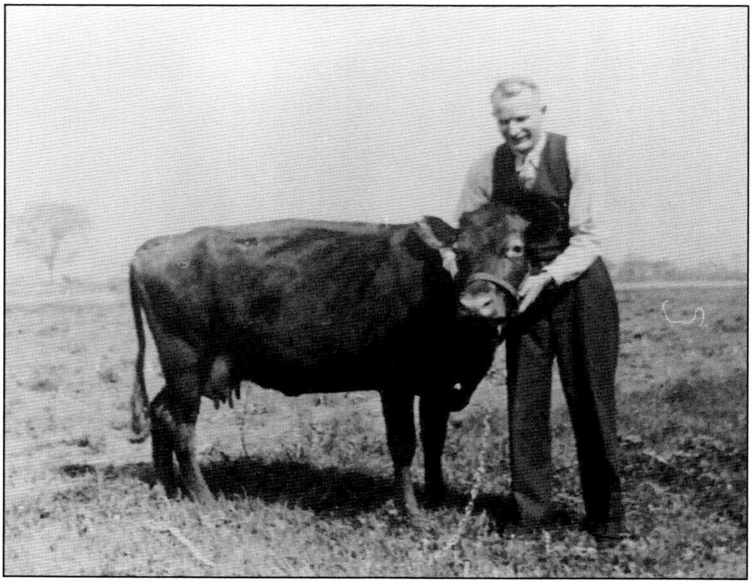

Sylvester Barbret, seen in 1939, shows off a cow on his farm. Barbret was born in 1892 and married Ethel Trombly in 1915 in Detroit. The couple eventually settled on a farm located on Bohn Street, near Town Hall Road (currently I-696). They raised five children: Alger, Clayton, Douglas, Gerald, and Joan. Barbret served the village as a fireman. He died in Roseville of natural causes at the age of 91.

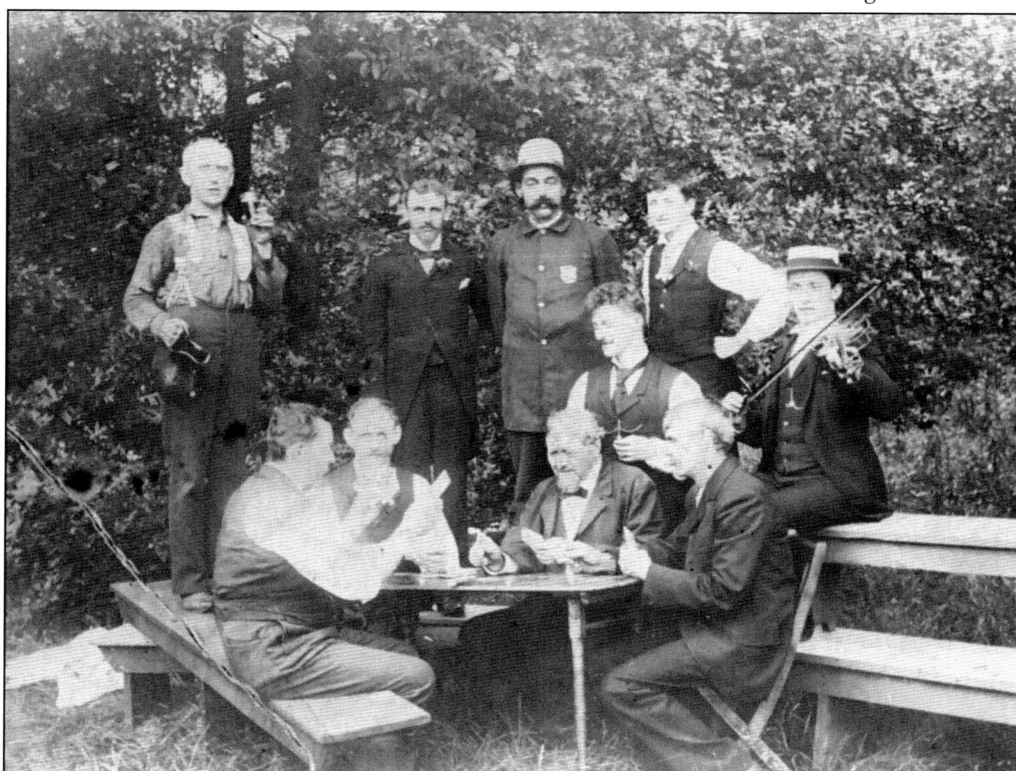

A group of Roseville gentlemen enjoys an afternoon card party and picnic. From left to right are (first row, playing cards) Fred Eibe, I.F. Cron, Frank Dueweke Sr., and Frank Dueweke Jr.; (second row) unidentified onlooker and David Van Howe (with violin); (third row, standing on bench) R. Bucher, Fred LaBelle, unidentified policeman, and Ollie Dueweke. Van Howe was a prominent Roseville businessman.

Two

A Community Takes Flight

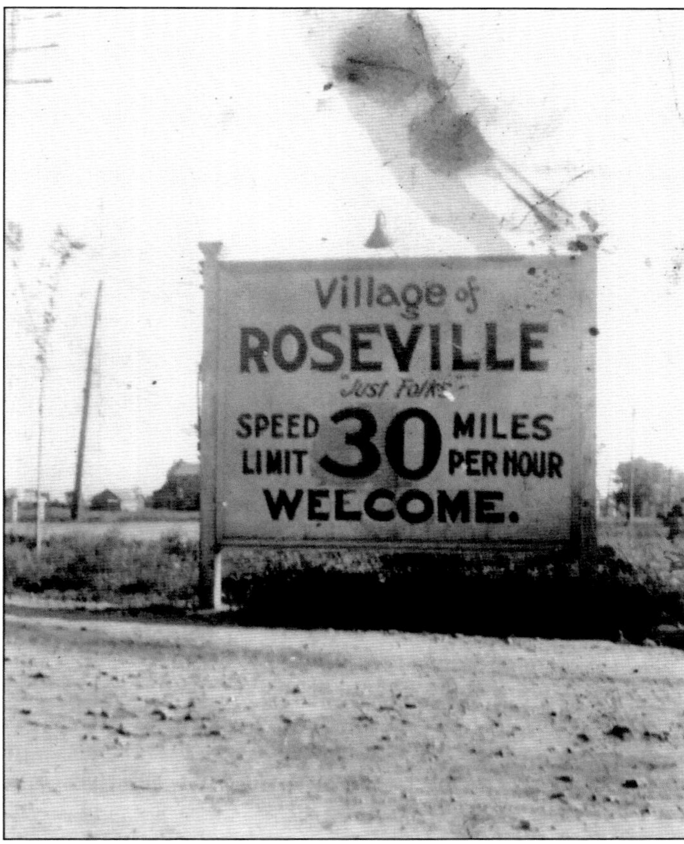

An early sign along Gratiot Avenue welcomes motorists to Roseville. The village of Roseville was formed and approved by Gov. Fred W. Green on February 12, 1926. John Asmus was elected the first village president. By 1930, the Roseville population had grown to more than 6,000 (6,836) from less than 3,000 in 1920.

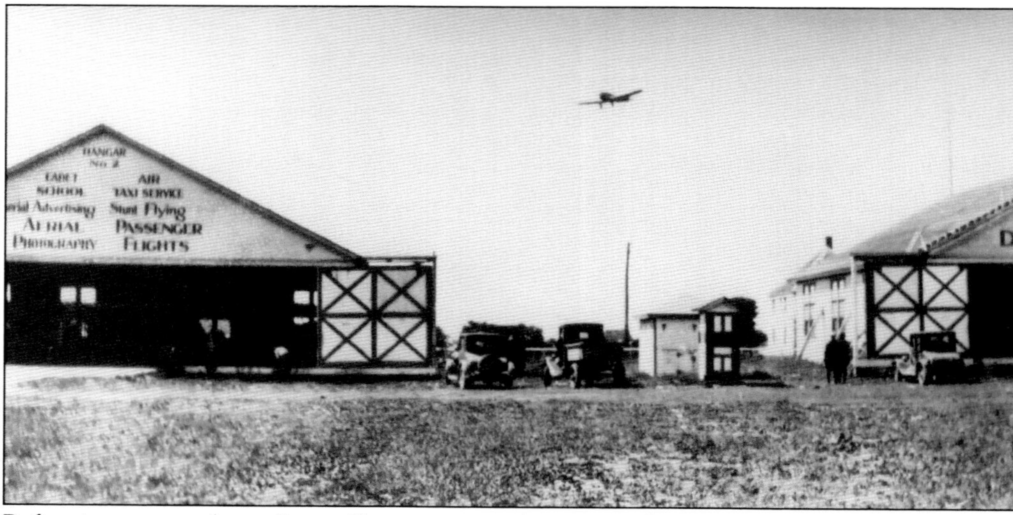

Before it was even born, Roseville was put on the map with its own airport. The airport was located on land at Gratiot Avenue and Frazho Road by the Packard Motor Car Company. The facility later became known as Hartung Gratiot Airport. It was operated by the Hartung Aircraft Corporation, which painted its name on the hangar roof, seen below. The facility began as Packard Field in 1919 and closed as Roseville Airport in 1951. In 1952, Adolph Komer, who had learned to fly at the Roseville Airport, studied an outdoor shopping center concept popular in the East and presented it to Roseville city officials.

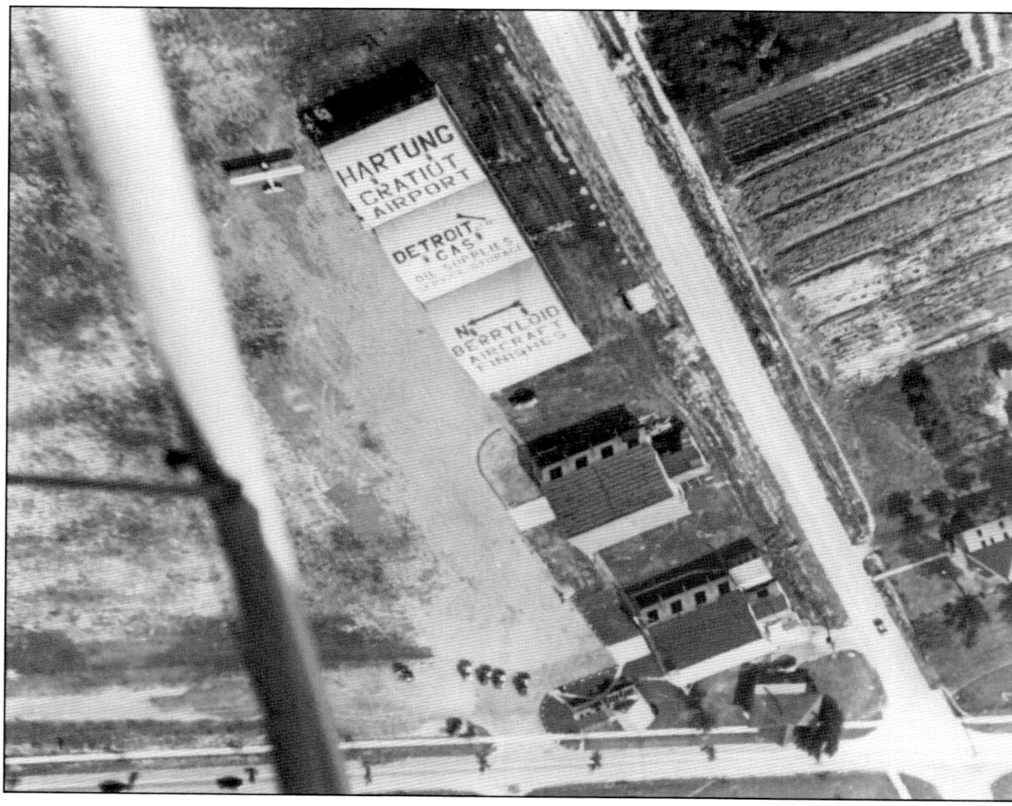

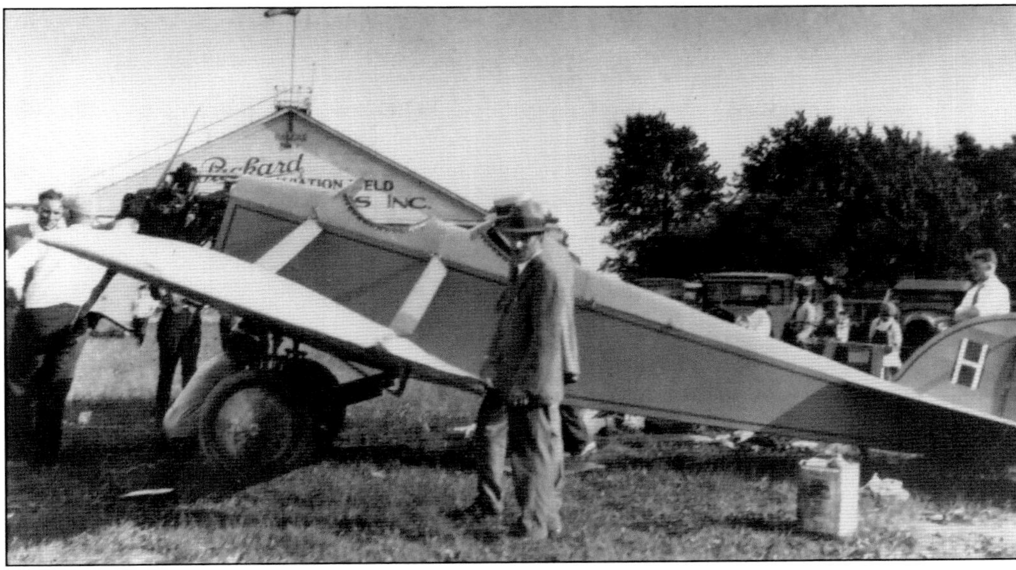

As seen in these photographs, nothing can attract men and boys like airplanes, in this case a Hurd aircraft built by E.P. Hurd, a Detroit manufacturer of locks and chains. The man in the image above is believed to be William B. Stout, Packard's chief aeronautical engineer in 1916–1917 and president of the Society of Automotive Engineers in 1935. He founded the Stout All-Metal Company in 1923, which was acquired by the Ford Motor Company in 1925. The boy pictured below dreams of becoming an ace pilot during the "Great War" (World War I). The Hurd had a top speed of 100 miles per hour, a cruising speed of 85 miles per hour, and a landing speed of 35 miles per hour. It had a maximum range of 340 miles.

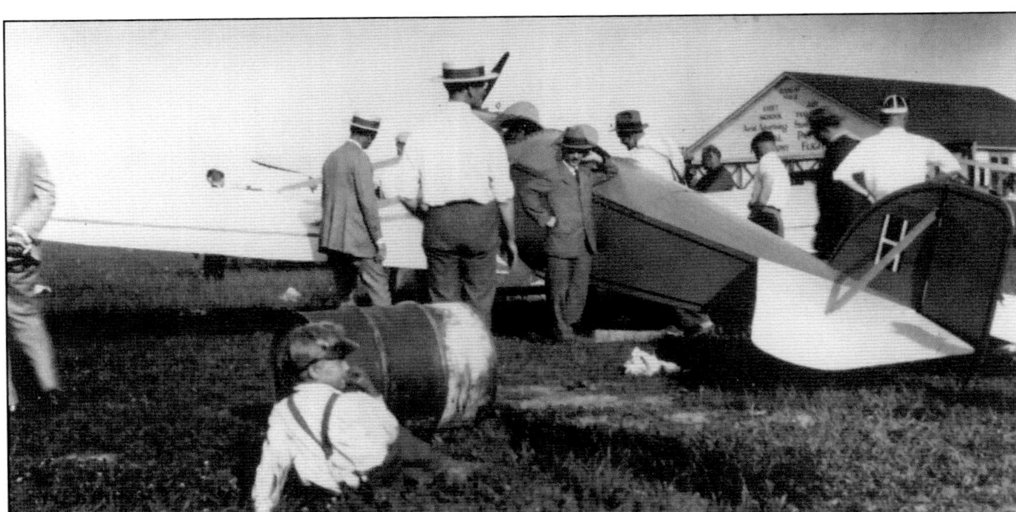

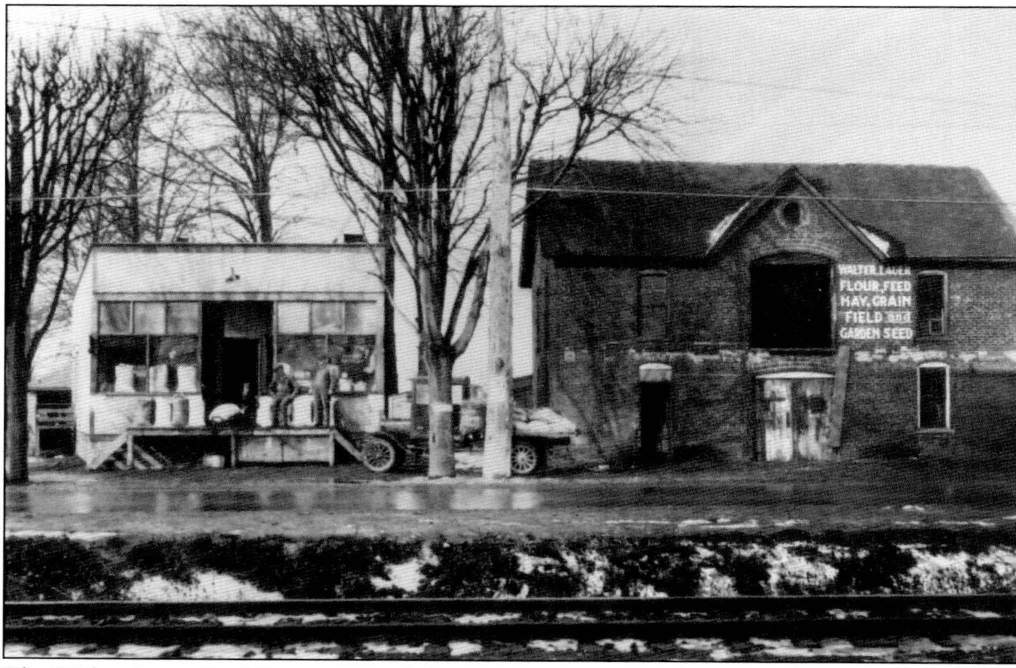

The Walter Lauer Feed Store, pictured above in 1926 and below in 1929, occupied two buildings on Gratiot Avenue. The small building to the left is in both photographs. The interurban tracks can be seen in front of the store as it stood in 1926. This block of Gratiot Avenue, between Martin and Utica Roads, developed into one of Roseville's busiest retail districts during the 1940s and 1950s. Over the years, and until recently, the Lauer family ran a beer store and novelty store in the same location. The Lauers sold the property in 2008. An antique store now occupies the space.

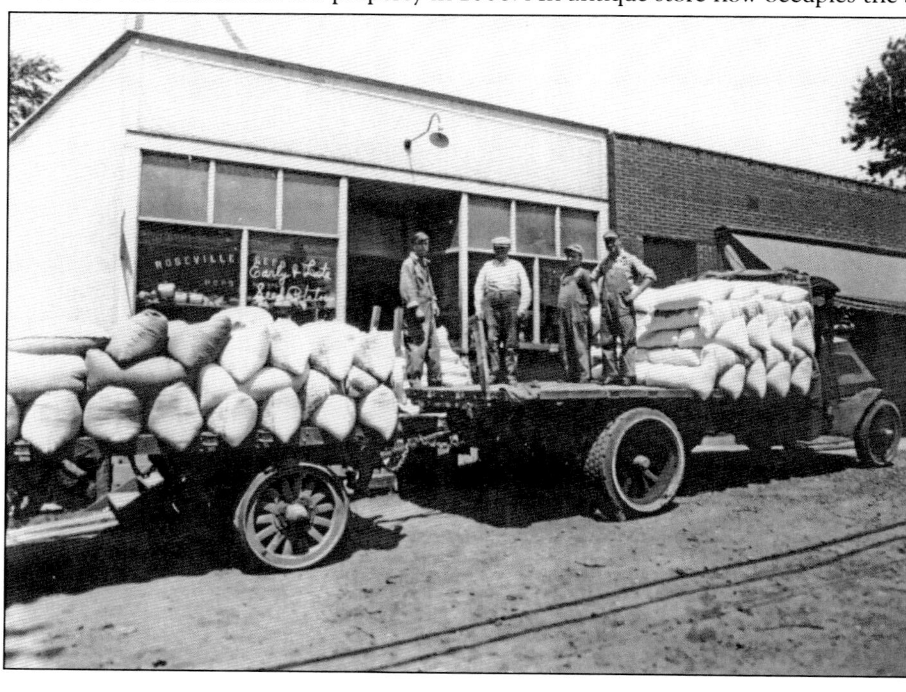

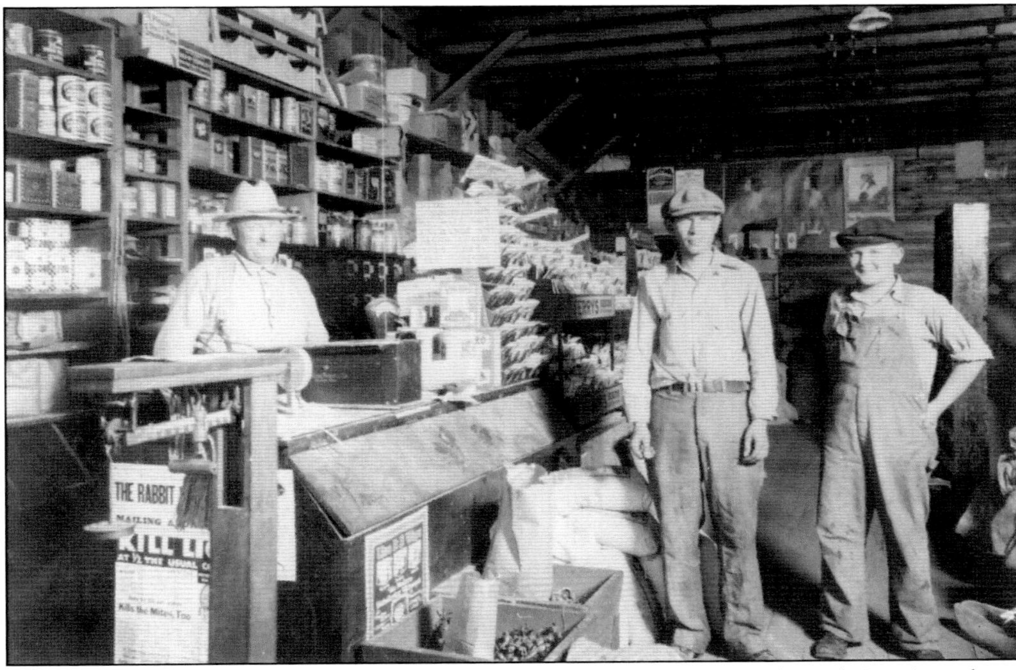

Owner Walter Lauer works behind the counter in this 1932 photograph, with Joe Ameel and Walter's young son, Vincent Lauer. Walter owned a store in Mount Clemens and worked at a mill prior to opening the feed store in Roseville sometime in the 1920s.

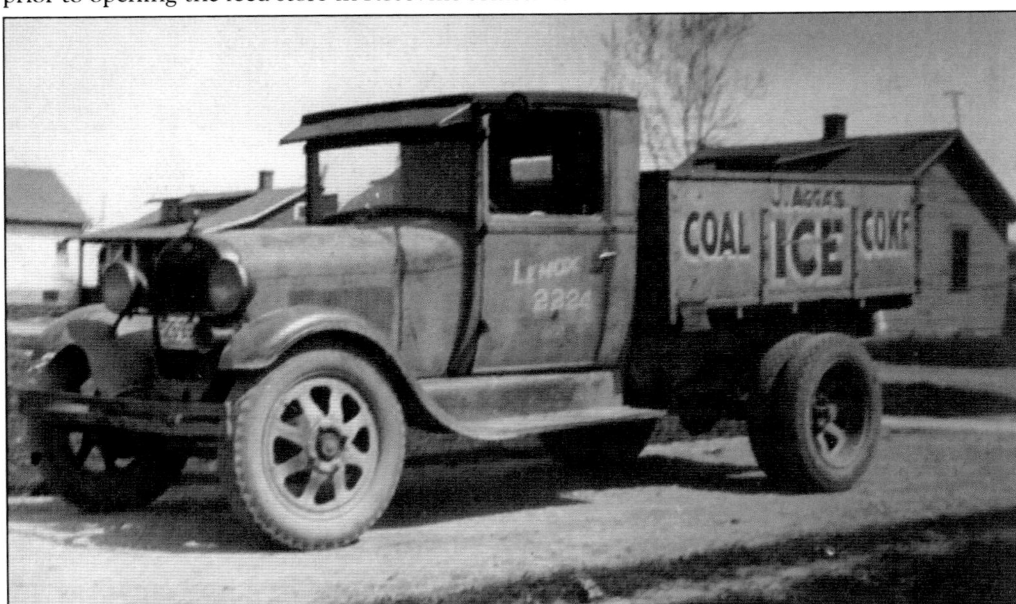

John Agga, of Agga's Ice, Coal & Coke, took this photograph of his truck on May 9, 1934. While the truck was no doubt delivering ice, the "Coke" referred to on the side of the truck was not the soft drink, but rather a fuel used commercially, while coal was used at the time to heat homes. Note the phone number, "Lenox 2224"; Lenox stood for "L-E" (5-3) on the rotary dial of the telephone.

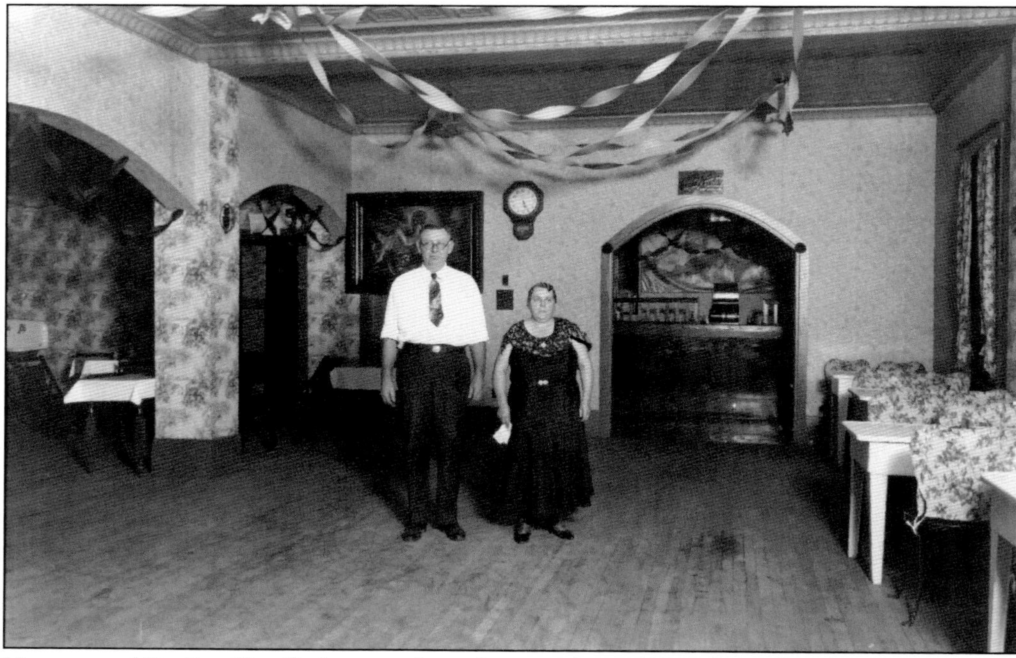

Herman and Pauline Haselhuhn pose for a photograph in 1933–1934 in their beer garden in the Roseville Inn, located on the west side of Gratiot Avenue at Frazho Road. The building, constructed in 1915, housed a saloon on the main level and a large dance hall upstairs. By 1946, the inn had been renamed the New Roseville Inn and was owned by Gus Henreau and Ed Howard. In 1950, seen below, the Roseville Inn is still standing—barely. The Haselhuhns continued to operate a tavern, Pleasant Grove Bar, located across the street, next door to their home. There is still a car wash located on the northwest corner of Gratiot Avenue and Frazho Road today.

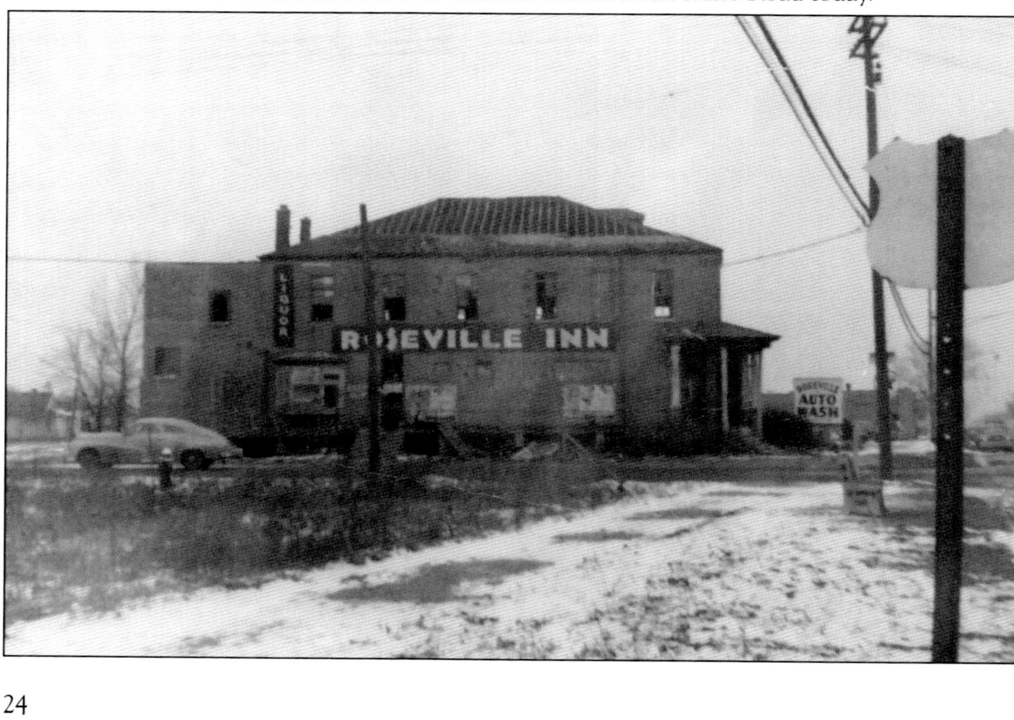

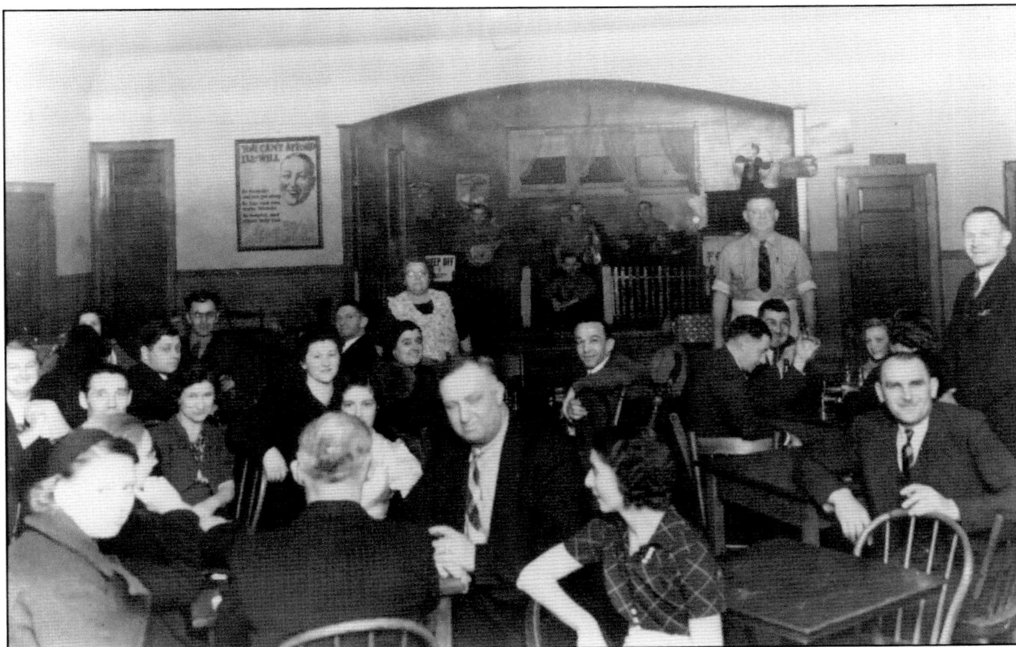

The Pleasant Grove Bar on Gratiot Avenue, south of Frazho Road, was a popular Saturday night hangout for square dancing and card playing, seen above, in 1941 and 1942. Formerly the St. Mark Lutheran Church social hall, the Pleasant Grove Bar (Pleasure Grove in some references) was opened by Herman and Pauline Haselhuhn shortly after Prohibition was repealed. It closed around 1955. A Hank Greenberg–endorsed Goebel Beer sign can be seen behind the band with the saying, "After the game I relax with Goebels." Goebel Brewing Company was a Detroit beer brewery from 1873 to 1964. Closed during Prohibition, from 1920 to 1932, the company was reorganized in 1932 and began operations again in 1934. Goebel was purchased by Stroh Brewing Company. Specials on the board in the photograph below indicate a chicken sandwich for just 25¢ and a bowl of chili for 15¢.

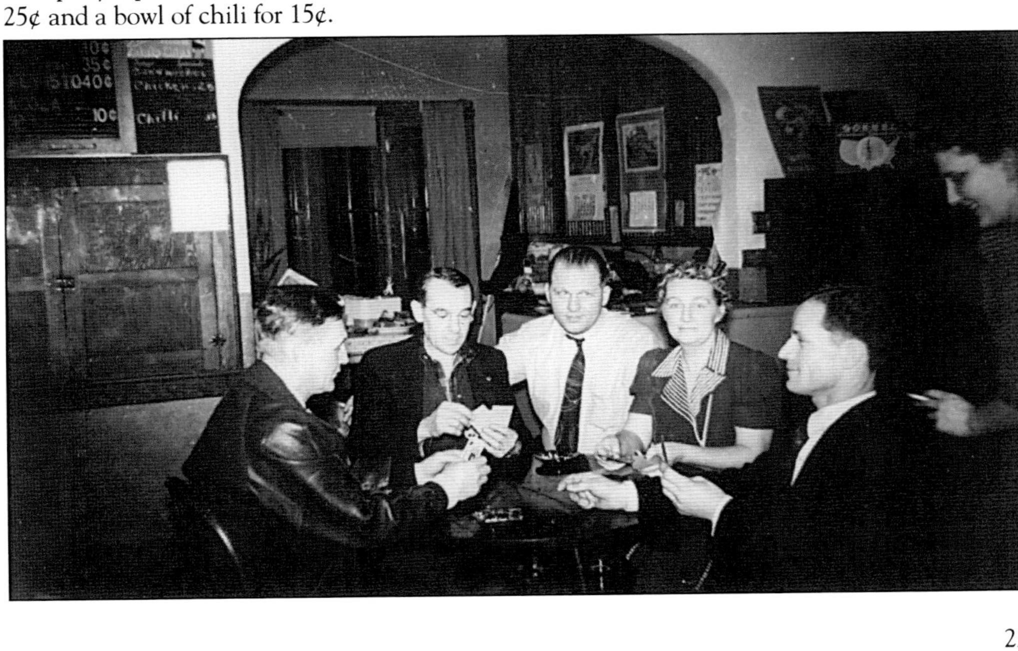

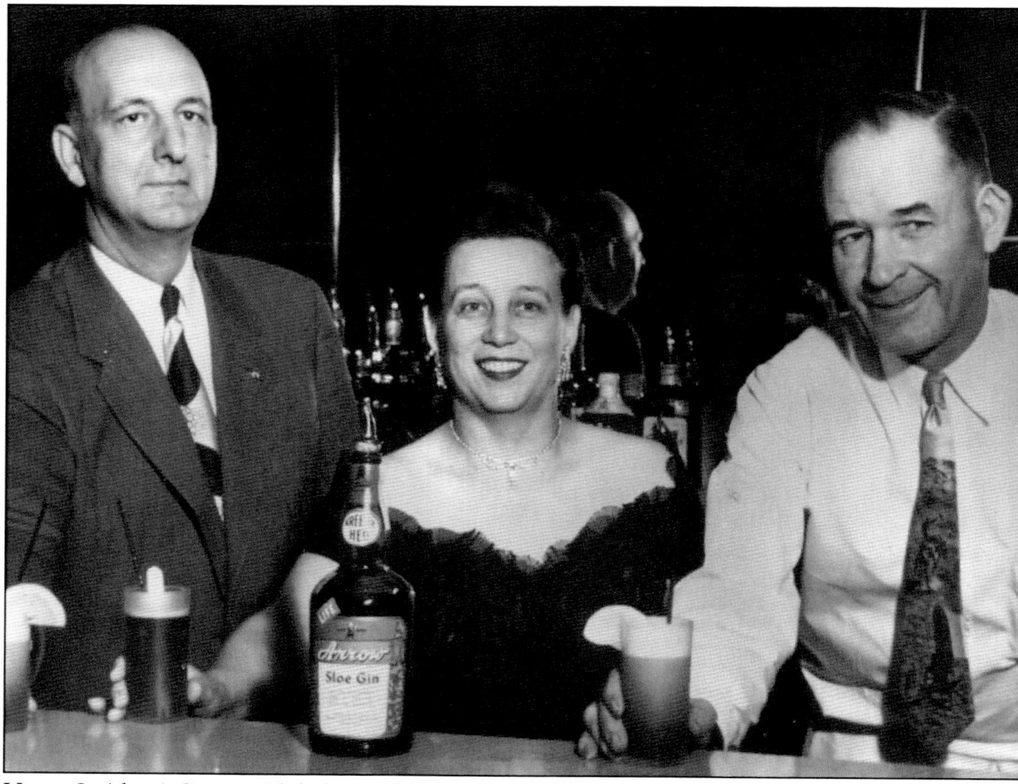

Harry & Alma's Supper Club, located on Gratiot Avenue near today's Eastgate Shopping Center, was the first nightclub of its kind to open in Roseville. Harry and Alma Marchant (left) are pictured here with Alex MacLellan, who was the first bartender at the club. Sloe gin was a popular liqueur in the 1950s. Arrow, the manufacturer, advertised the Sloe Gin Fizz as a drink that "Looks Cool! Tastes Cool!" (Courtesy of Dwain Lusk.)

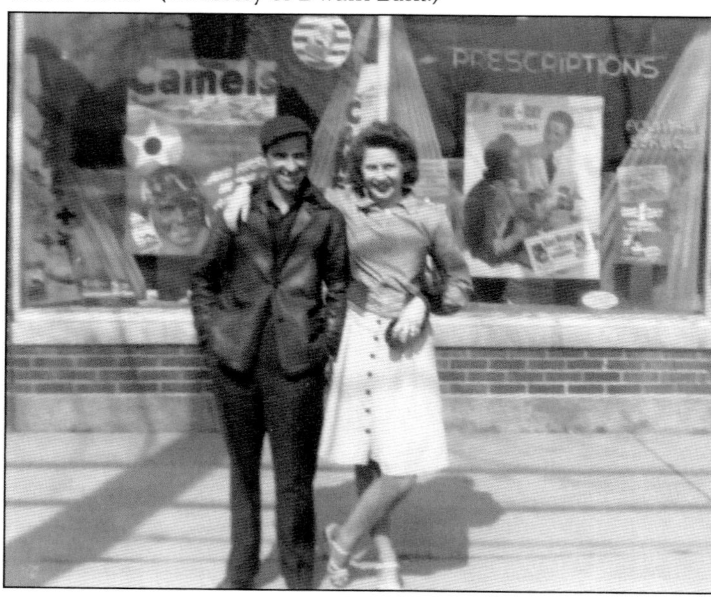

Frank Sabo and Elizabeth Jacobs are pictured here in the early 1940s in front of Donnelly's Drug Store. The store was located on Gratiot Avenue on the same block as Harry & Alma's Supper Club. The store window advertising offers equal space for cigarettes and prescriptions. The drugstore also offered fountain service, popular among drugstores in the 1940s and 1950s. Donnelly's motto was "Good Service and Good Prices!" (Courtesy of Dwain Lusk.)

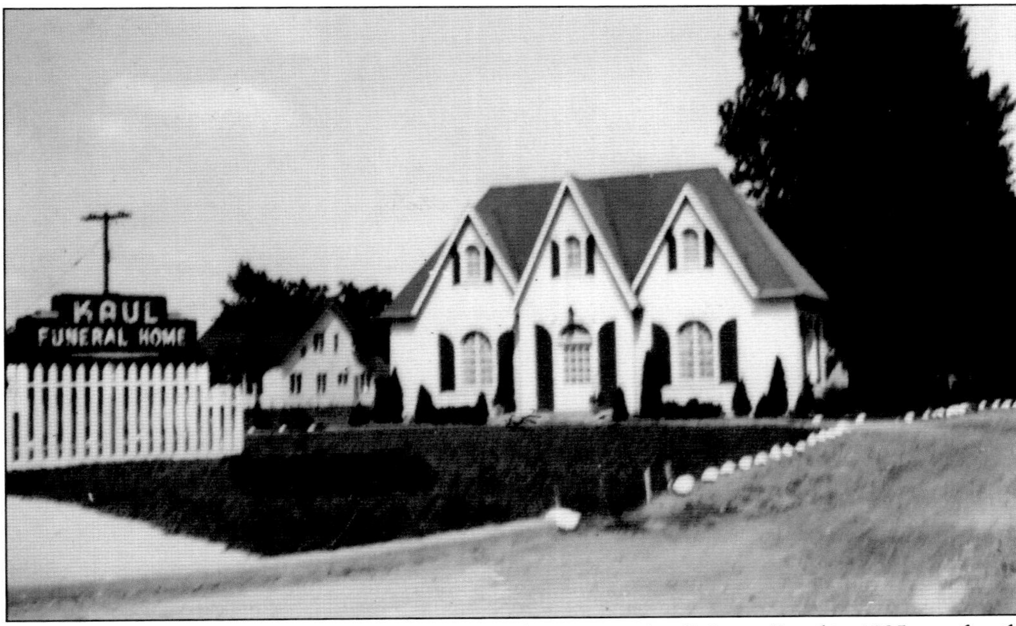

Founded in 1927, Kaul Funeral Home, on Gratiot Avenue south of Martin Road in 1935, was family owned and operated. Kaul Funeral Homes expanded to meet the needs of its communities in St. Clair Shores, Clinton Township, and Roseville. It is now part of the Dignity Memorial network of more than 2,000 licensed providers, North America's largest purveyor of funeral, cremation, and cemetery needs.

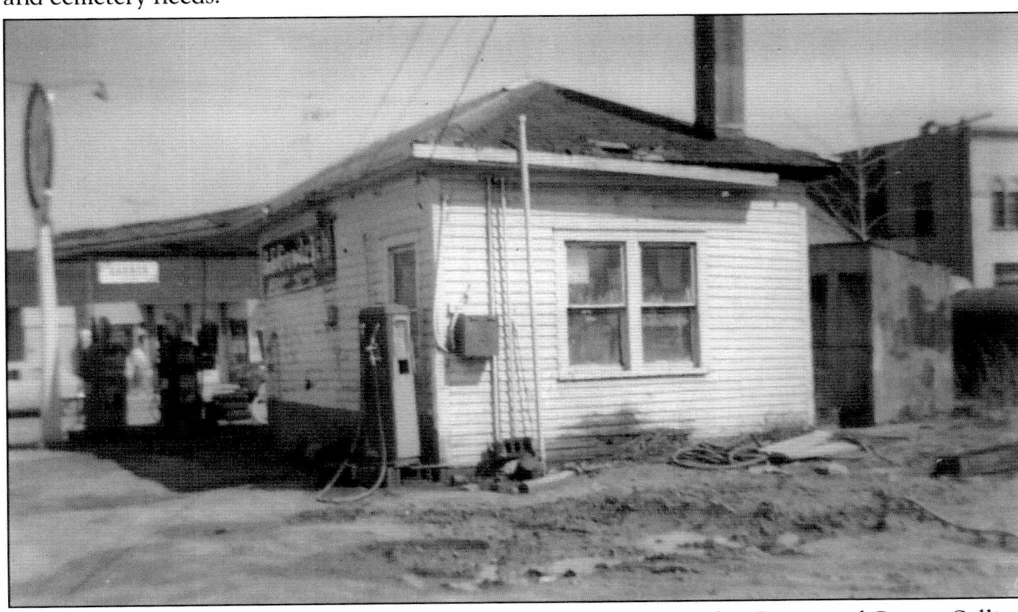

In 1937, H. Brothers Service Station was located on 11 Mile Road at Rosewood Street. Selling Texaco gasoline and oils, the station was owned and operated by Hasenauer brothers Bob, Bud, and Don. The Texas Company, Texaco's parent company, was founded in Beaumont, Texas, in 1901 when oil was discovered in Spindletop. Many will remember Texaco's long-running jingle, "You can trust your car to the man who wears the star."

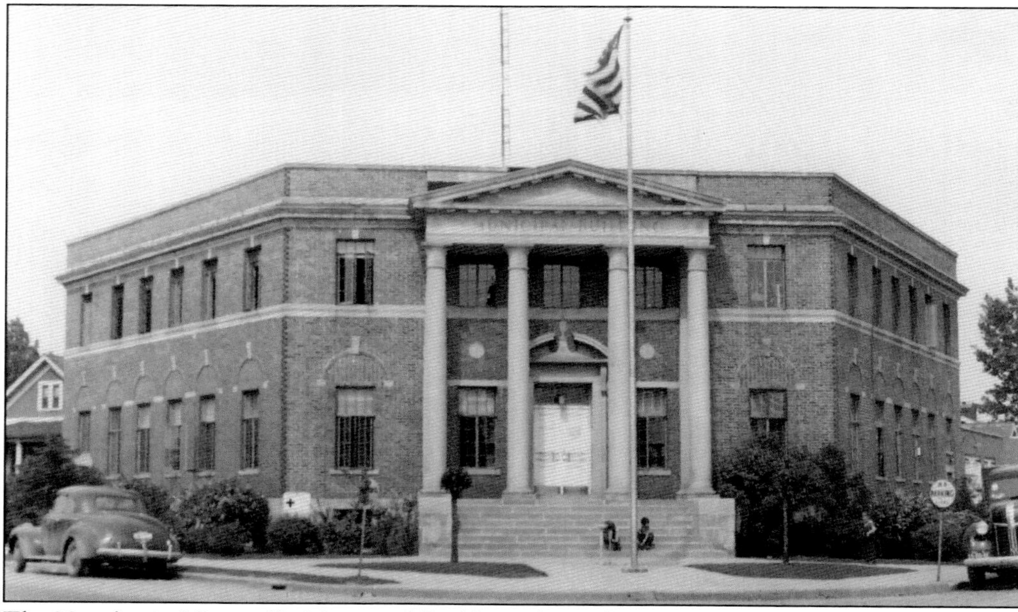

The Neoclassical Roseville Municipal Building, shown here in 1940, was constructed in 1929, shortly after Roseville became a village. The building not only housed the municipal offices but also those of Erin Township and the village police and fire departments and the public library. When Roseville constructed its new municipal complex on Gratiot Avenue at Common Road in 1974, the old building was sold to the Talon Group. Today, Fox Portrait Studios operates out of the building on Gratiot Avenue at Meier Road.

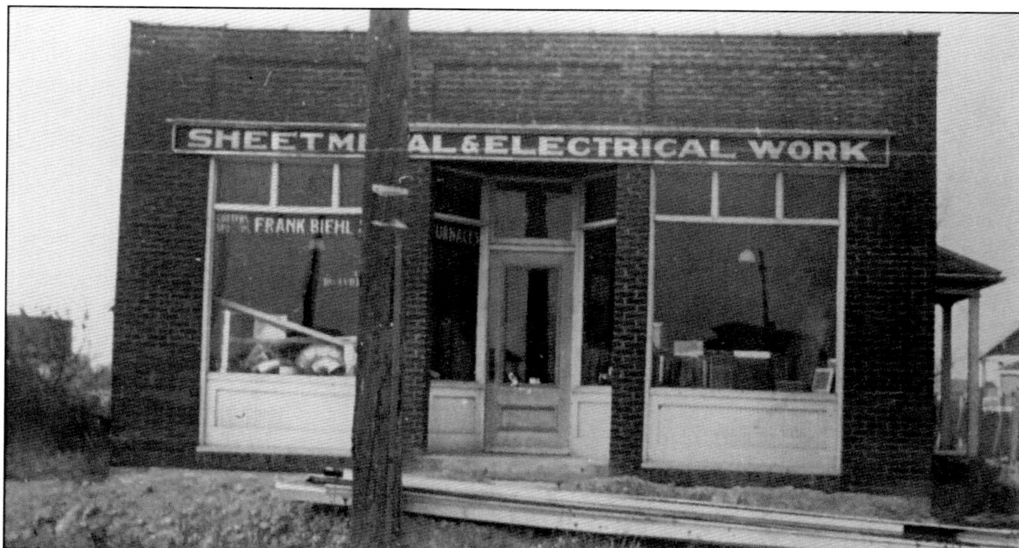

Frank Biehl Sheet Metal & Electrical Work, pictured here in 1926, was located at 28541 Gratiot Avenue, between Utica and 12 Mile Roads. The Biehl family lived in an apartment at the back of the building during the 1920s—note the side porch in the photograph—and Frank Biehl eventually became Roseville village president. The building went on to become Tony's Bar, the Flanagan Restaurant, Jo-Jo's, and the Canton Inn, a Chinese restaurant that has been at the location for decades and is still there today.

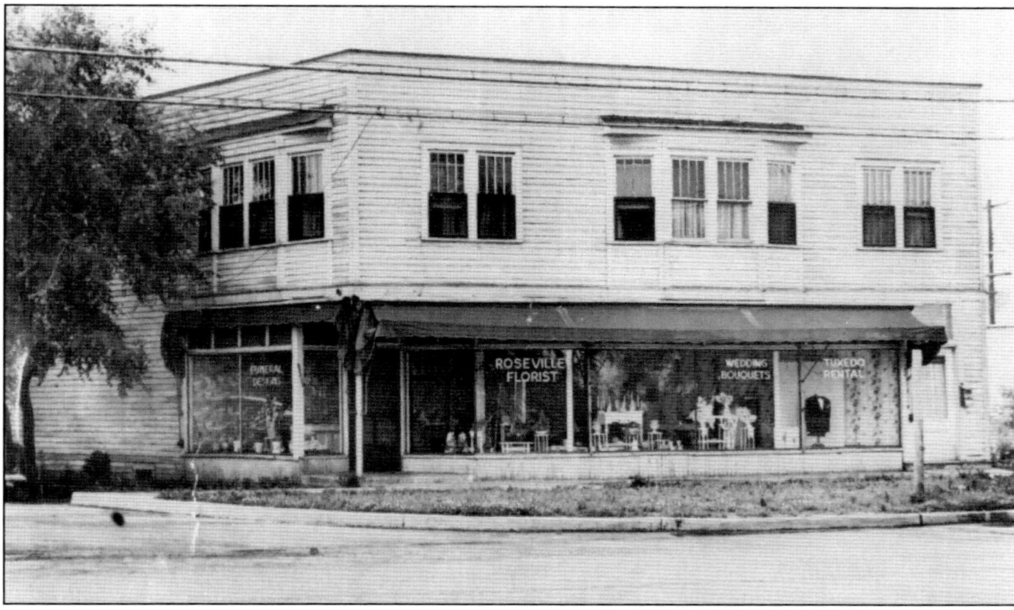

In 1951, Walter and Jenny Jasen bought the former Roseville Florist building at 27603 Gratiot Avenue, south of Martin Road, and started Jasen's Furniture & Appliance Company. The Jasens began selling fans at cost to get to know the people in the neighborhood. In the 1960s, they began carrying living room sets, along with washers, dryers, televisions, and other major appliances. Eventually, Jasen's shifted to fine furniture exclusively. Wally, Jim, Diane, Joe, and Chris Jasen managed Jasen's Fine Furniture, and it is still run by the Jasen family to this day.

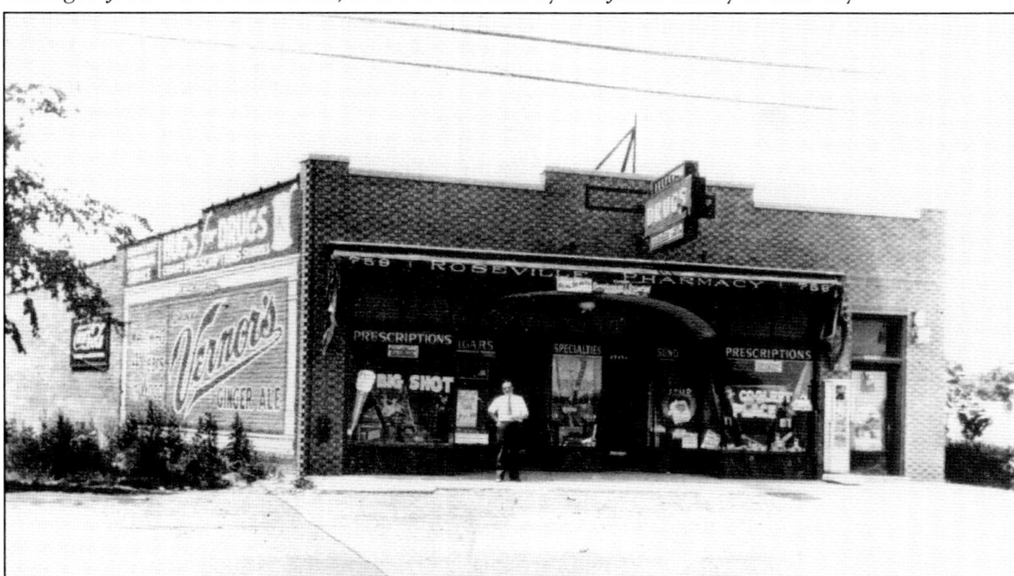

In 1925, Hug's Drug Store, "Hug's for Drugs," located at 27453 Gratiot Avenue between 11 Mile and Martin Roads, was also known as Roseville Pharmacy and later operated as Read's Drug Store for many years. Vernor's Ginger Ale, advertised on the side of the building, originated in Detroit in 1866. The former Hug's/Roseville Pharmacy building still stands today under the auspices of the Rainbow Jewelers.

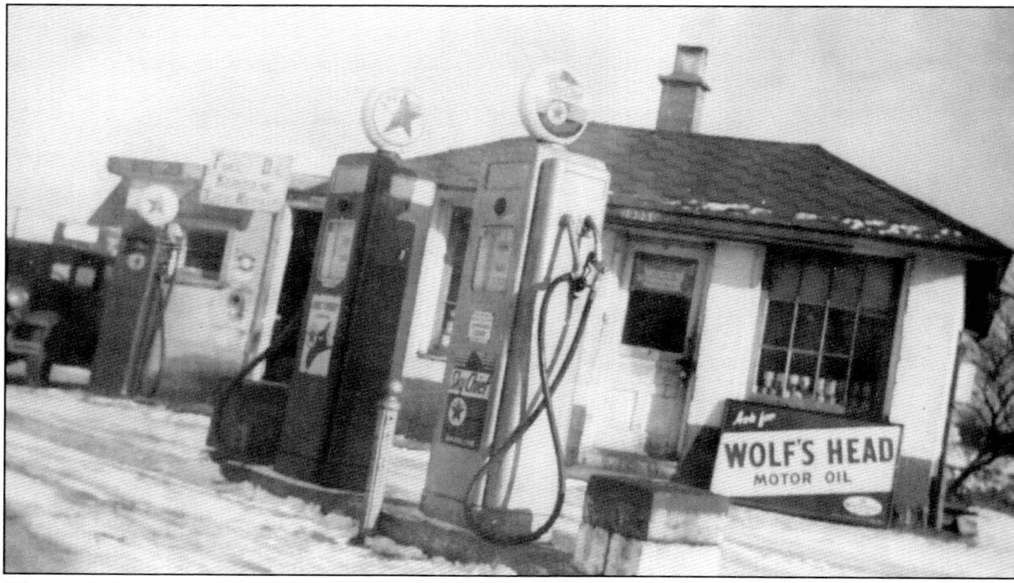

Chownyk Service operated for some 20 years on Gratiot Avenue at Glenn Street. John and Florence Chownyk purchased the station in the 1940s. Gene Chownyk recalls as a teenager working at the station after school with his brother Ralph. The Chownyks also had two daughters, Arlene and Lois. In 1951, Gene would go on to marry Pat Delmotte, daughter of Theophiel and Amelia Delmotte. The Delmottes and Chownyks were all lifelong Roseville residents. Today, Pat Chownyk is president of the Roseville Historical and Genealogical Society. Below, a service station attendant, possibly one of the Chownyk men, fills a tire for a customer. (Courtesy of Pat Chownyk.)

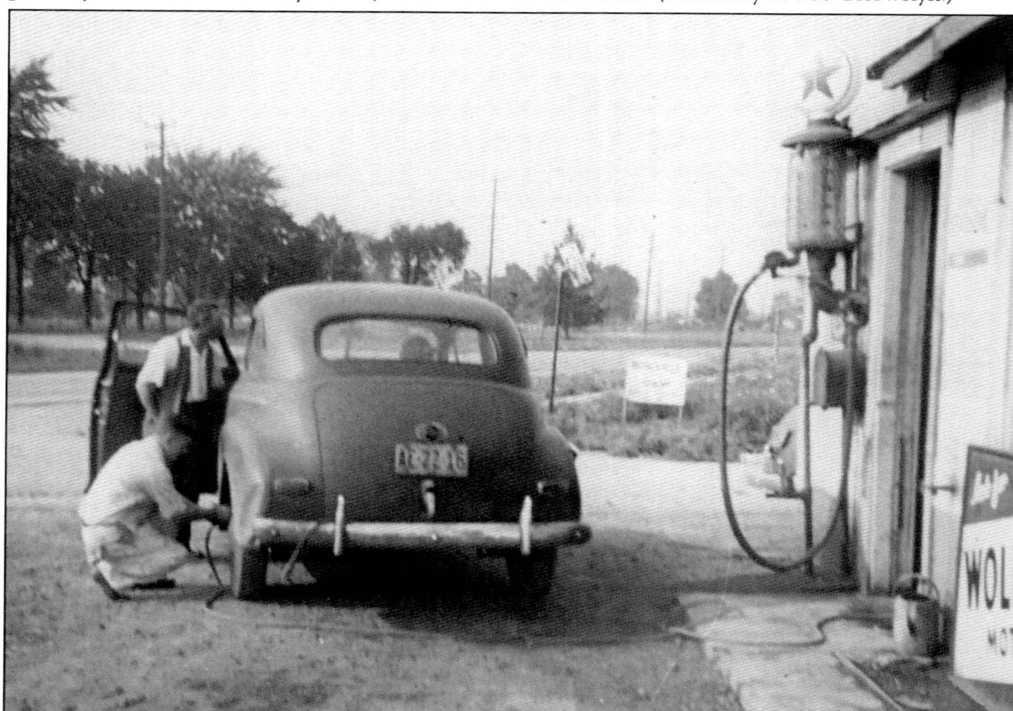

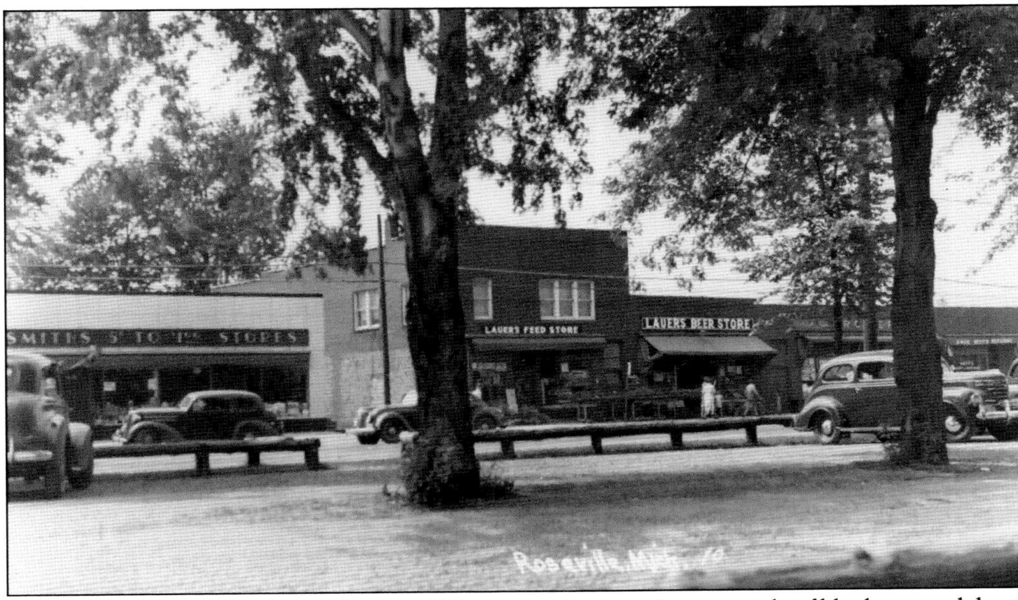

Downtown Roseville in the 1940s was still located at the junction, a couple of blocks up and down Gratiot Avenue at Utica Road. Pictured above, south of Utica Road, are Smiths 5¢ to $1 Store, Lauers Feed and Beer Stores side by side, Kroger Grocery, and Neff's Shoes & Repairing. Below, north of Utica Road, are the Roseville State Savings Bank, Suburban Drug Company, Vollegar's Bakery, Quality Meat Market, and Famous Cleaners. Note also that parking was provided in the median of Gratiot Avenue. Roseville's downtown buildings still stand today and are slated for revitalization as a Town Center Overlay District. The Michigan Economic Development Corporation announced in August 2014 that Roseville and Allegan were named the first communities in the state to receive Redevelopment Ready Communities certification.

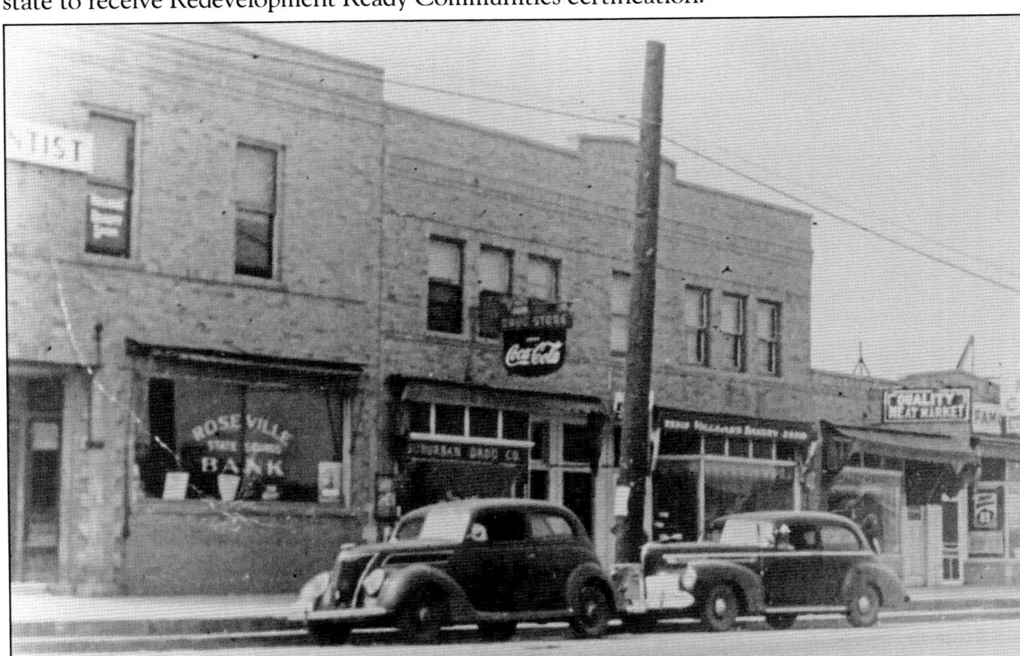

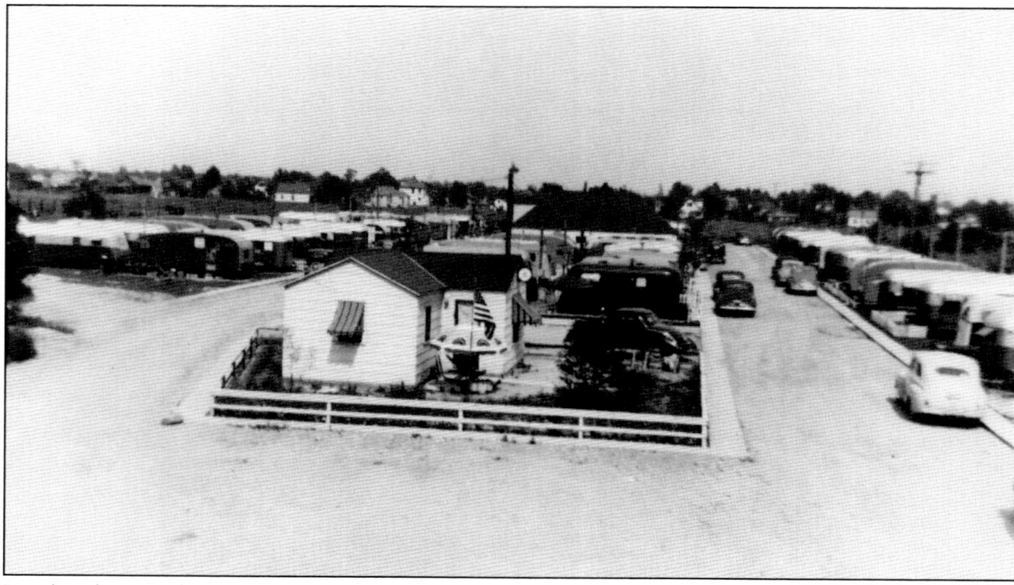

Lambrecht's Trailer City, pictured here in 1942, was developed by the Lambrecht Lumber Company on Gratiot Avenue, just north of 10 Mile Road. Purchased by Leslie Maliskey in 1951, the park then passed to his brother Larry, son Terry, and then Terry's widow, Joanne, who, with daughter Karla (the fourth generation), manages the mobile-home community today. Grandfathered in in 1955, Leslie's remains Roseville's only mobile-home community.

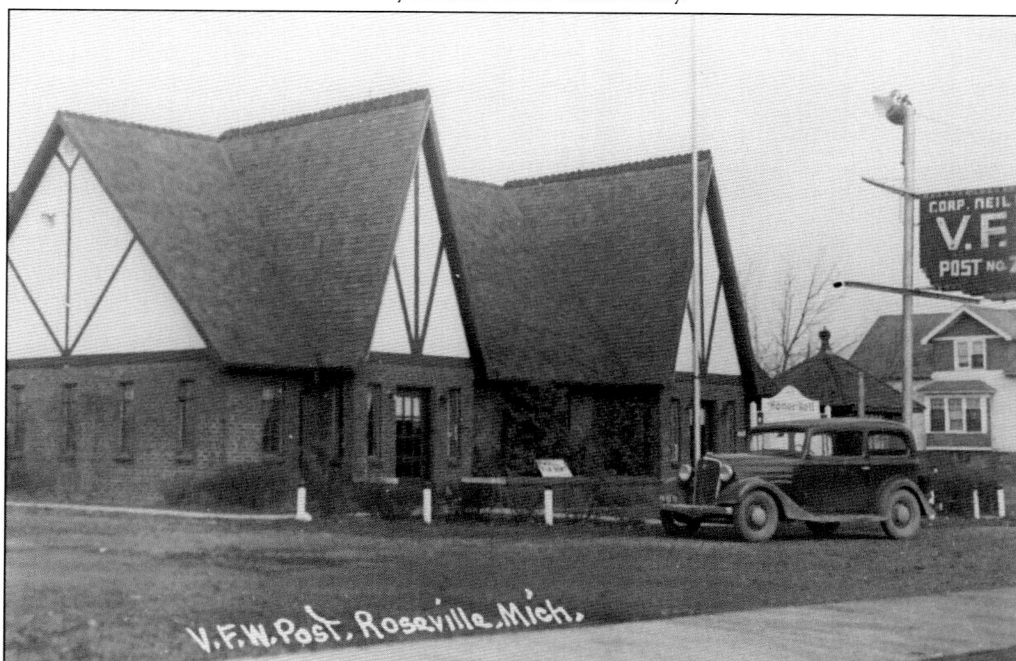

Roseville's iconic VFW Hall on Gratiot Avenue continues as a landmark in Roseville today; however, the Neil W. Reid Post 2358 announced that it is looking to sell the property. The Veterans of Foreign Wars post was founded 1936 and bought its building, the Old Burgher Inn, in 1941. The post was named for the first soldier from Macomb County to be killed in World War I.

Siblings John and Anne Lano (pictured), along with sister Mary Lano, operated a florist shop and greenhouse on Maple Street in Roseville. John Lano Florist was operated full-time by John, while both sisters held other jobs. Anne worked as a comptometer operator. A comptometer was the first commercially successful key-driven mechanical calculator. Mary worked as a stenographer for an architectural company. John lived in Roseville until his death in 1983.

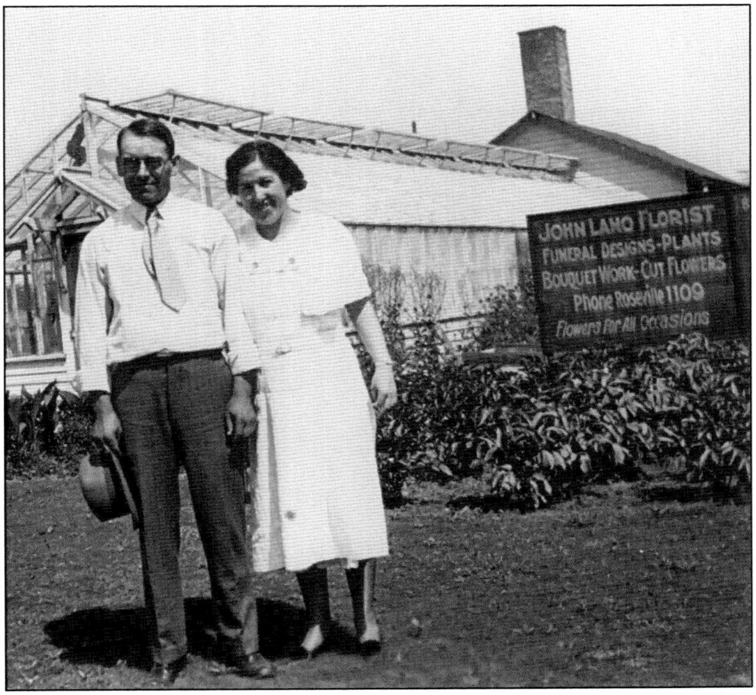

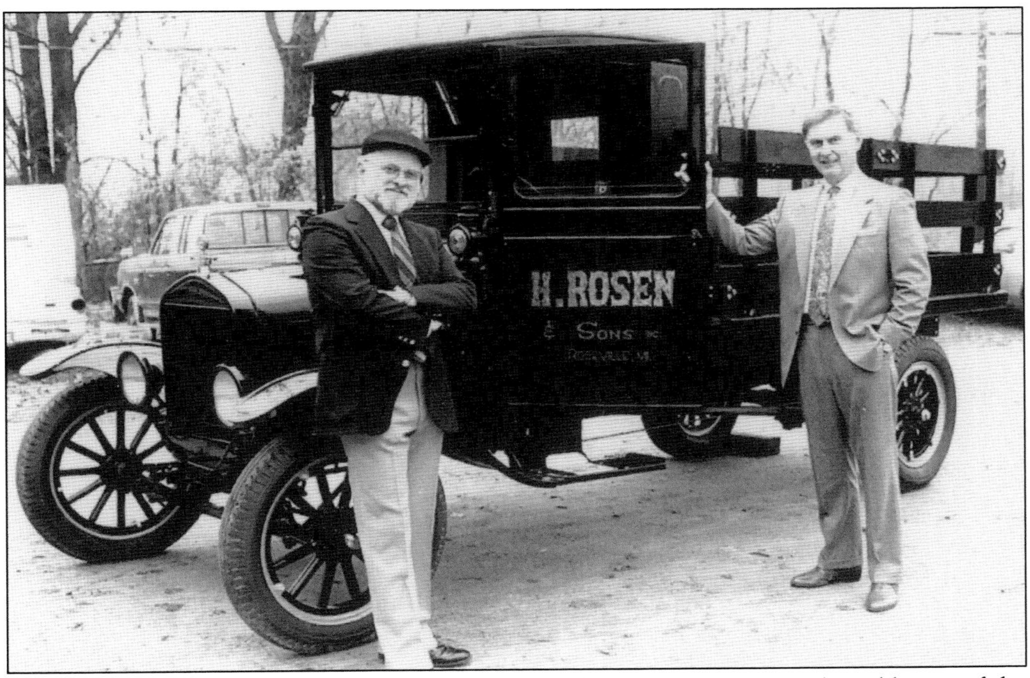

The roots of H. Rosen & Sons, Inc., date back to 1927, when Henry Rosen (possibly one of the men showing off a new truck) began salvaging old newspapers and rags in Detroit. The business grew so much that before long he needed two of his sons to help him keep up. The company still operates today in Roseville as Great Lakes Recycling and is managed by the third generation of the Rosen family, Henry's grandchildren.

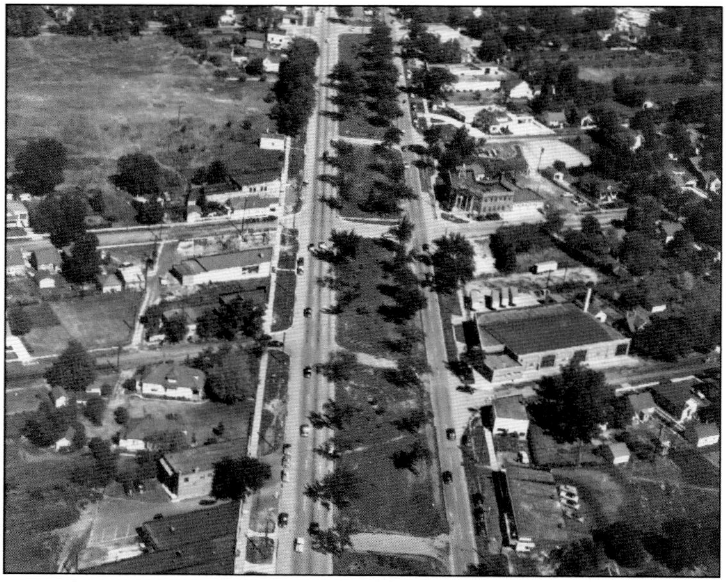

Roseville's majestic city hall stands out in this 1954 aerial view of Gratiot Avenue. The large flat-roofed building in the right foreground is the former Pfeiffer beer distributor, owned by Peter Tocco and Joseph Zerilli. Joe Randazzo's Fruit & Vegetable Market operates out of the building today. Conrad Pfeiffer began brewing beer in Detroit in 1889. Founded in 1953, Randazzo's has stores in Detroit, Dearborn Heights, Roseville, and Westland.

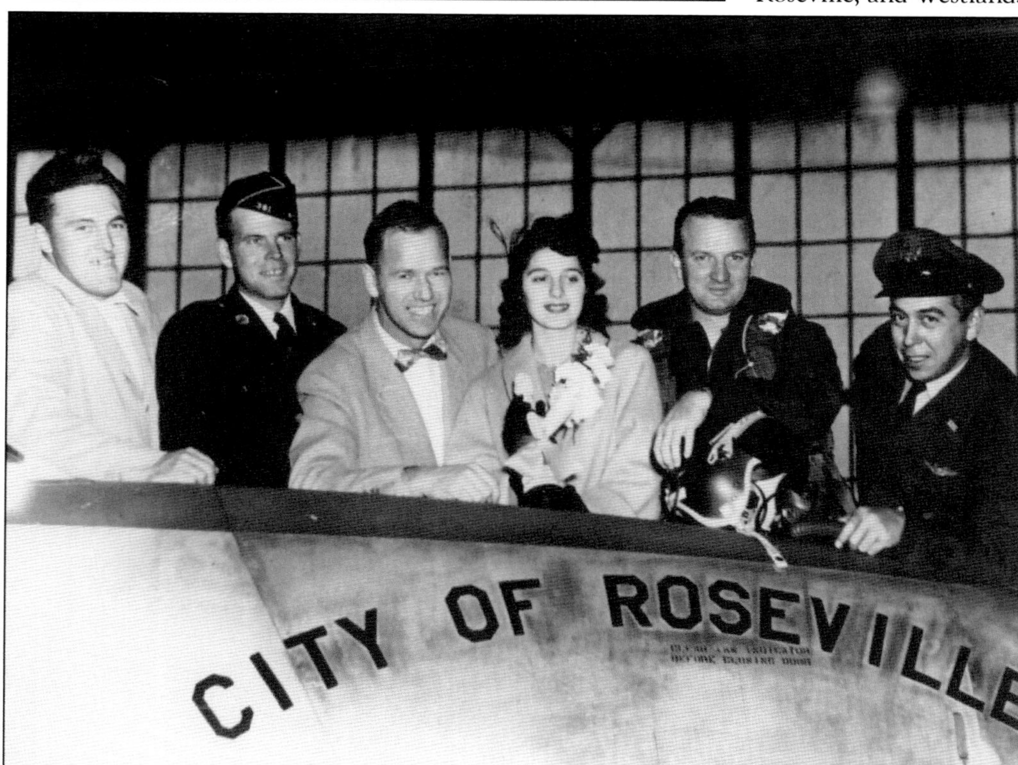

The City of Roseville had its own airplane in 1954 and 1955. At a photo opportunity with the plane are, from left to right, Harvey Bannasch, department of public works employee; American Legion commander Blair Rudd; Glen Alsip; Miss Roseville; unidentified pilot (a major at Selfridge Air Base, where the photograph was taken); and Air Force captain Harold Kirkwood Sr.

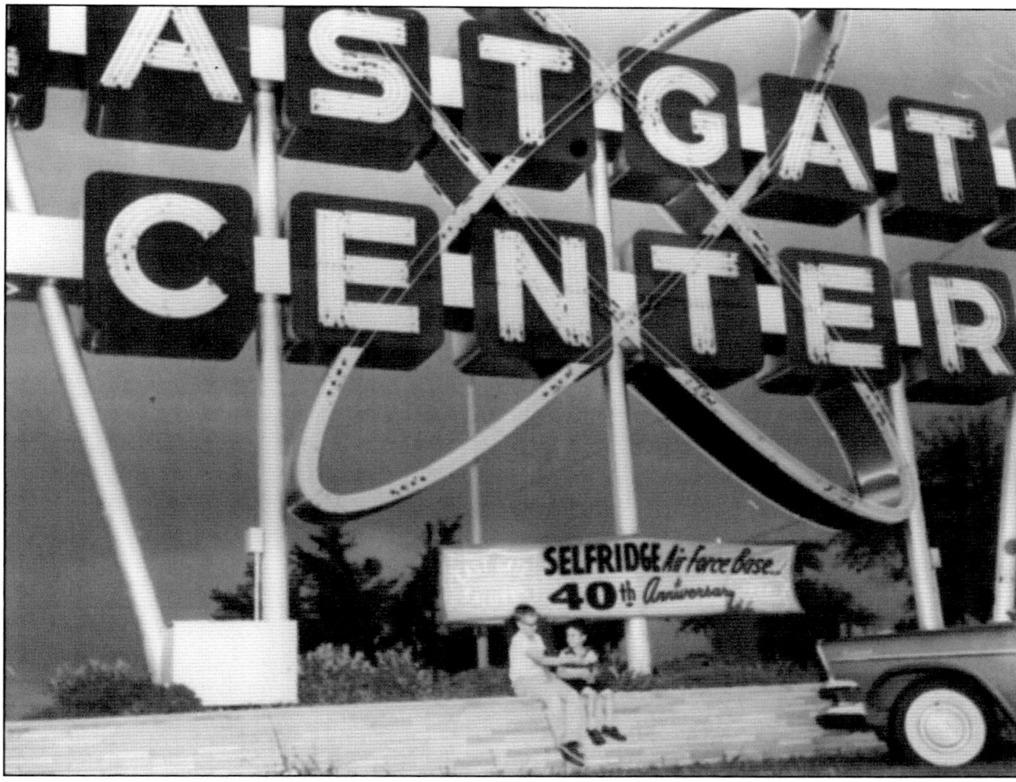

Above, a couple of youngsters take a rest under the atomic Eastgate sign. Eastgate, Macomb County's first shopping center, was built in the 1950s on the site of the former Hartung Airport (originally Packard Field). The Eastgate Shopping Center in Roseville attracted big-name Detroit retailers, seen below, including the S.S. Kresge Co. and, at the end of the strip, a Wrigley Food Store, one of Detroit's largest grocery chains at the time. Sebastian Spering Kresge founded his company in 1899 with two five-and-dime stores, one in Detroit. In 1977, the company was renamed Kmart Corporation. In 1955, ACF-Brill, a former streetcar manufacturer, purchased 60 Michigan Wrigley Food Stores to form the ACF-Wrigley Stores Inc., later acquired by Allied Supermarkets. Incidentally, Wrigley-Allied operated all Kmart Food Stores.

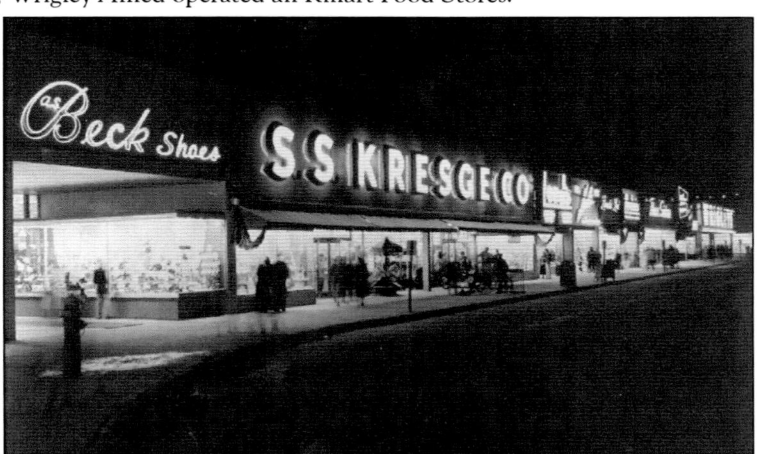

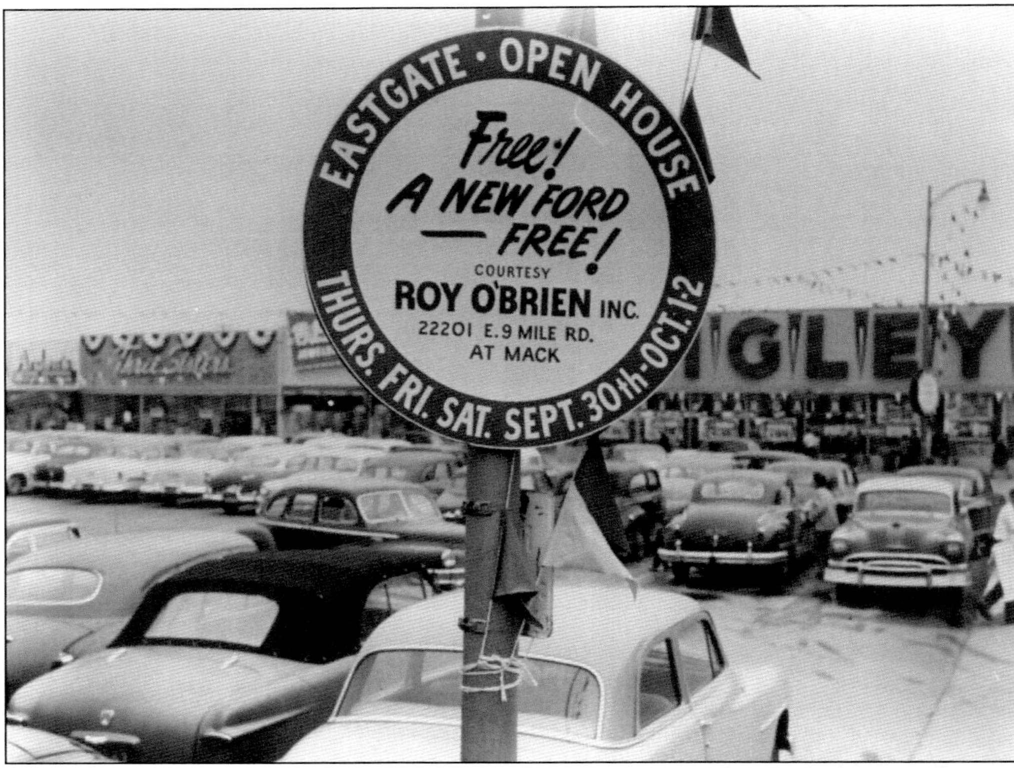

The Eastgate Shopping Center, in conjunction with Roy O'Brien Ford, sponsored an open house in 1954, with all the stores selling raffle tickets to win a new Ford Crestline. The Ford Crestline, and its standard V-8 engine, was a popular model during its run, with more than half a million being produced. The 1954 model year was the last of its generation, as a major redesign was scheduled for 1955. Roy O'Brien Ford became a household name with its advertising jingle, "Stay on the right track to Nine Mile and Mack," where the dealership was located. The jingle was sung by the Gaylords—before they became famous as well. Family owned and operated since 1946, Roy O'Brien Ford is still on the right track at Nine Mile and Mack.

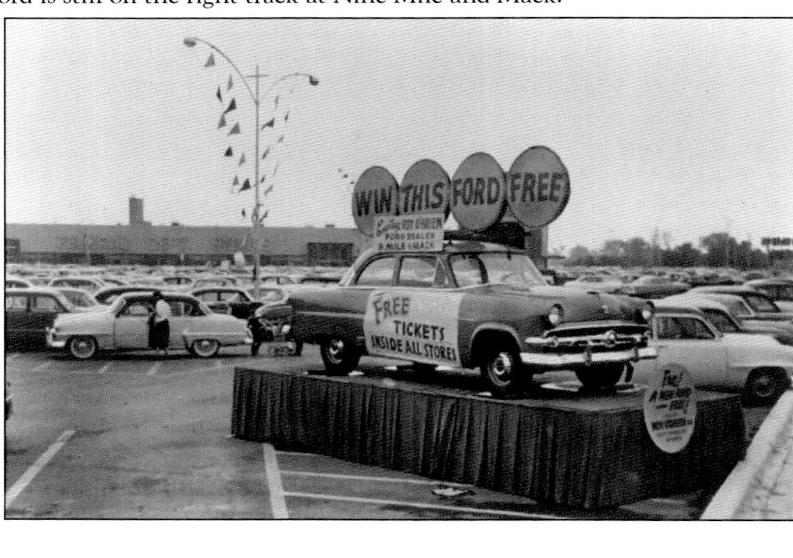

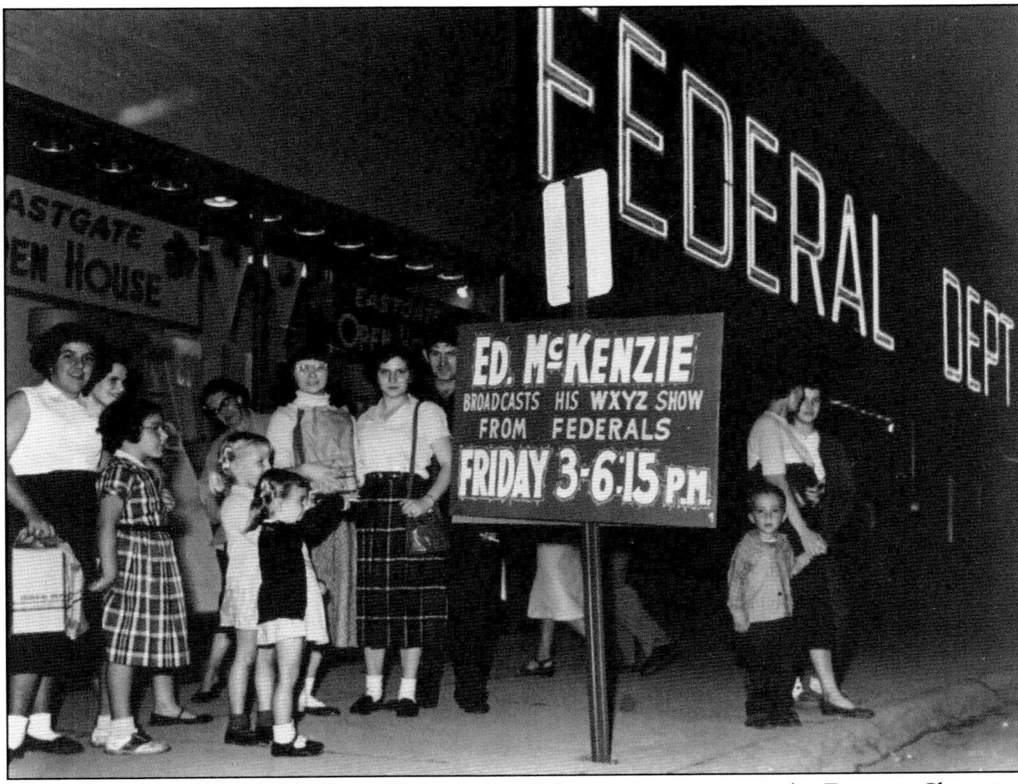

Above, at an open house in front of the Federal Department Store at the Eastgate Shopping Center are, from left to right, (back row, standing) Sharon McRill, Dorothy McRill, and Evelyn McRill, aunt, mother, and grandmother, respectively, of author Terry Minnis. The trio on the far right includes, from left to right, Ray Miller, Lillian Bittern, and Joanne Miller. The Federal Department Store was a popular destination for both adults and teenagers—and buses, as seen below. Federal's, as it was commonly known, was a department store chain founded in Detroit with stores in Lansing and Kalamazoo as well. The chain filed for bankruptcy in 1972. Steven Watstein, also known as Steven West, purchased Federal's in 1978, the same year the Roseville store burned to the ground in February.

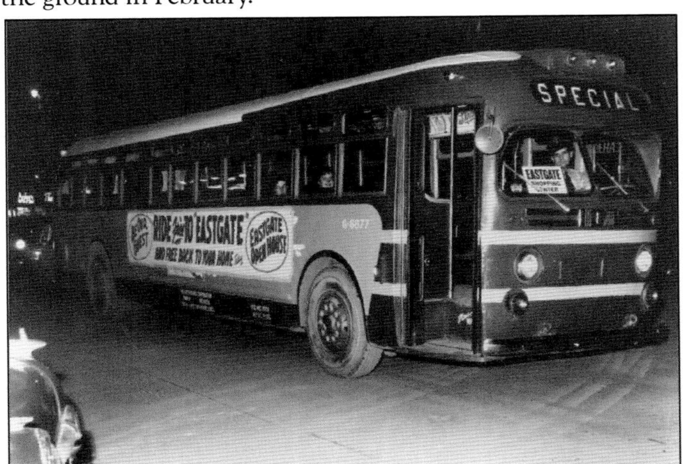

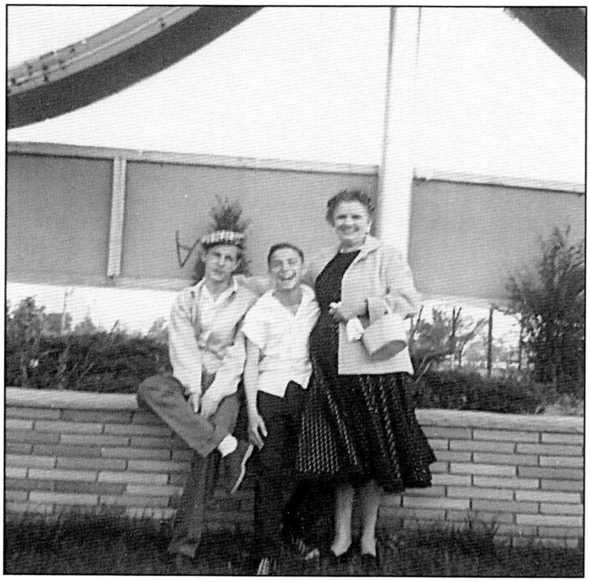

From left to right, Johnny and Eddie Garnett, with their mother, Mary Garnett, pose under the Eastgate Shopping Center sign in the spring of 1958. The atomic age Eastgate sign was a popular Roseville spot for photographs. The boys and mother are the uncles and grandmother of author Terry Minnis. Joe Niedzielski purchased the Eastgate sign in 2013 with plans to restore it. Niedzielski also owns the old Gratiot Drive-In sign. (Courtesy of Dorothy McRill.)

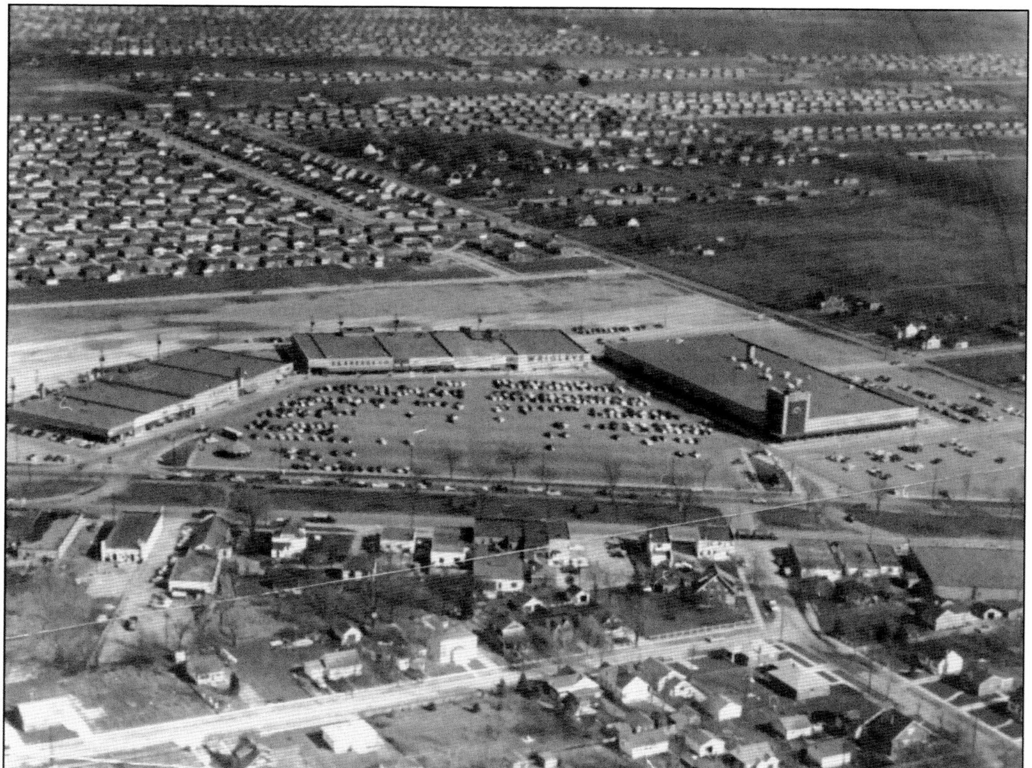

Adolph "Jimmy" Komer, who had learned to fly at the former Roseville Airport site, proposed developing the 104 acres for 400 homes, 650 apartments, and 1.2 million square feet of retail space. The shopping center, the first of its kind in Michigan, was to be named Eastgate. An aerial photograph of the Eastgate Shopping Center clearly shows the Federal Department Store anchoring the right, the southern end of the shopping center.

Three

HOUSES OF WORSHIP

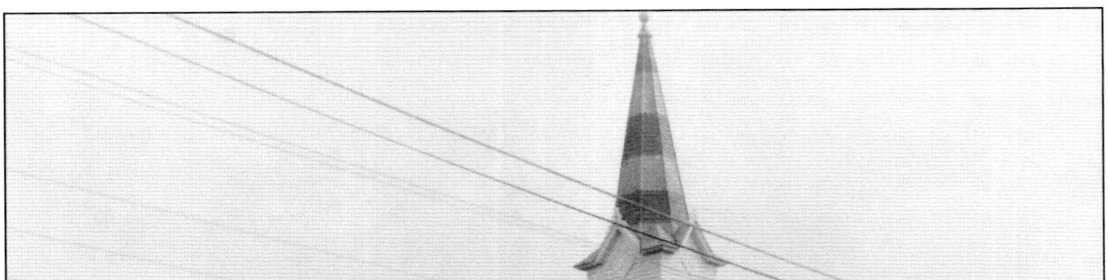

By the mid-19th century, Germans had replaced the former Irish population in the area that was to become Roseville. The first church in Roseville was St. Peter German Evangelical Lutheran Church, established in 1853. The church building seen here, located at about 10 ½ Mile Road on the east side of Gratiot Avenue, across from the former VFW building, was dedicated on the Monday following Easter, March 28, 1853.

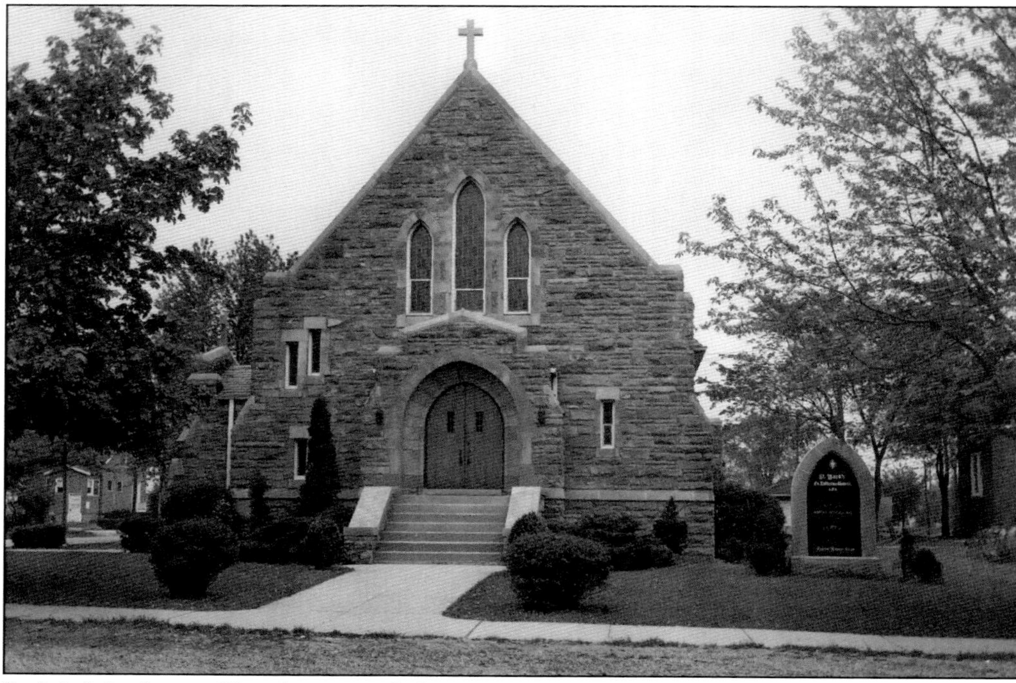

St. Mark Lutheran Church, pictured above in 1945, grew out of what was the former St. Peter congregation. Originally in German, the first English service was spoken on June 20, 1920. In 1926, St. Peter's was reorganized as St. Mark's. The original stone edifice was dedicated on February 12, 1933, at 26830 West Park Street at 11 Mile Road, west of Gratiot Avenue. During its centennial celebration in 1953, the congregation voted to raise $125,000 to expand and build a new sanctuary, tripling the church's footprint to its current size, pictured below. The original church, the southern wing, is now used for social gatherings after services. (Above, courtesy of St. Mark Lutheran Church; below, photograph by John Minnis.)

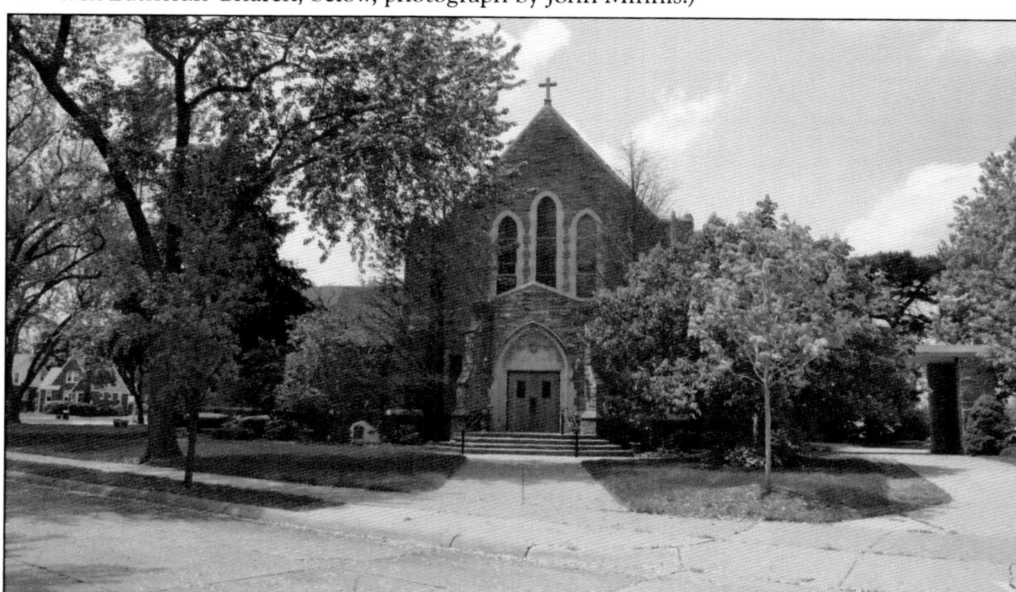

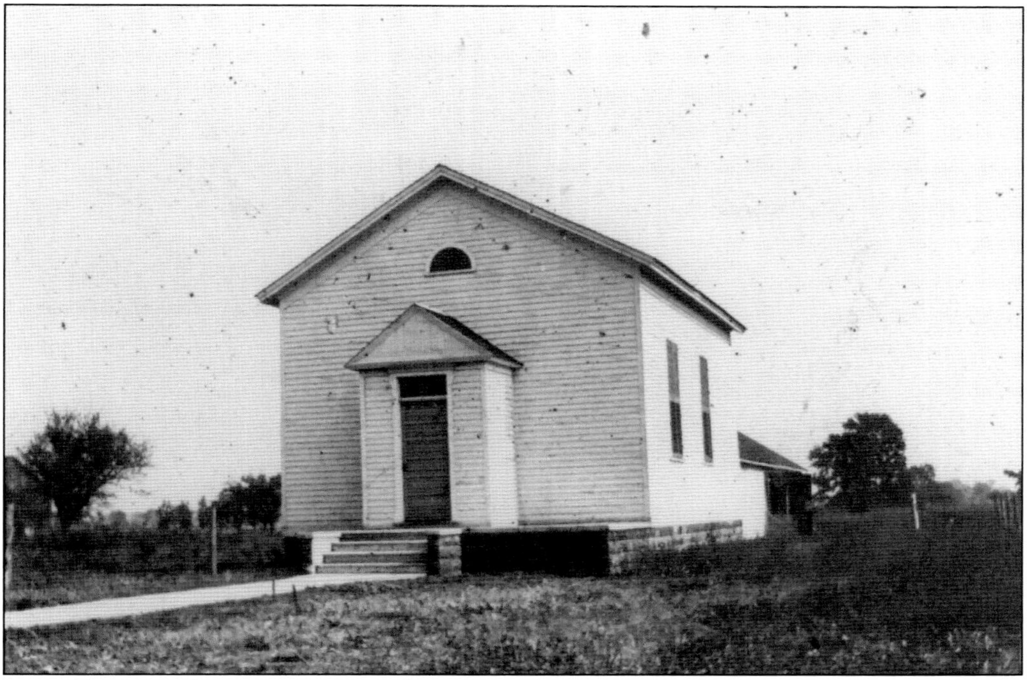

Roseville's second congregation was the First Presbyterian Church of Erin in 1860. In 1857, the Common brothers, Thomas and John, settled on two side-by-side 60-acre farms of land purchased by their father. Just after settling in with his young wife in 1861, Thomas Common donated land on the east side of Gratiot Avenue at the foot of what is now Common Road to establish the church (above), which was completed in October 1861 at a cost of $487.88. The church's first pastor was the Reverend Harry N. Bissell, who regularly came down from Mount Clemens to conduct services. The first church elders were James Bottomley, George Moorhouse, and John Common. The "new" church (below) was built in 1930.

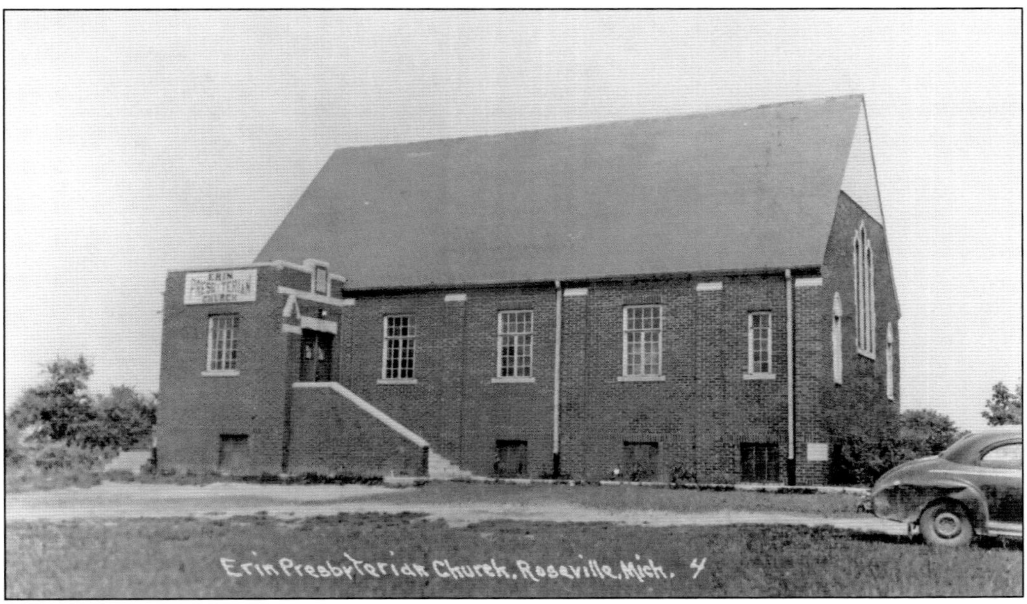

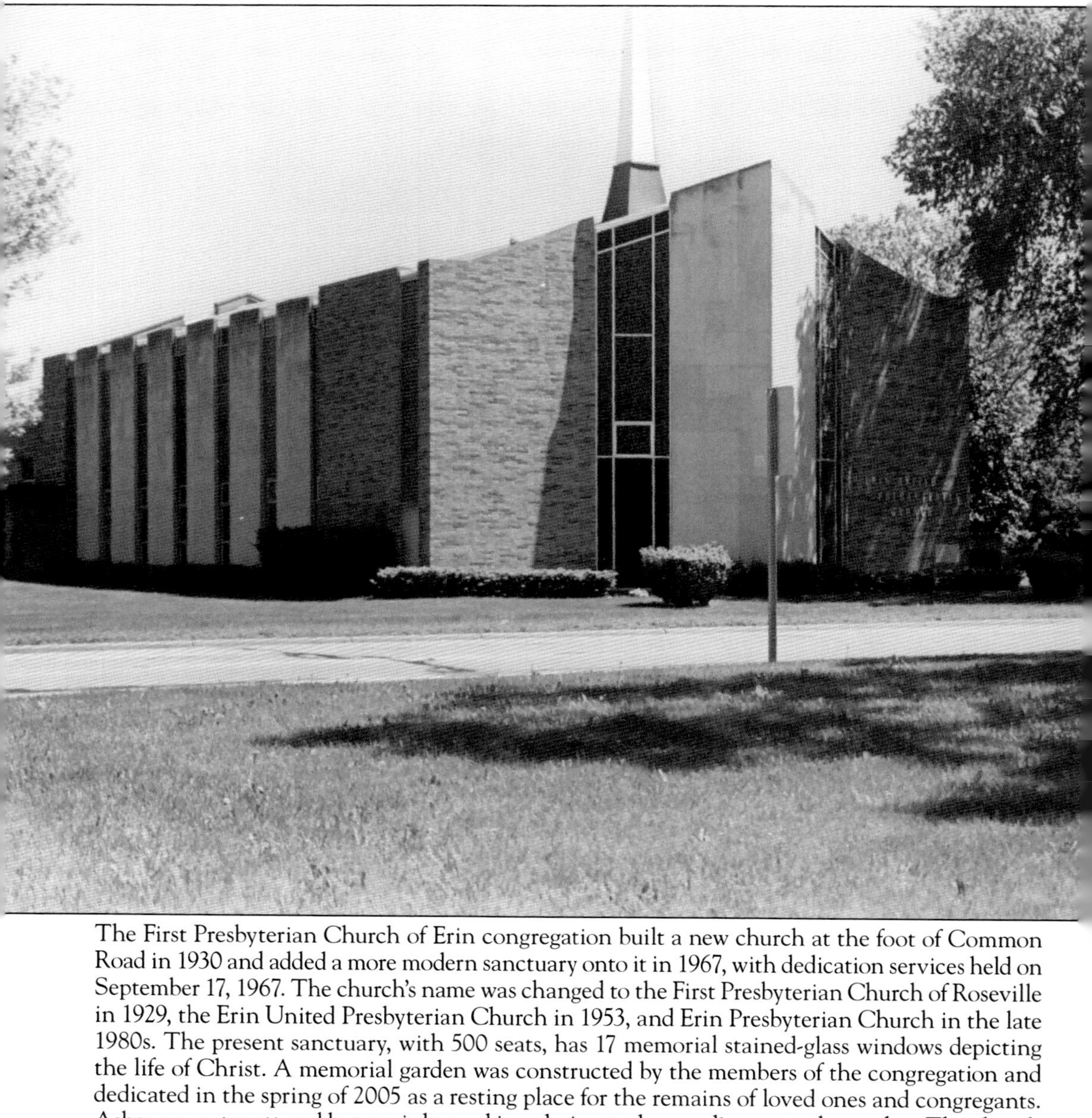

The First Presbyterian Church of Erin congregation built a new church at the foot of Common Road in 1930 and added a more modern sanctuary onto it in 1967, with dedication services held on September 17, 1967. The church's name was changed to the First Presbyterian Church of Roseville in 1929, the Erin United Presbyterian Church in 1953, and Erin Presbyterian Church in the late 1980s. The present sanctuary, with 500 seats, has 17 memorial stained-glass windows depicting the life of Christ. A memorial garden was constructed by the members of the congregation and dedicated in the spring of 2005 as a resting place for the remains of loved ones and congregants. Ashes are not scattered but are inhumed in a designated area adjacent to the garden. The church grounds are designated as a Michigan Historical Site.

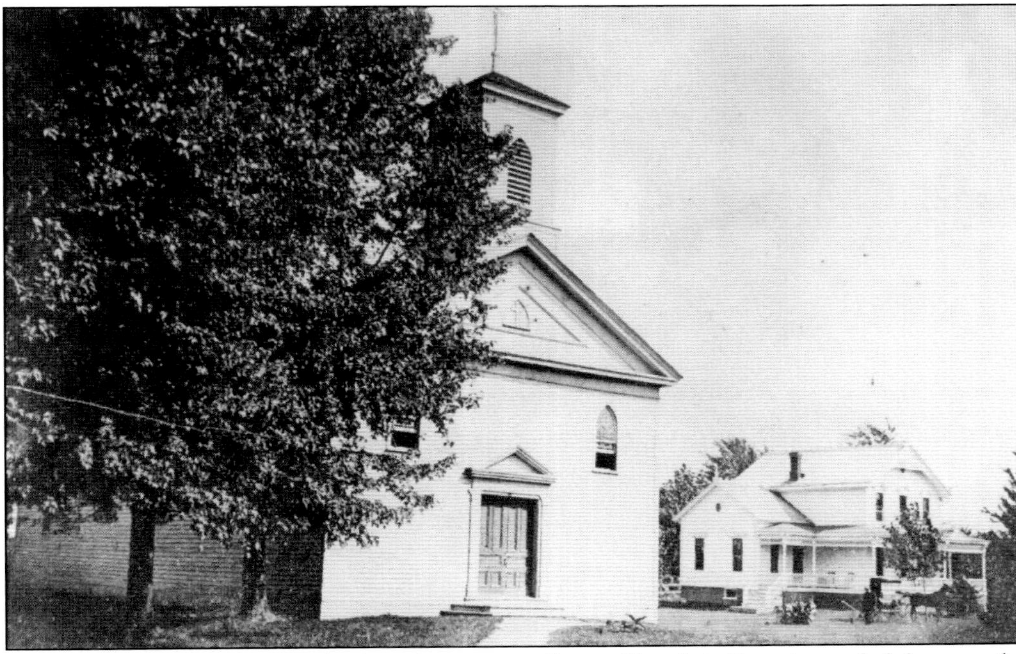

In 1861, Father VanDenDriessche from Assumption Grotto Church in Detroit traveled the turnpike to establish a mission for the Catholics in Roseville. Daniel and Margaret Corby contributed three acres of their land for the purpose of building the church. Sacred Heart Church was a small wooden structure located near the Junction. Note the clean, Greek Revival architectural elements common in the early to mid-19th century. Corby's niece Margaret was one of the first to be married at Sacred Heart. By 1915, below, the entry addition was added, no doubt to prevent cold air from rushing into the sanctuary.

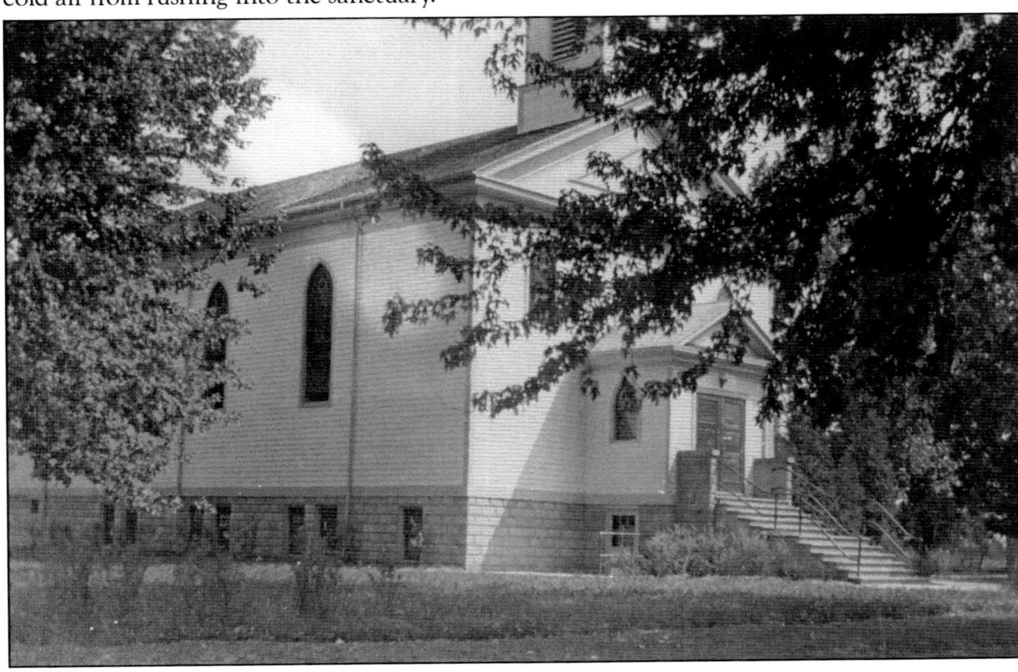

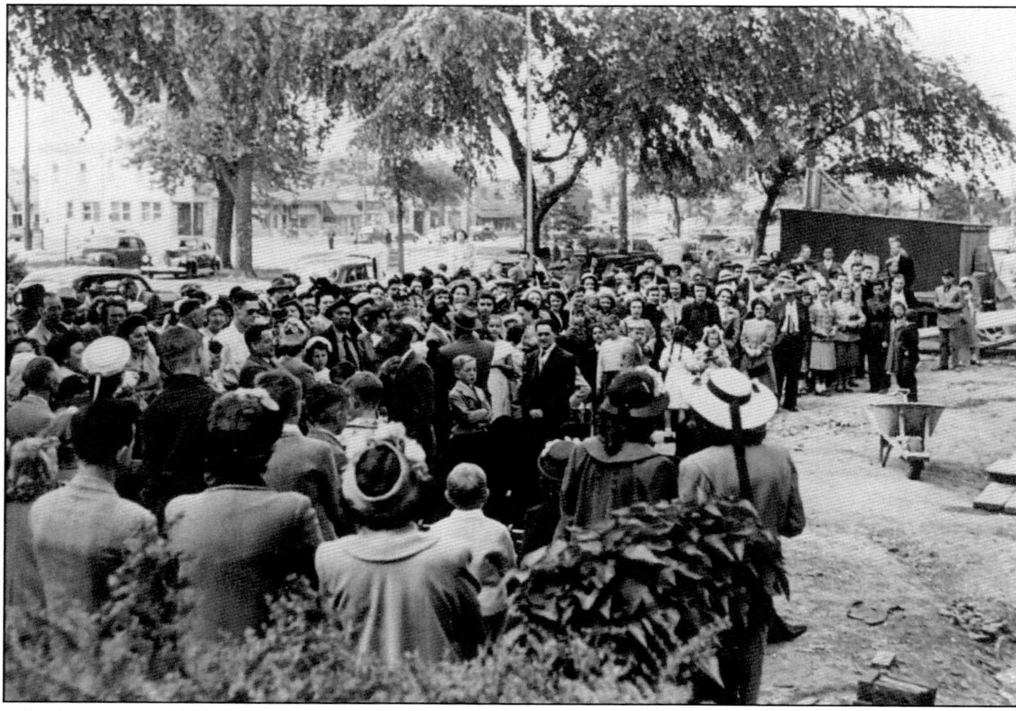

The frame church had been moved twice over the years, and Fr. Dennis Tighe did not think the structure could survive a third relocation when Gratiot Avenue was widened in 1928. Construction on the new building had begun, and only the basement could be completed before the Great Depression began. With construction projects on hold until after World War II, the basement served as the church's sanctuary. Above, a large crowd is present at the ground-breaking in 1949. Below are the two white frame entrances that led to the steps to the basement church.

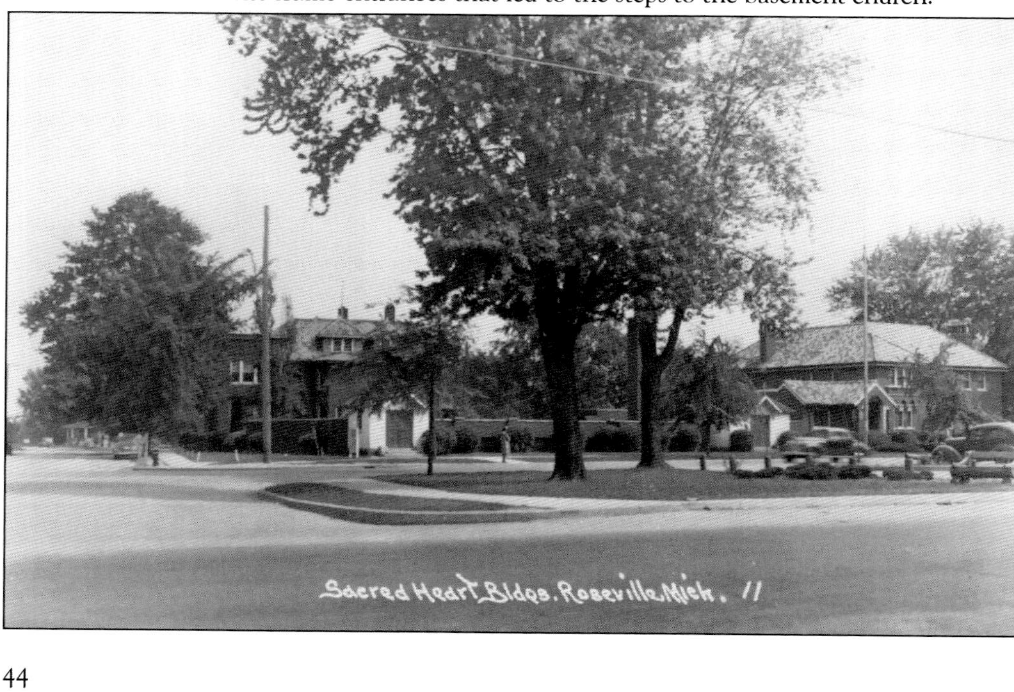

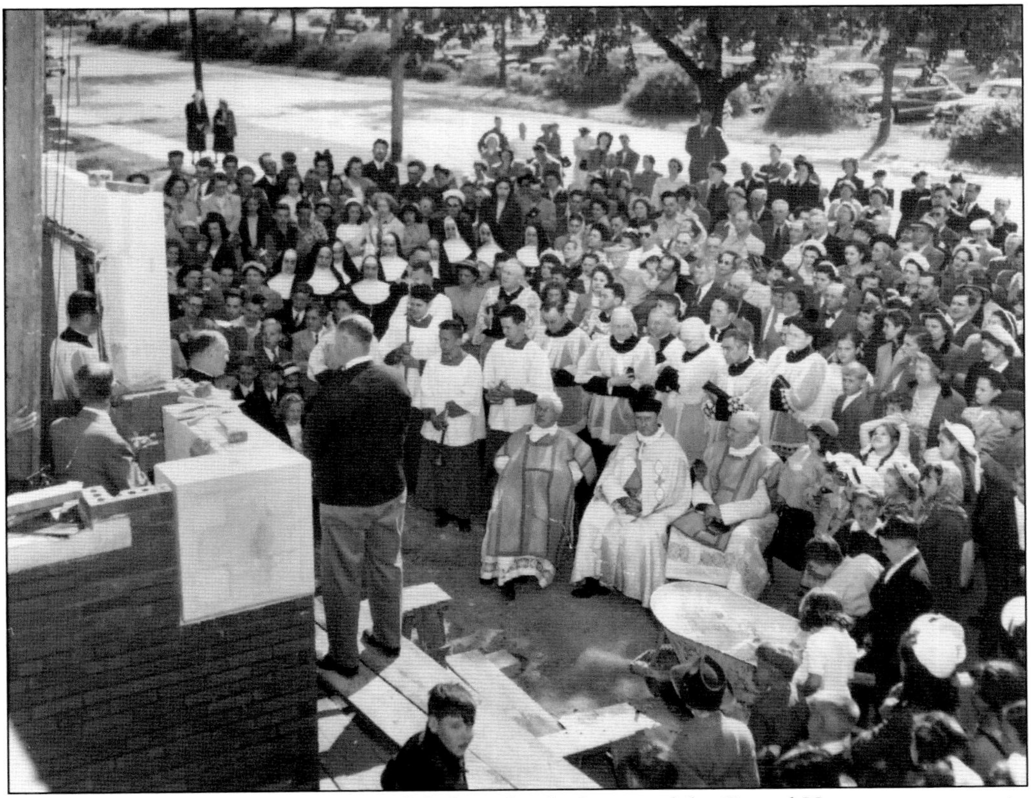

High Church officials turned out in full dress for the laying of the Sacred Heart cornerstone in 1950. Over the years, 22 new Catholic churches formed out of what was the original Sacred Heart parish. In the mid-21st century, the trend reversed itself with church closings and consolidations. After the 2014 mandated merger with St. Athanasius and Our Lady Queen of All Saints, the church's name was changed to St. Pio of Pietrelcina. In 2015, it was announced that Sacred Heart would close once renovations to St. Athanasius were completed, and the property would be offered for sale. All that will remain is the cemetery.

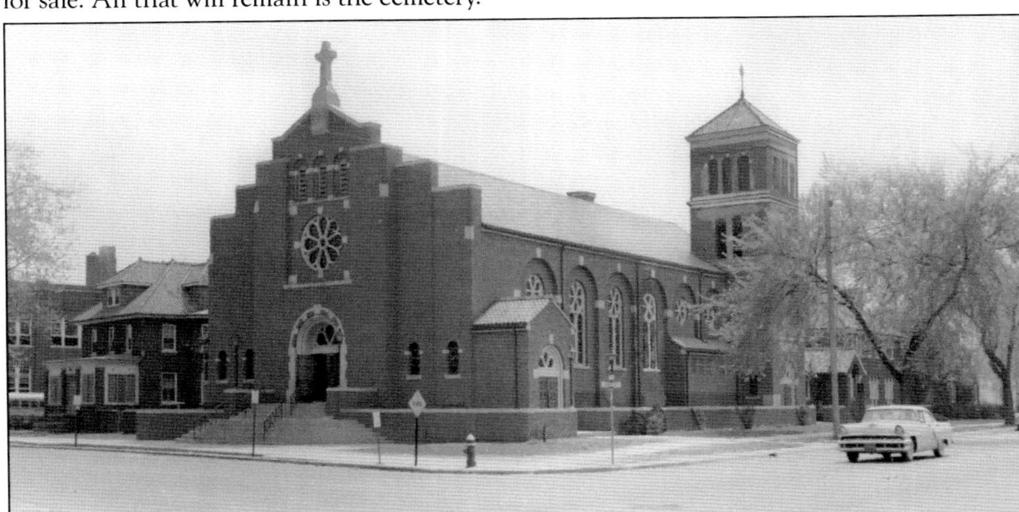

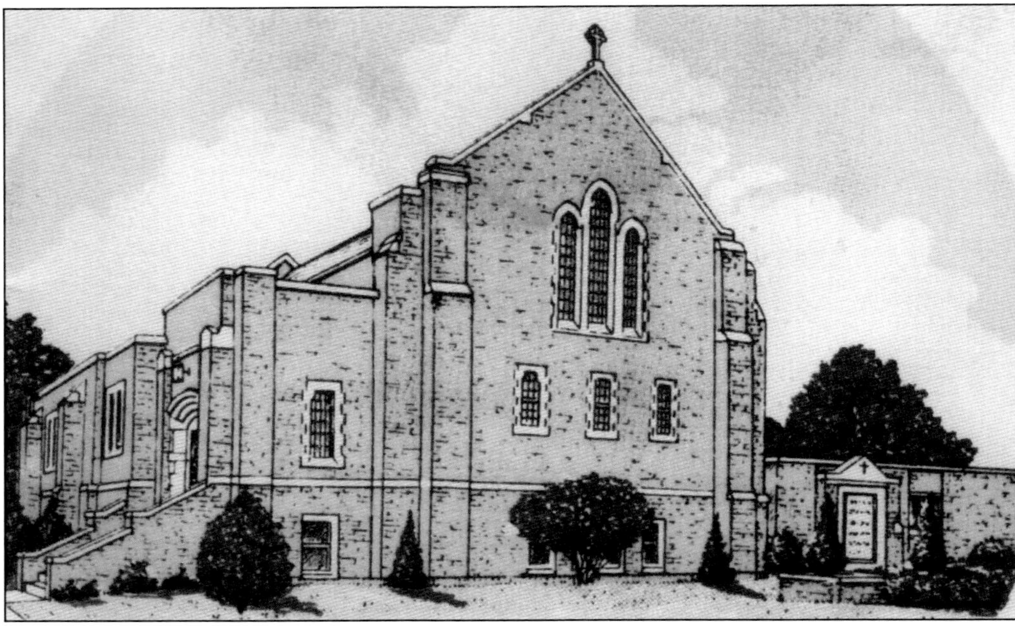

Originally organized in 1923 as a German Methodist Church, Trinity's first services were held in William Apps's Hardware Store at 11 Mile Road and Gratiot Avenue using a barrel for a pulpit. Trinity Methodist Episcopal Church, pictured above around 1925 in the artist's rendering, was destroyed by fire shortly after it was built. Devoted members began building a new church with a basement on 11 Mile Road at Fernwood. Services were held in the basement for many years until the sanctuary, below, was completed in 1949. Fate would deal another blow to the church and congregation with the arrival of the I-696 freeway, which forced the congregation to relocate and the church razed. Over the span of 92 years, the congregation has worshipped under three denominational names: Methodist Episcopal Church, Trinity Methodist Church, and Trinity United Methodist Church, as it is known today. (Both courtesy of Doreen Tavernier-Evans Baughn.)

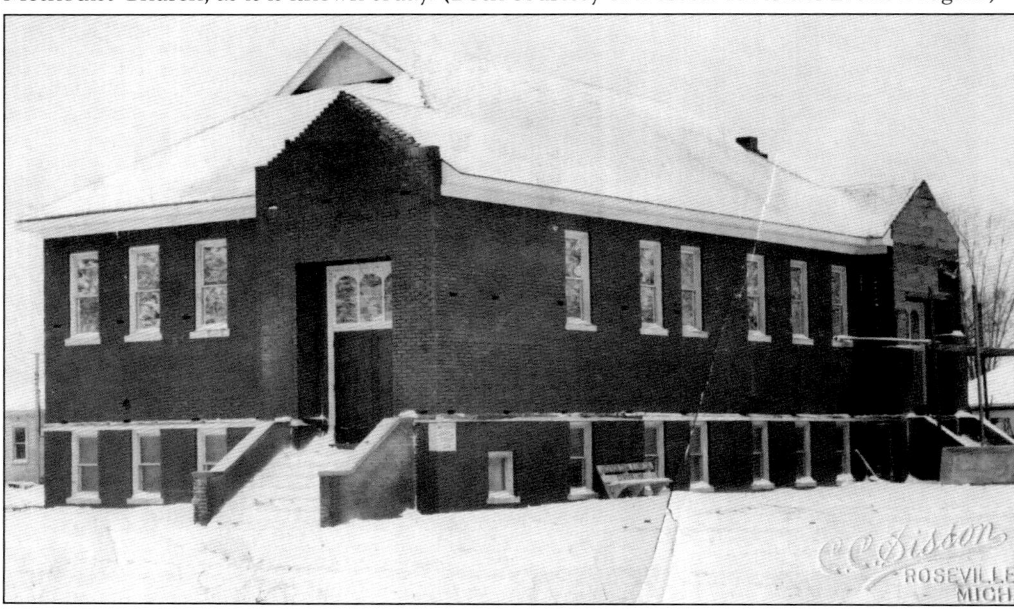

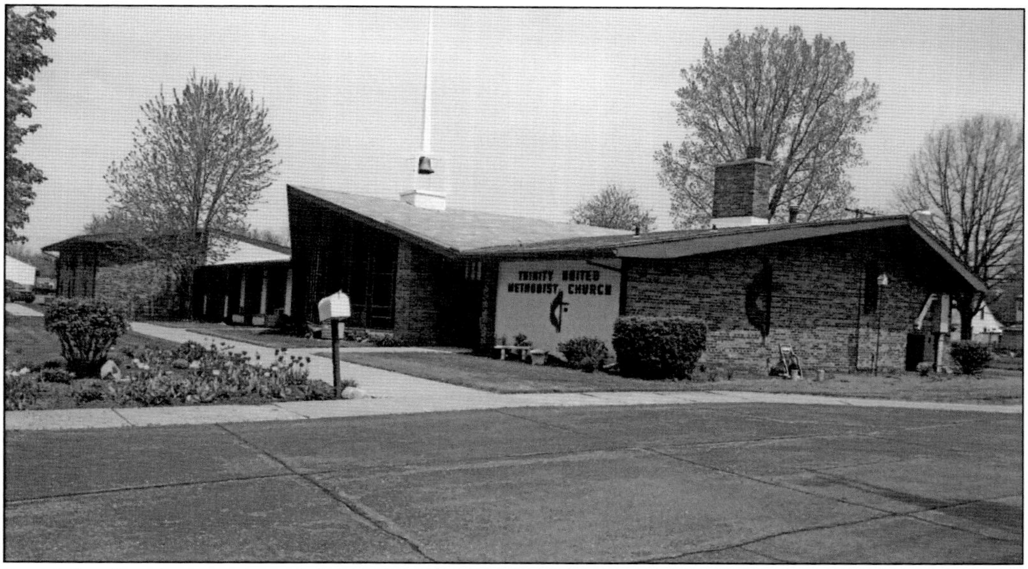

In 1971, after being evicted from their home to make room for the I-696 expressway, Trinity Methodist Church congregants purchased a small church, Lakeside Christian, on Common Road at Quinkert Street. Since then, a large addition with a kitchen, fellowship hall, restrooms, and classrooms was added. In 2002, Trinity added "United" to its name when Warren Wesley United Methodist Church joined its fold. (Courtesy of Doreen Tavernier-Evans Baughn.)

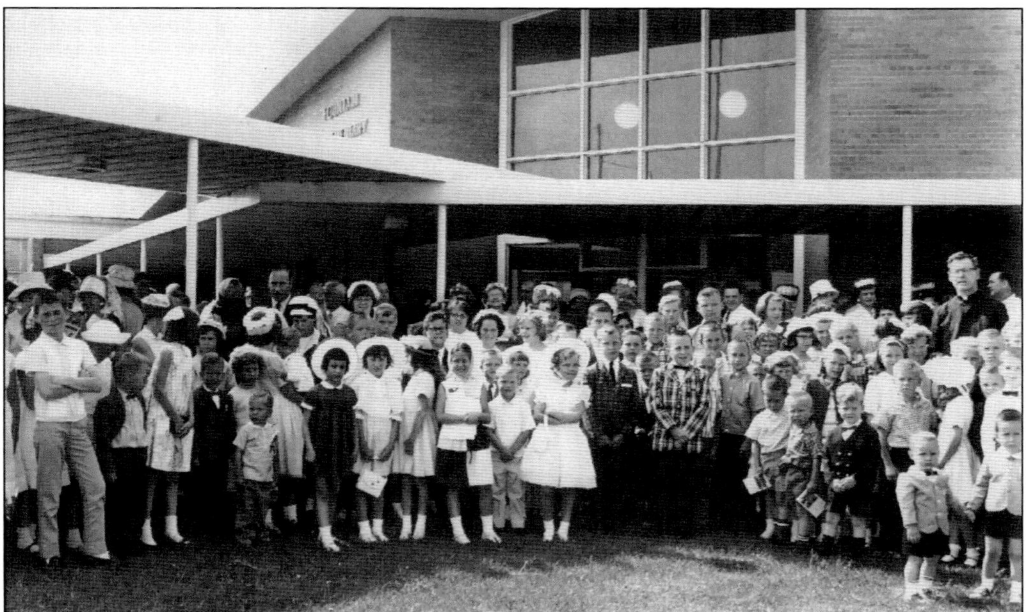

St. Donald Catholic Church, one of 22 spin-off parishes to come out of Sacred Heart, celebrated its first Mass on June 27, 1965, at Fountain Elementary School. Fr. Erwin J. Bauer (far right) was St. Donald's first pastor. St. Donald's, on 12 Mile Road near Groesbeck Highway, was dedicated on May 28, 1966. The parish had two other pastors before it closed on July 1, 2012: Fr. Edwin A. Schroeder and Fr. Michael Donovan. (Courtesy of St. Donald Catholic Church.)

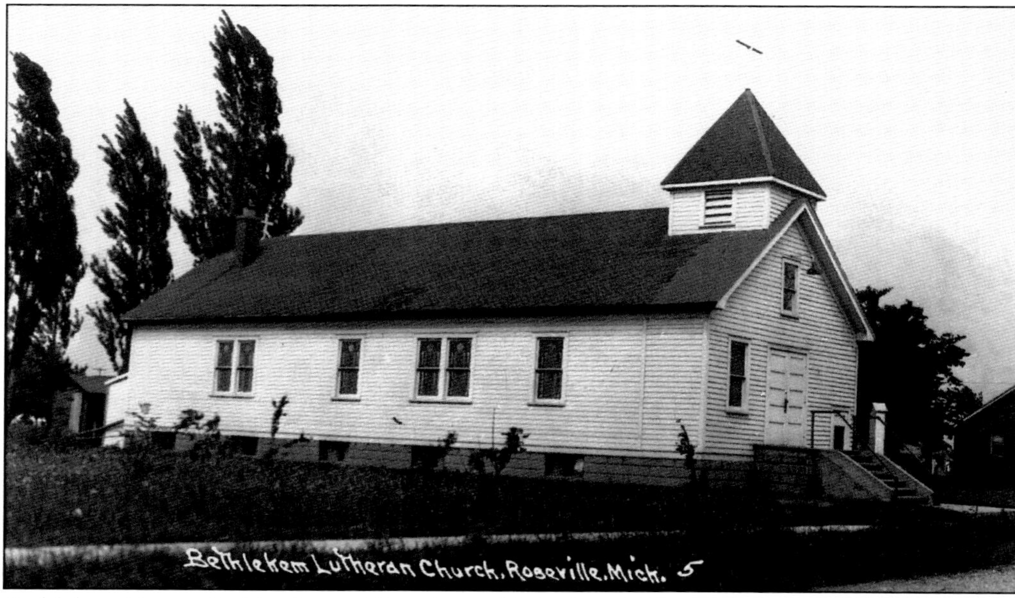

Bethlehem Evangelical Lutheran Church, established in 1925 under pastor Forest Friese, is one of Roseville's oldest parishes. Above is a photograph of the old church before the current church, pictured below around 1970, was built in 1948 on Gratiot Avenue next to the future Roseville municipal complex. The existing school wing was added in 1957, and at one time it was the third-largest Lutheran school in Michigan. The school closed in 2000. Today, it serves as the Bethlehem Early Learning Center. The Bethlehem flock today is served by Rev. Jeffrey D. Frechette Sr., pastor, and Rev. Jeffrey F. Fritz, emeritus. The old church building moved to Eastland and Ruthdale Streets and serves as the South Macomb Church of Christ, whose motto is "Serving Christ in our community for over 50 years."

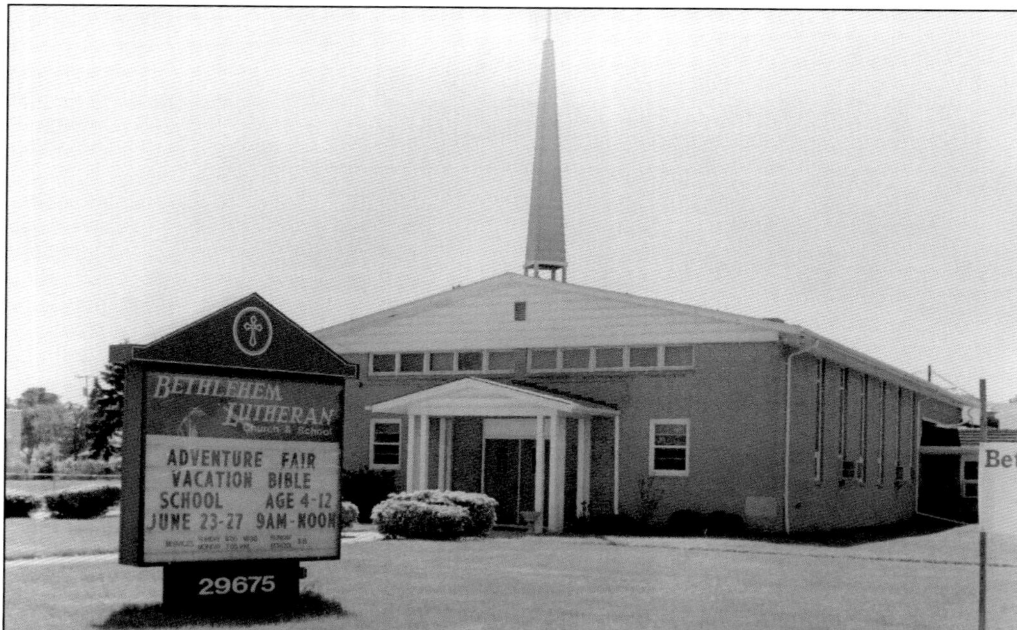

Four

Book Learnin'

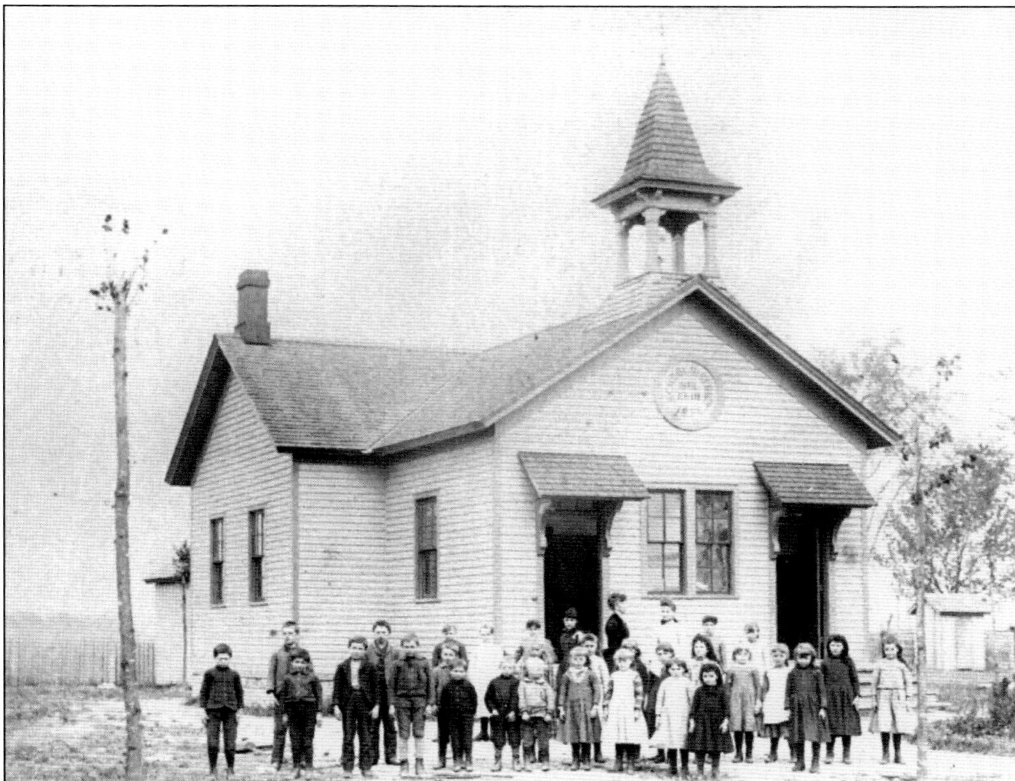

A new schoolhouse with a steeple was built in 1870 to replace the old log structure that had been in use since 1851. Erin Township was divided into six different school districts. The District 6 school was named Burton School. Schoolteacher Jennie Templeton, shown here with her students outside the school, taught at Burton for six years in the 1880s. She was remembered by her septuagenarian former students well into the 1950s and 1960s.

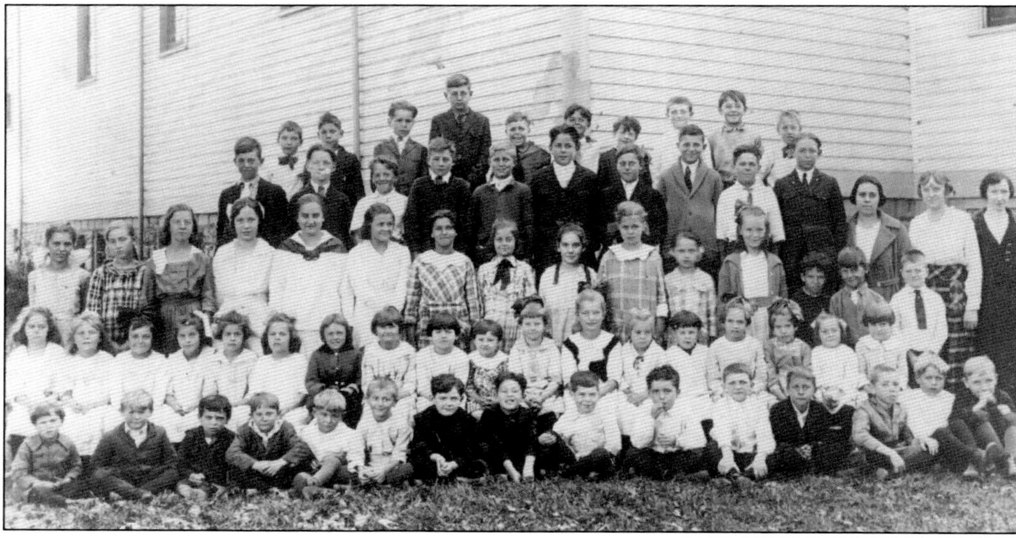

In September 1882, Sacred Heart opened its new schoolhouse to 12 students in grades one through eight. When Fr. Van Straelan was transferred, the school program ended. In 1918, new pastor Fr. Dennis P. Tighe, recognizing the need for a school, had the church basement divided into classrooms and hired three lay instructors. Sacred Heart schoolchildren pose outside the church for a photograph in 1919.

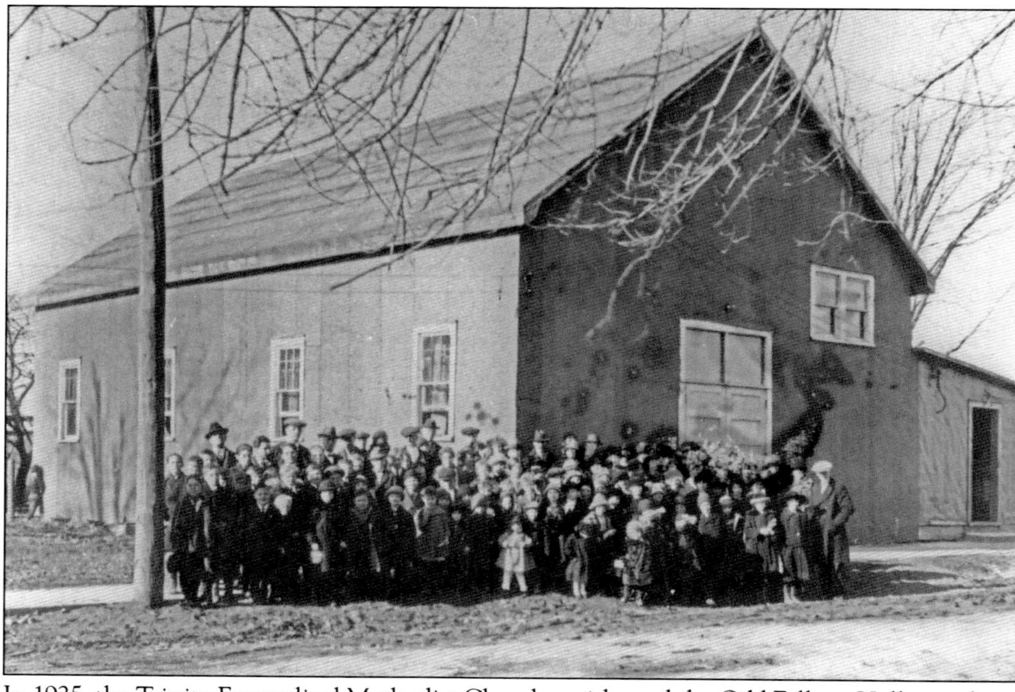

In 1925, the Trinity Evangelical Methodist Church parish used the Odd Fellows Hall, seen here, while its church was being built. The Odd Fellows Hall was the home of the local lodge of the Independent Order of Odd Fellows, a British fraternal organization exported to the United States in 1819. Its members were called "Odd Fellows" because, in 18th-century England, it was thought odd for people to organize to help others.

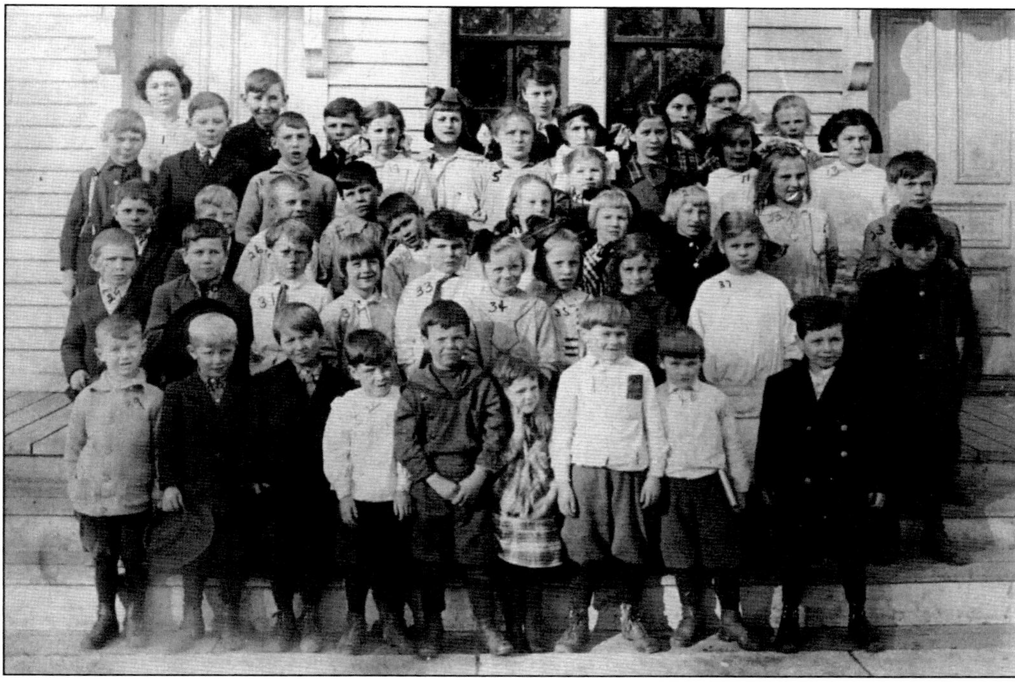

Some 46 children attended Eleanor Geis's class in 1916. Roseville's pioneer family names such as Van Howe, Flechsig, Brohl, Demerick, and Jahn were all represented. In 1917, Roseville's one-room schoolhouse on 11 Mile Road (Town Hall Road), east of Gratiot Avenue, was moved from the site and converted into a private home. A 1946 city directory lists Eleanor Geis as a piano teacher living at 27315 Bohn Street.

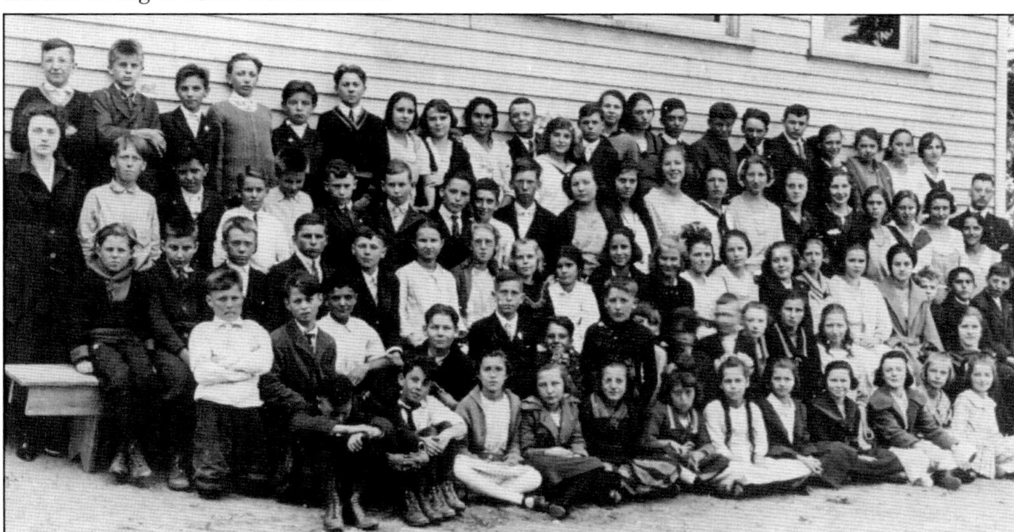

Pictured here is the Burton High School class of 1920. Principal Duvall stands on the far right, and teacher Marion Hall on the far left. Roseville founding family names represented in the class were Apps, Peters, Flechsig, and Kaiser. With the introduction of the automobile, Roseville attracted many newcomers. Between 1922 and 1928, Roseville's school enrollment was less than 350; by 1928, it grew to almost 1,000.

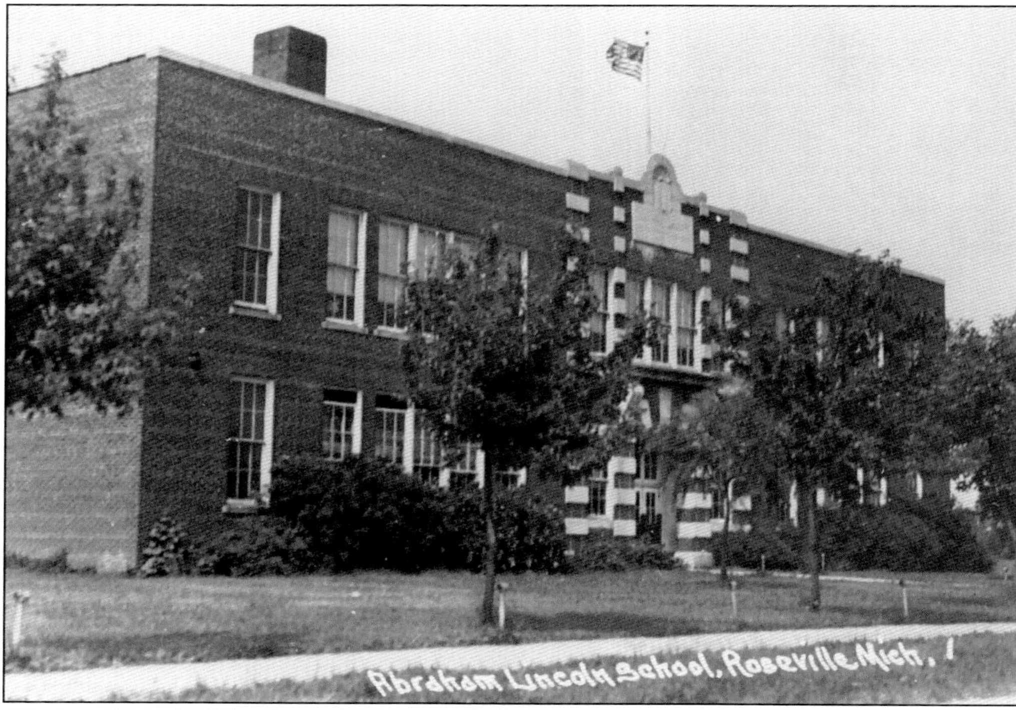

Abraham Lincoln School, on the corner of Chestnut and Blum Streets in Roseville, was built in 1925. The community was growing, and along with it public schools were being built to accommodate the student population. By 1930, the village of Roseville's population was 6,836. Just 10 years prior, all of Erin Township's population, including Roseville, was 2,791.

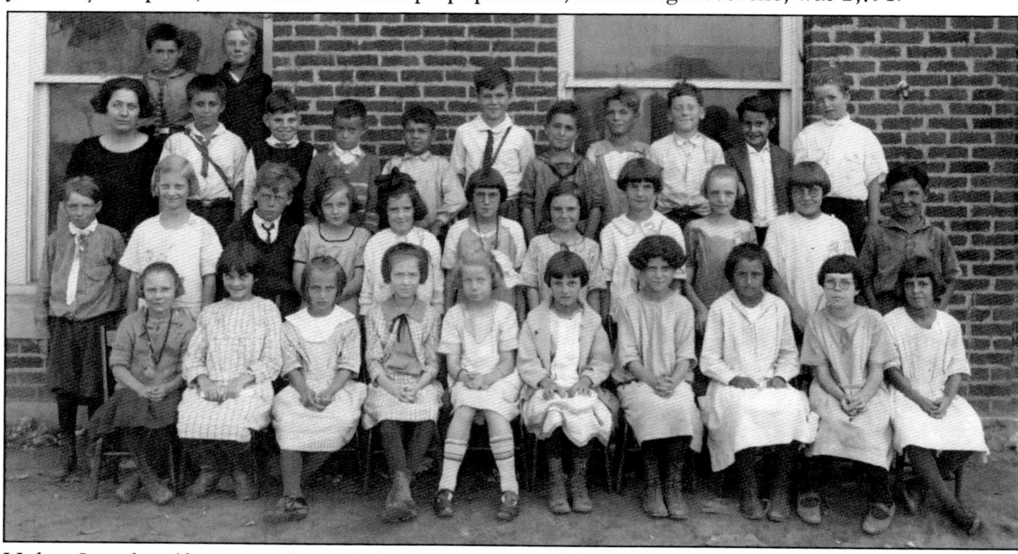

Helen Lumley (first row, far right) was 11 years old when this class photograph at Lincoln Elementary was taken in 1925. The teacher, Mrs. Neverth, is pictured in the third row on the far left. According to the 1930 Census, Lila Neverth ran a boardinghouse for schoolteachers on nearby Town Hall Road with her husband, Albert, who was also a teacher. Lincoln School was closed permanently in 2010 and demolished a few years later. (Courtesy of Janice Carter.)

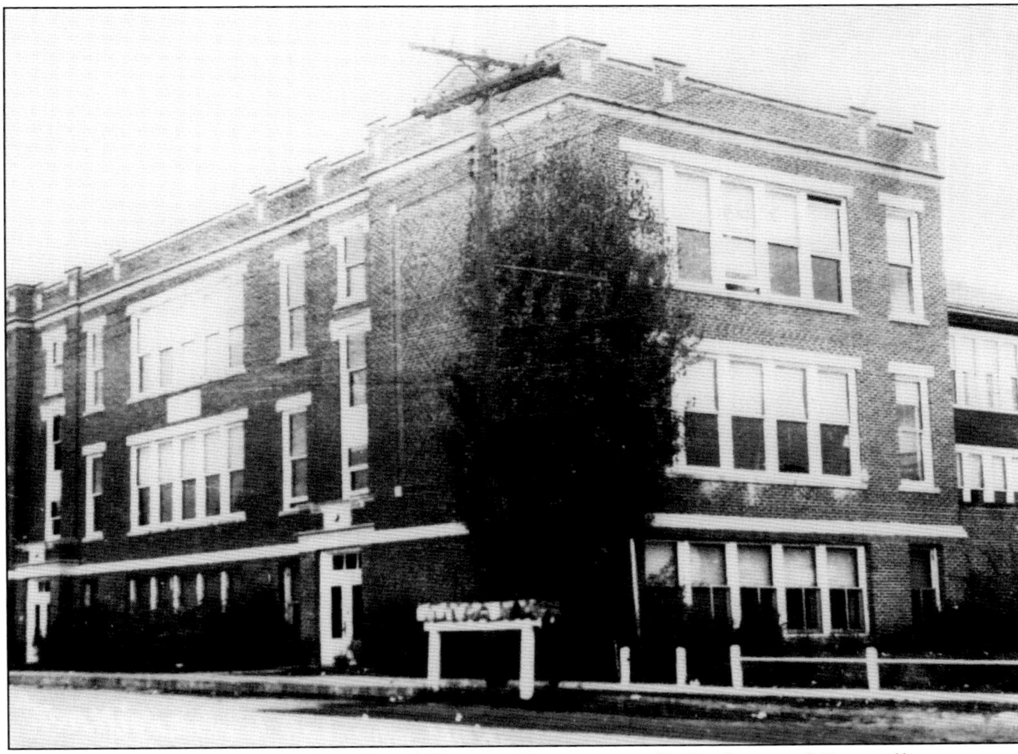

The Burton High School (above) and Burton Gymnasium (below) served Roseville teenagers for many years. The school was built in 1922, and the gymnasium was added in 1927. The 1922 version included 10 classrooms, administrative offices, and a basement gymnasium. When the new 60-foot-by-90-foot brick gymnasium adjacent to the school was completed, it was hailed as one of the finest sporting facilities in Macomb County. It allowed the school district to host district and regional basketball tournaments. In 1956, when Roseville High School was completed on Barkman at Martin Road, Burton became a junior high school. In 1966, the old Burton school was torn down and replaced by a newer structure.

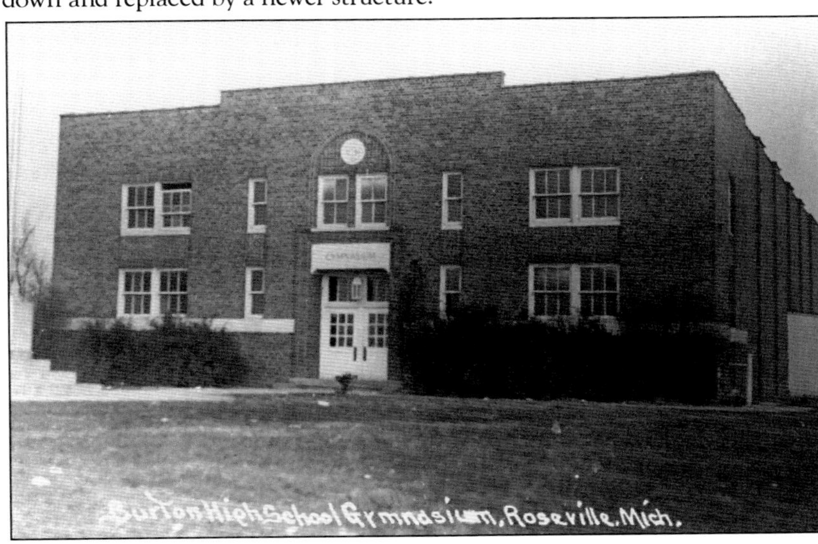

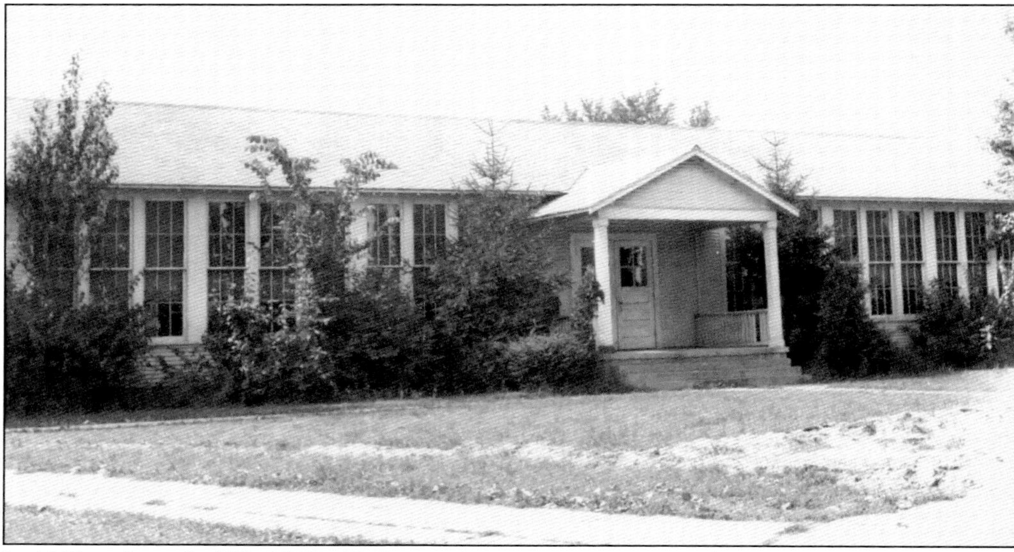

In 1947, at the end of World War II, Burton Annex was necessary to handle the increasing number of students in Roseville. In 1943, during World War II, Roseville added one school, MacArthur Elementary School, on 11 Mile Road near the present I-94 expressway. Between 1940 and 1950, Roseville's population grew from 9,023 to 15,816.

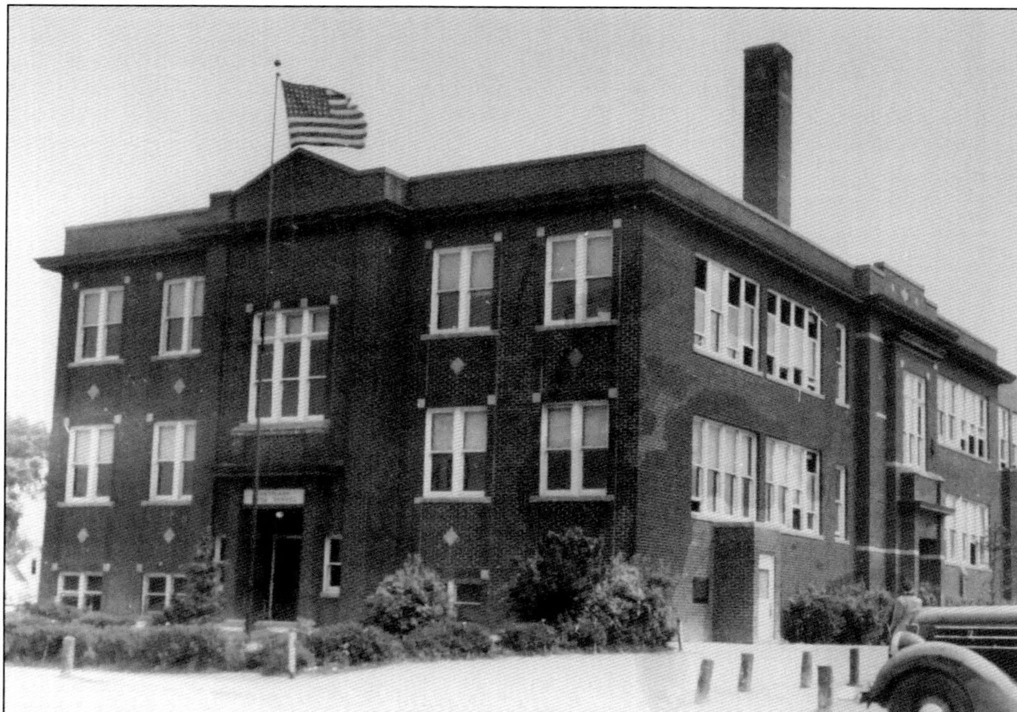

Originally part of the Eastland School District, Eastland High School was located on Eastland Street at Park Street. Built in 1922, the school was limited to 10 grades until 1934. The first graduating class was in 1935. In 1956, the district merged with Roseville. The last superintendent was John McLeod. The building also served as a middle school and middle school annex.

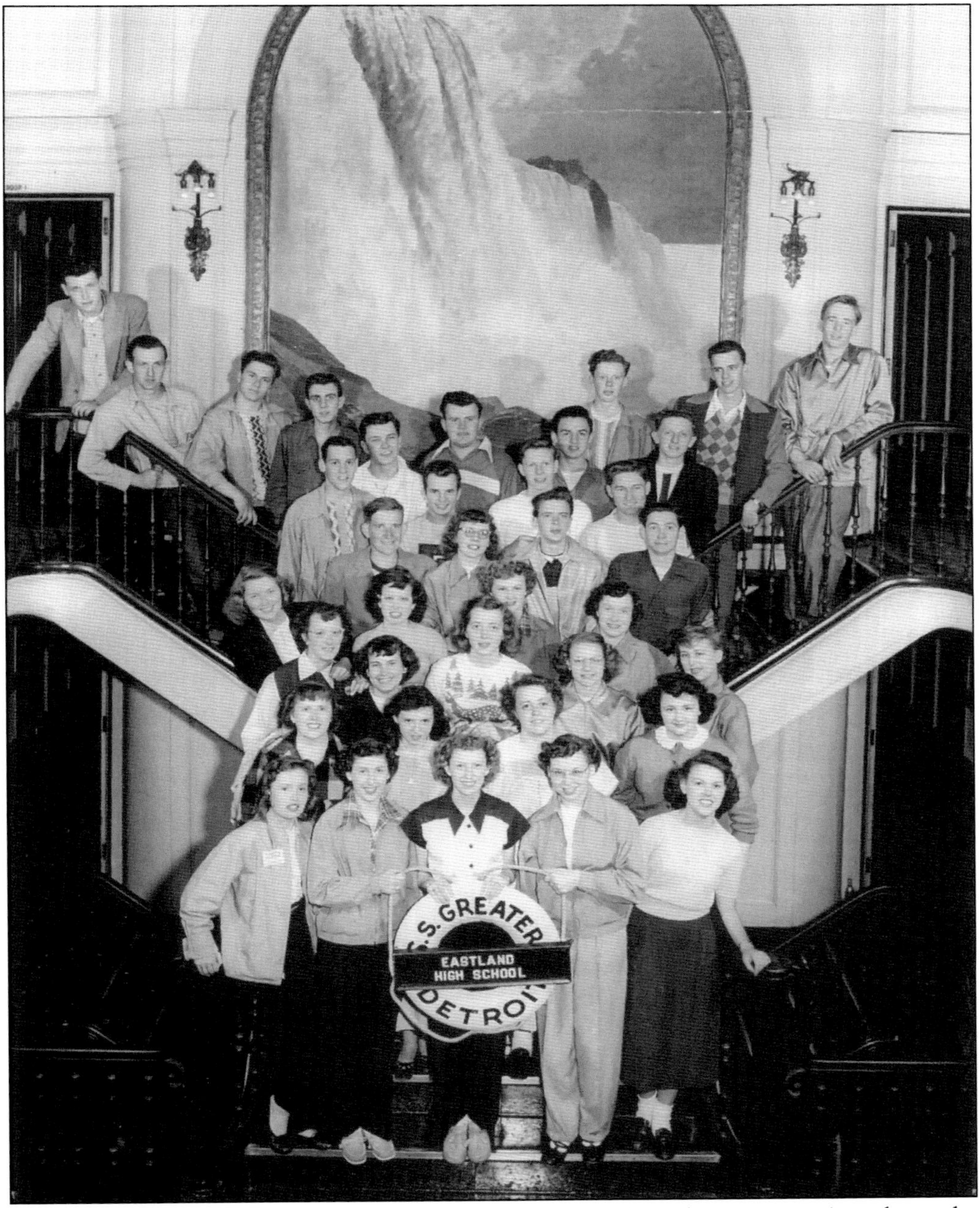

The Eastland High School class of 1950 got creative with their class portrait. At right in the first row is Pat Chownyk (Delmotte), the 2014–2015 president of the Roseville Historical and Genealogical Society. Two rooms were added over the auditorium in 1935 with the assistance of the government's Federal Workers Agency. The total cost was $10,277, with the school contributing $2,216. The first graduating class in 1935 consisted of eight students and the last in 1956 had 56 graduates. The school was torn down to make way for a senior-housing complex that remains to this day. (Courtesy of Pat Chownyk.)

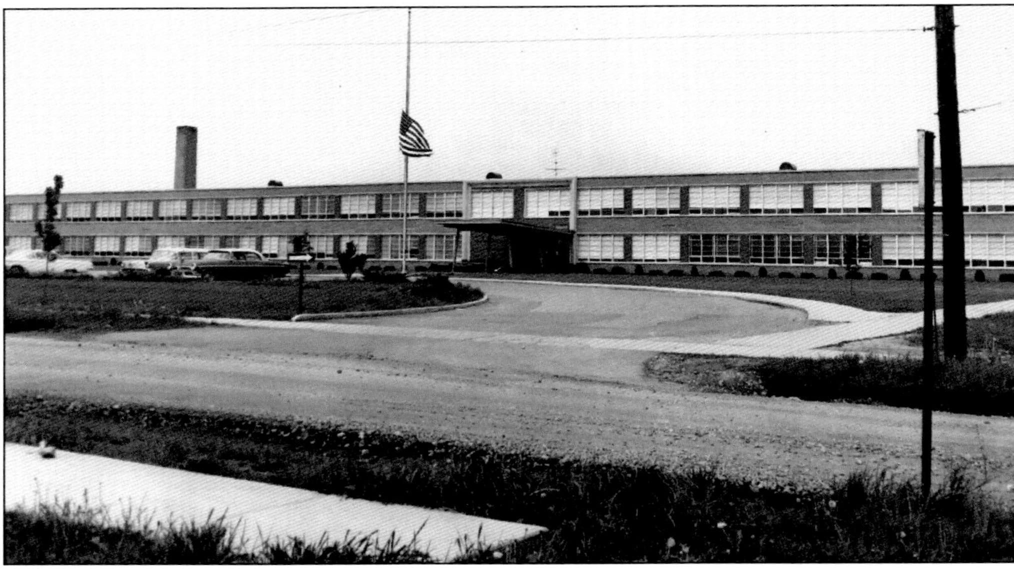

Roseville High School, seen above, on Barkman at Martin Road, was built in 1956 and served as the city's only high school until Carl Brablec High School was established in 1967. Roseville High School housed both schools until the completion of Carl Brablec in 1969. Though housed in the same building, each school maintained separate personnel. Below, school superintendent Carl Brablec (far right) is attending an early-1950s dance at Roseville High School. The other men in front are, from left to right, Ralph Erickson (with mustache), Glen Alsip, and in the center looking serious is band teacher Seraphime Mike. School dances in the 1950s were typically held in the gymnasium and well attended by students, teachers, and administrators.

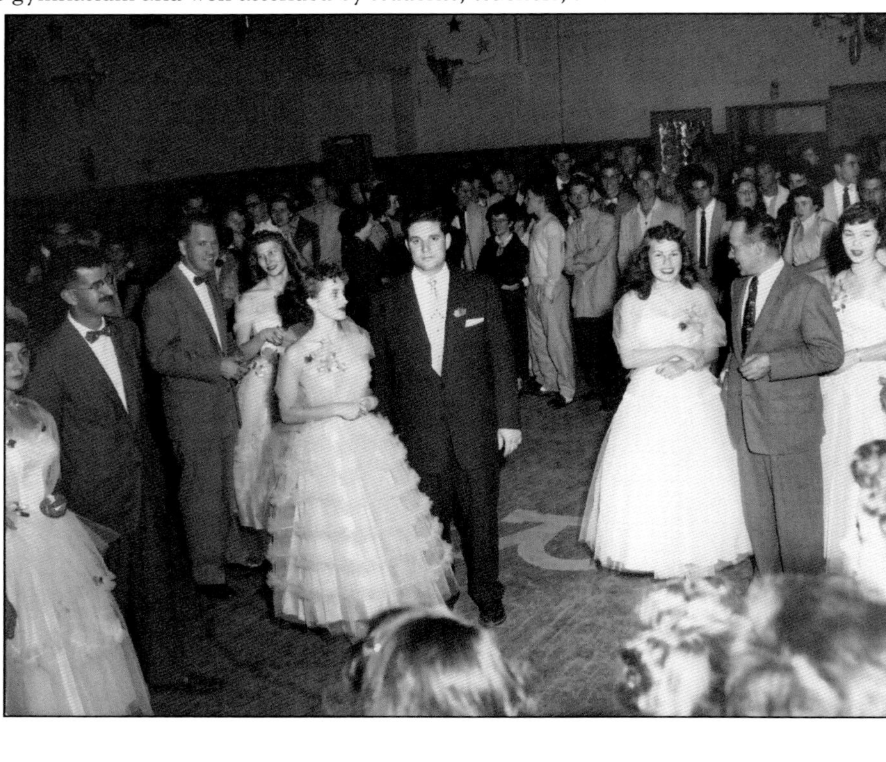

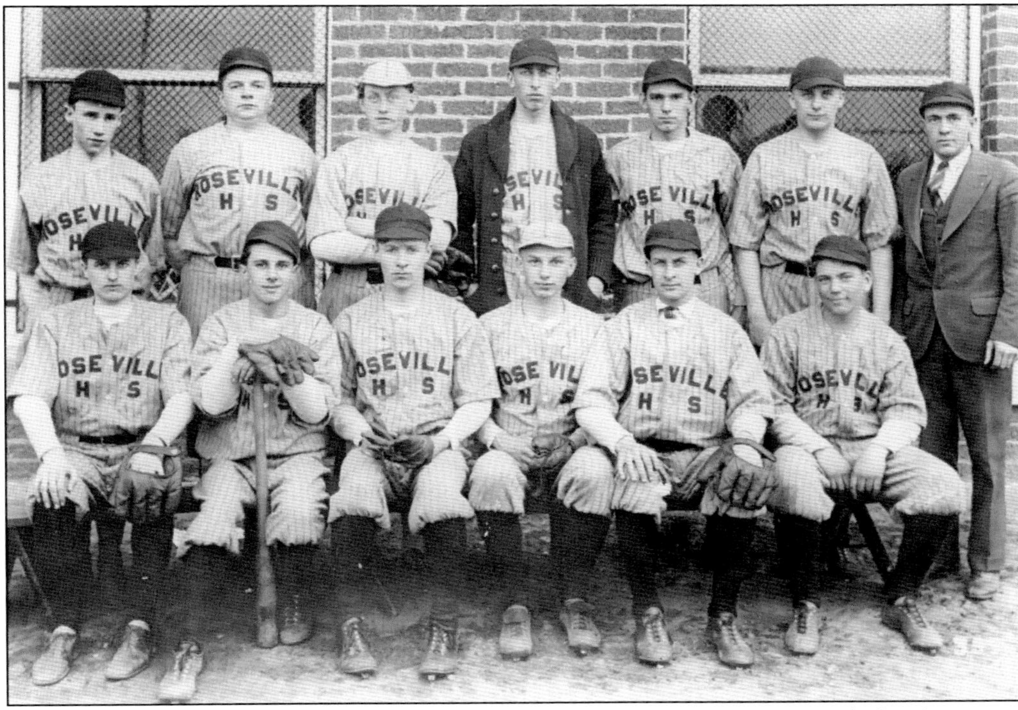

Coach Robert Nunn was also a Roseville High School teacher for many years before becoming Roseville's first city clerk. Robert and Vera Nunn (née Kennedy) had two children, Larry and Patricia. Both parents were well educated, and they encouraged their children to pursue their educations. Pat graduated with a teaching certificate from Eastern Michigan University and taught in the Roseville Community Schools for a few years before moving to Farmington Hills, Michigan.

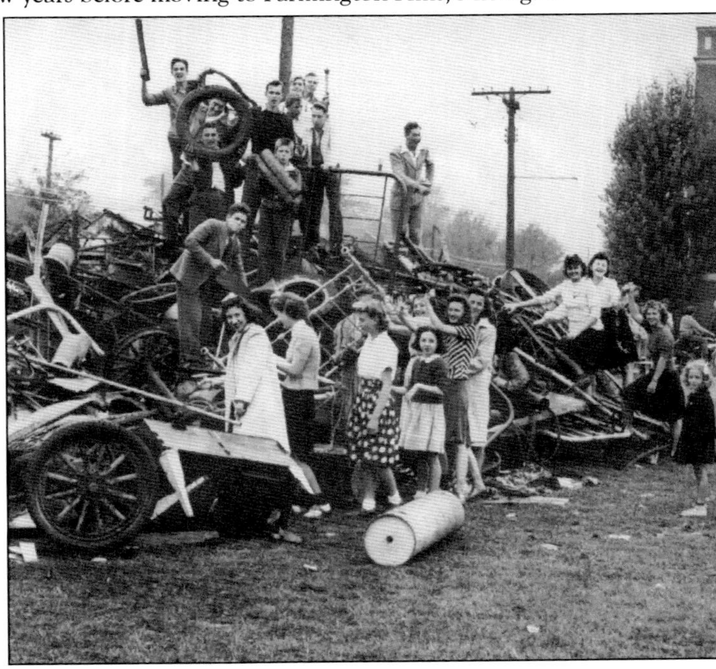

According to Roseville High School's 1943 yearbook, *The Tower*, "The highly successful scrap drive is a symbol of the students' ability, cooperation and willingness which characterizes all their participation in the war effort." Scrap drives proved to be a huge morale booster for civilians during the war. In 1943, pennies made from zinc-coated steel were issued so that copper could be reserved for the war effort. (Courtesy of Dwain Lusk.)

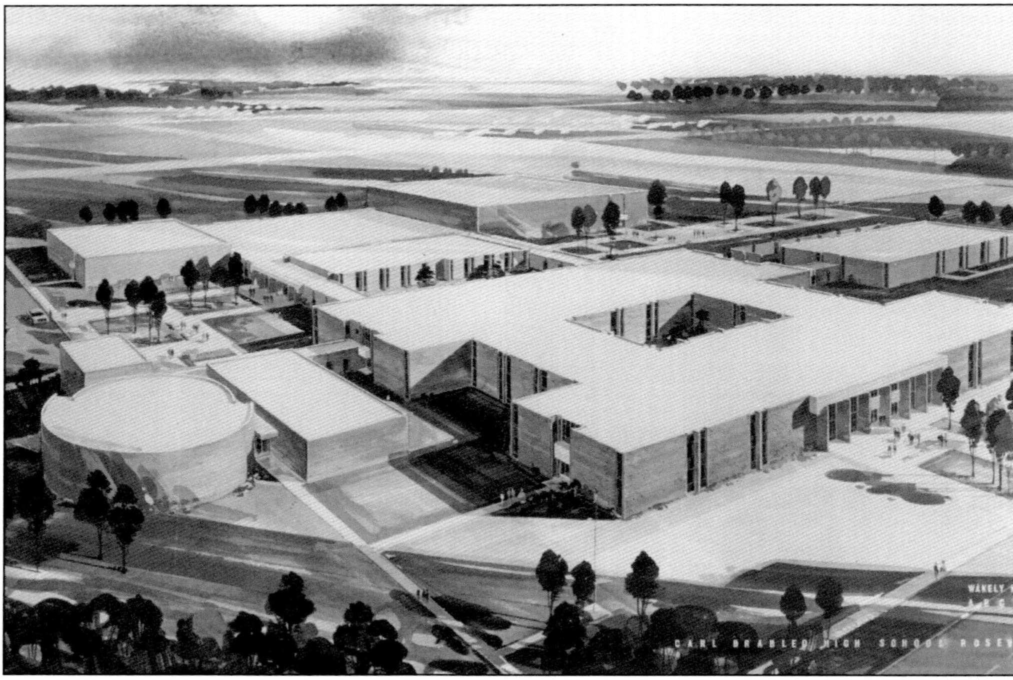

Carl Brablec High School, shown here in a rendering by Wakely Kushner Associates Architects, became Roseville's "new, modern" high school when it opened in 1969. The new school included a planetarium and was built on the north end of town at the intersection of Common Road and Normal Street. The school was named after the former school superintendent.

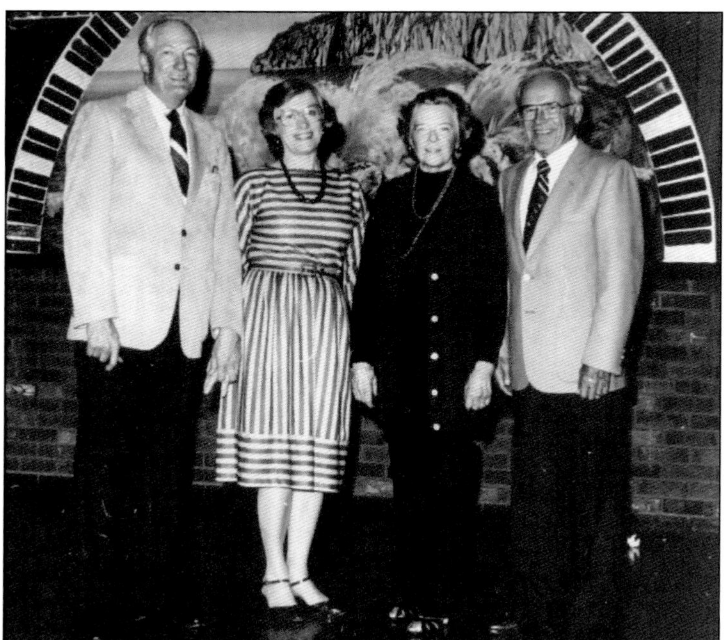

Longtime superintendent of schools Carl Brablec (far right) is pictured with his wife, Dorothy, and John and Maxine McLeod. John, a 1940 graduate of Eastland High School, spent many years as a Roseville Community Schools employee, holding positions as teacher and later the first principal at Carl Brablec High School. After retiring, he served on the Roseville Board of Education for nine years.

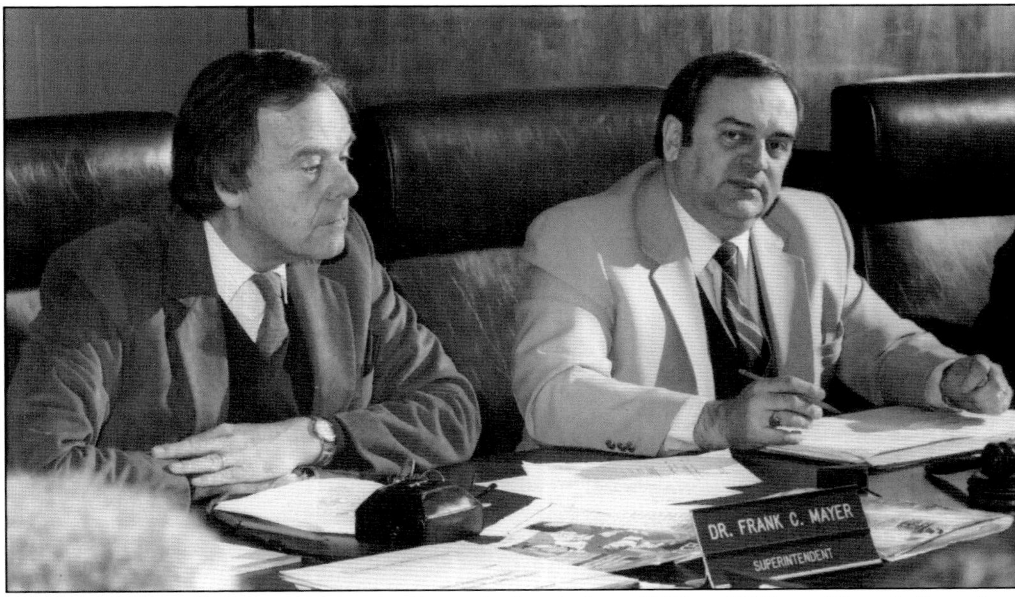

Dr. Frank Mayer (left) was superintendent of schools from 1973 to 1988, and Joseph Steenland (right) served as president of the Roseville Board of Education for 29 years. Steenland was first elected to the board in 1976; he served as trustee, treasurer, and secretary before becoming president. Joseph G. Steenland Elementary School, located on the corner of Barkman and Chestnut Streets, was built and named in his honor.

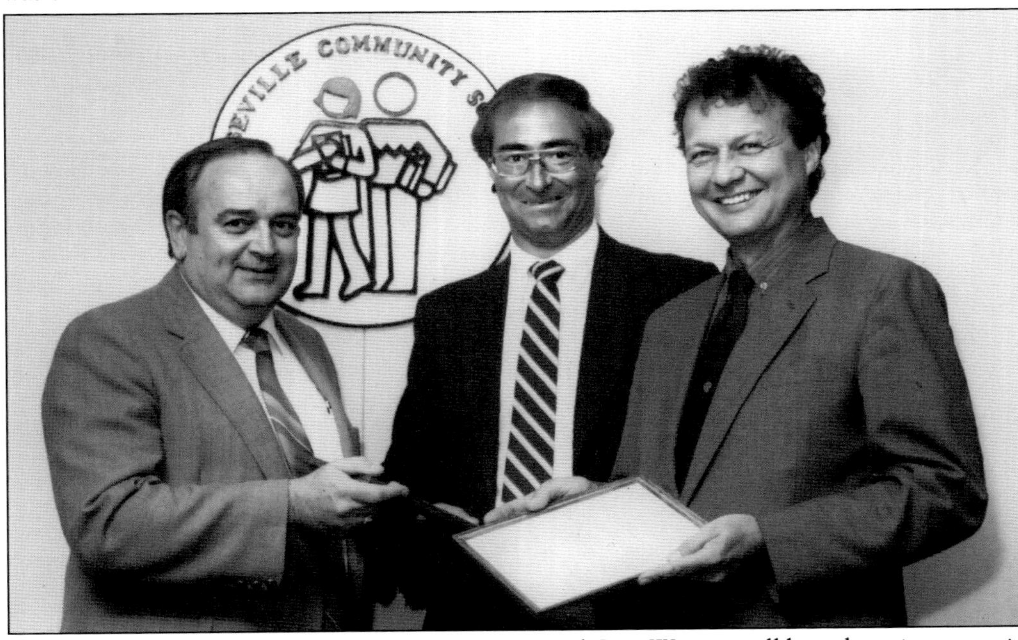

From left to right, Joseph Steenland, John Kment, and Curt Winnega all have longtime roots in the Roseville Community Schools. Kment, a longtime employee of the district, began teaching in it in 1968 and was appointed superintendent in August 1988; he continues to serve in that role. In 2009, both Kment and Steenland were honored when two new elementary schools, the first new schools built in 40 years, were named for them.

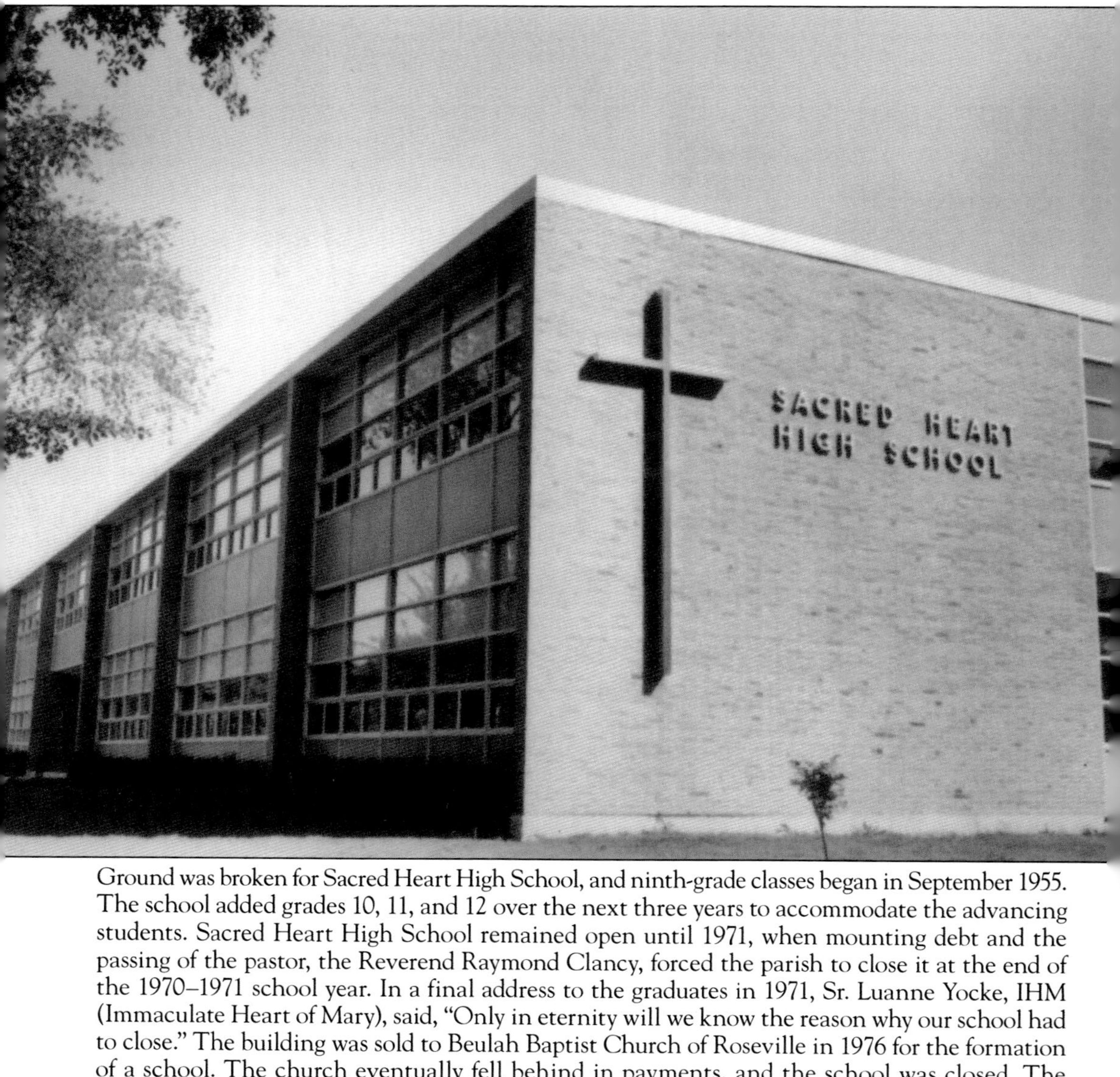

Ground was broken for Sacred Heart High School, and ninth-grade classes began in September 1955. The school added grades 10, 11, and 12 over the next three years to accommodate the advancing students. Sacred Heart High School remained open until 1971, when mounting debt and the passing of the pastor, the Reverend Raymond Clancy, forced the parish to close it at the end of the 1970–1971 school year. In a final address to the graduates in 1971, Sr. Luanne Yocke, IHM (Immaculate Heart of Mary), said, "Only in eternity will we know the reason why our school had to close." The building was sold to Beulah Baptist Church of Roseville in 1976 for the formation of a school. The church eventually fell behind in payments, and the school was closed. The building stood following a fire in 1981 for another four years before being demolished in 1985. The adjacent cemetery has since been expanded and now resides on the property.

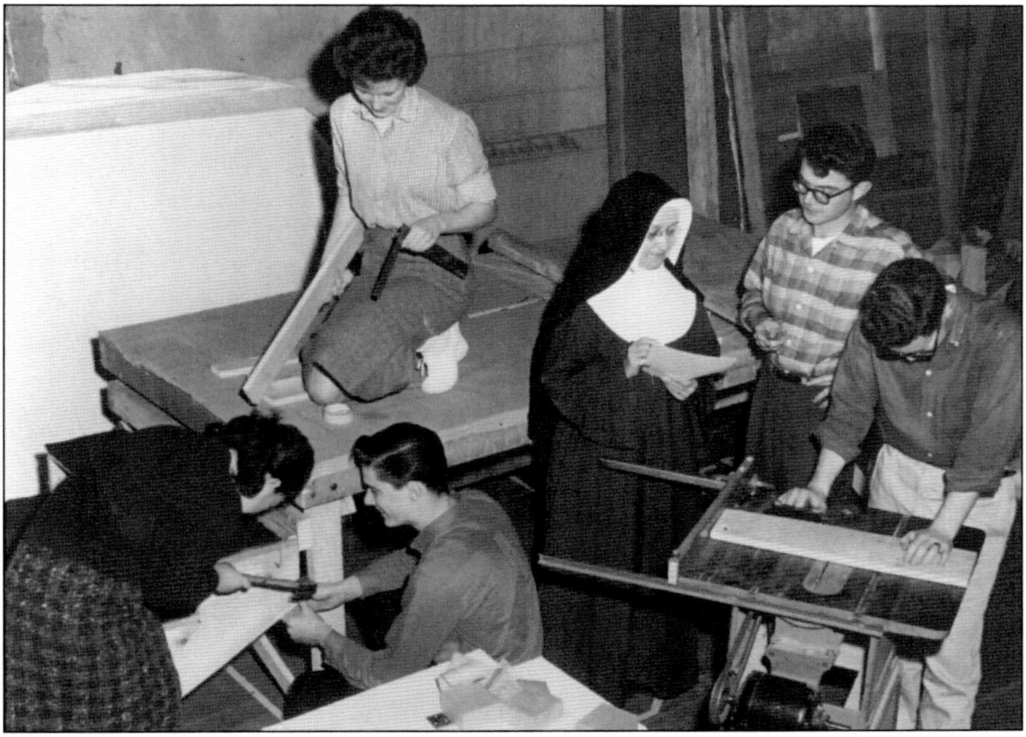

More than 1,700 students in first through twelfth grade were enrolled at Sacred Heart in 1961. The school's Little Theater presented the play *Harvey*, for which students built the set under the watchful eye of the nuns. Senior teachers were IHM Sisters Rosalie and Rebecca and James Zimmerman. Mother Mary Clotilde Schrage was principal. All 99 members of the senior class graduated on June 11.

In 1920, Sacred Heart pastor Fr. Dennis P. Tighe received permission to construct a new school and contacted the Sisters, Servants of the Immaculate Heart of Mary for permission to have three nuns teach at the new school. In 1921, with the school built, the nuns began teaching 130 students in grades one through eight.

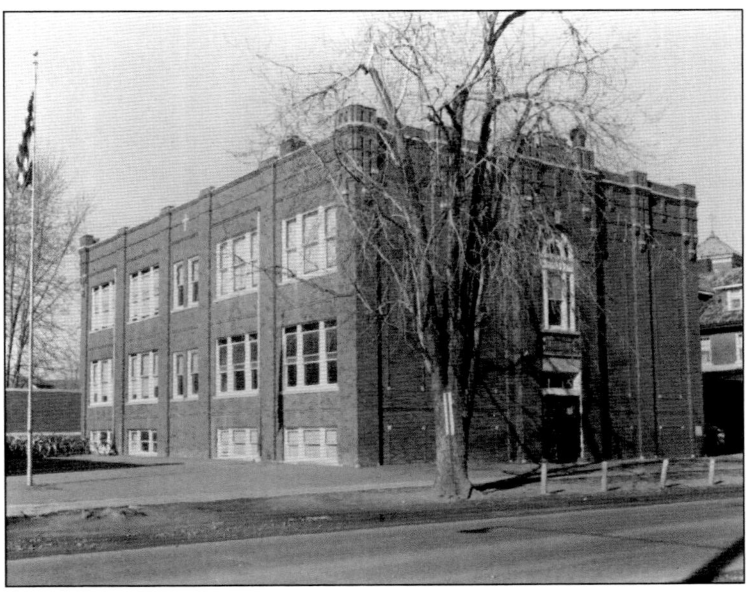

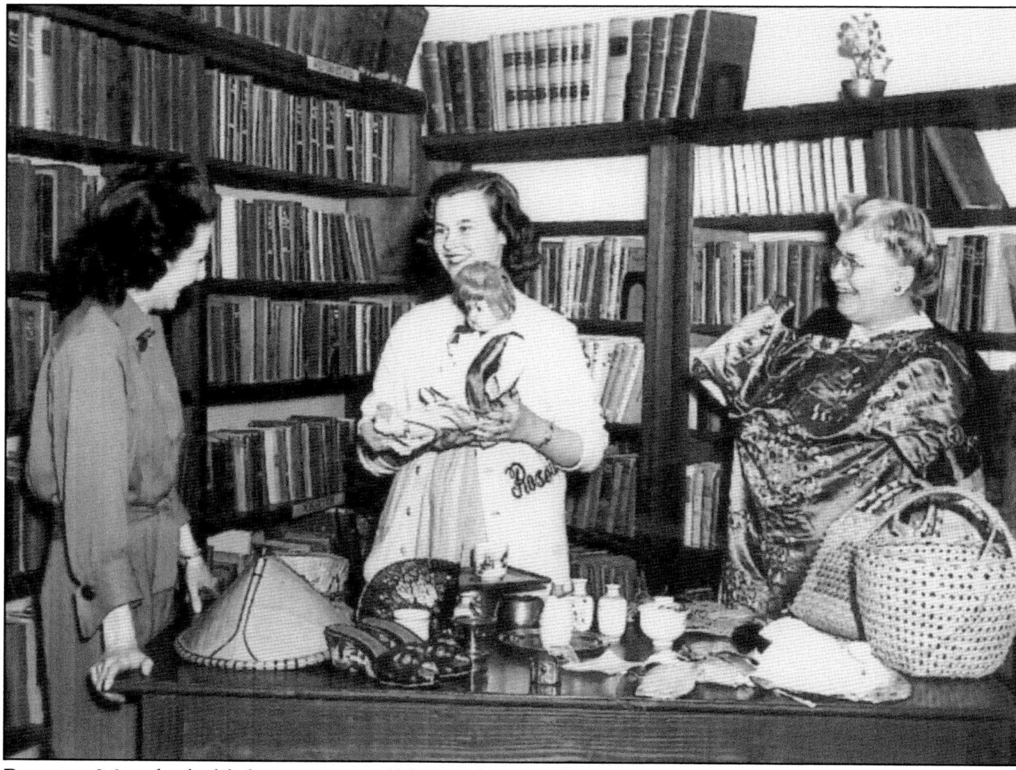

Beatrice Murphy held the position of library director from 1937 to 1961. Murphy (at right, holding a Korean gown) is pictured with Sally Clark (center), a high school intern, and Julie Cooper, also a library employee. Murphy was born on January 19, 1895. She died in September 1970 at the age of 75.

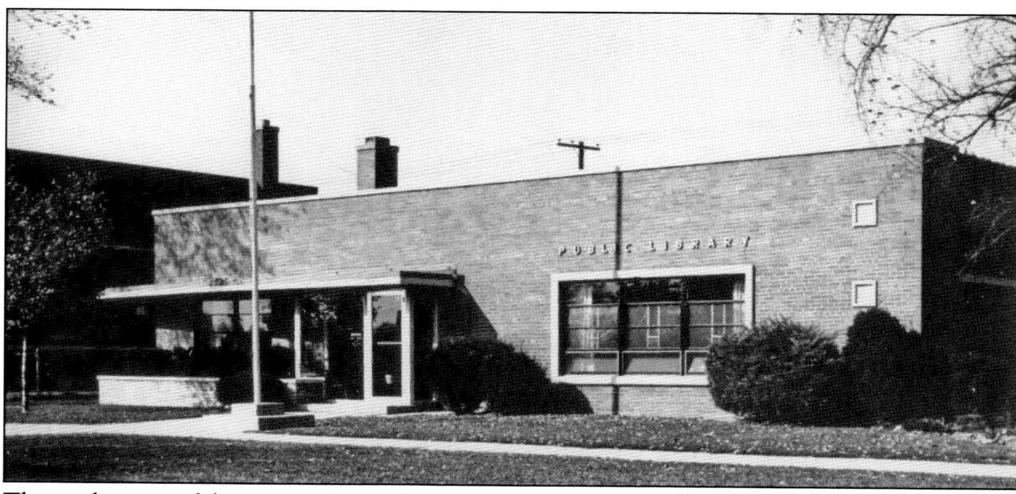

The predecessor of the current Roseville Public Library was a small, low-profile building on Gratiot Avenue, just north of 11 Mile Road, from 1958 to 1975, when the new library and municipal complex were built off Common Road, just west of Gratiot. The public library dates back to 1936 with the formation of the Roseville-Erin Township Library Association and the one-room Erin Township Library in the then new Roseville Municipal Building.

Library clerk Irene Wingate is seen in the library building on Gratiot Avenue around the Christmas holidays in the 1960s. The aluminum Christmas tree was popular in the United States in the late 1950s to mid-1960s. The trees were traditionally illuminated from below by a rotating color wheel. Wingate retired as a library assistant in 1995 and was presented with a retirement watch from Mayor Gerald Alsip.

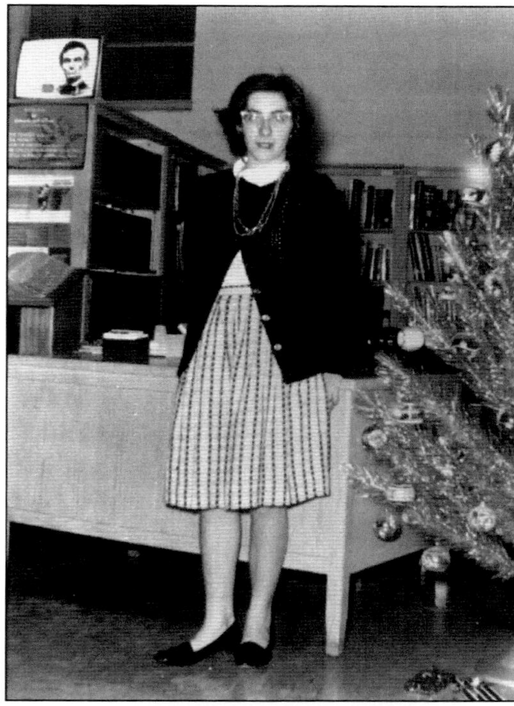

Roseville Library director Rose Kollmorgen (seated on the floor) enjoys a gathering with the library commission and staff. She served as director for 31 years: 1973 to 2002. With the retirement of Beatrice Murphy in 1961, Shirley V. Brabant became Roseville's first professionally trained director. She was succeeded by Mildred Borkowski in 1971 and Marilyn J. Sharrow in 1972. Kollmorgen was succeeded by Rita Valade. The current director is Jacalynn Harvey.

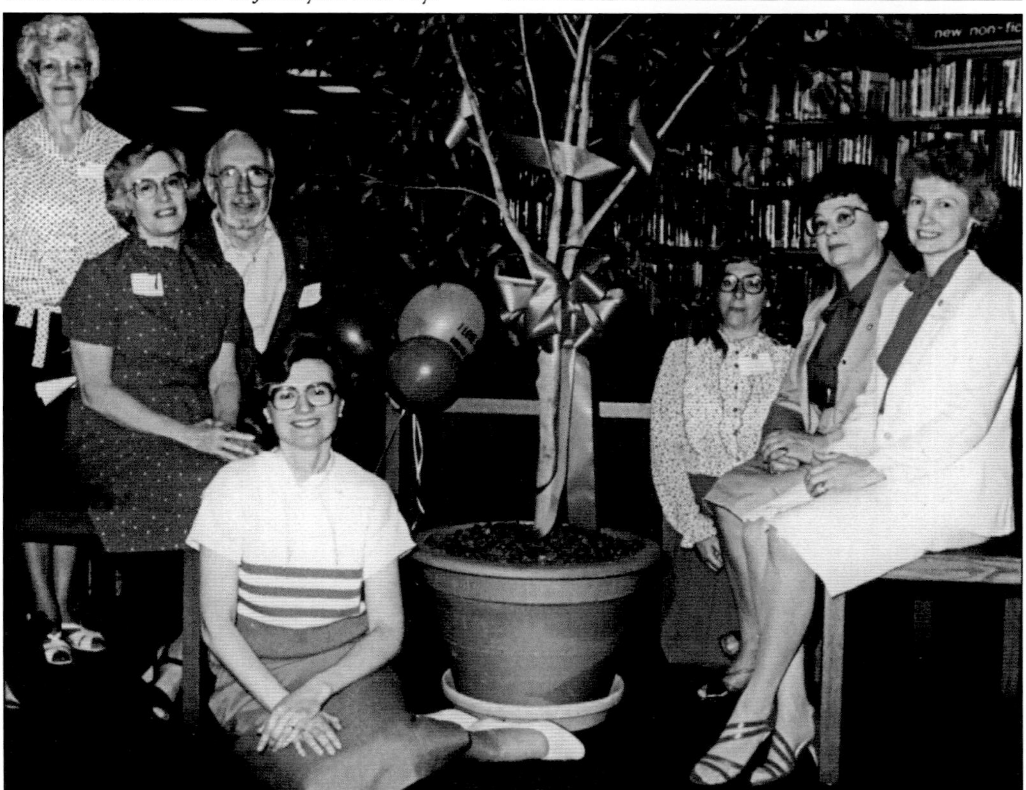

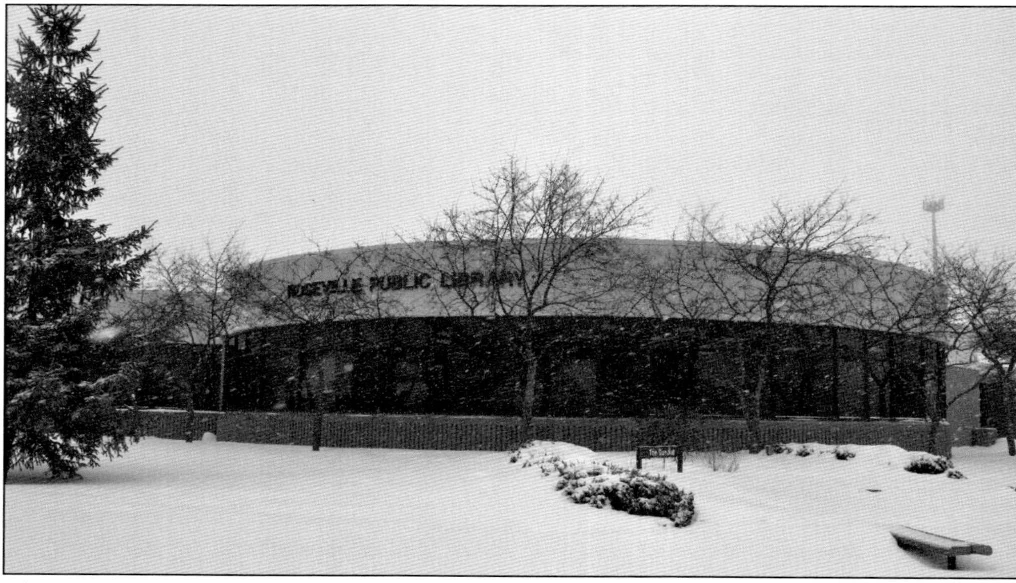

The Roseville Public Library has grown considerably since its humble days, from the old municipal building and the one-story building on Gratiot Avenue to the modern facility at the civic complex next to city hall. The new library and civic center were dedicated in 1975. In 1998, in great need of space, another 14,000 square feet were added to the library. (Photograph by John Minnis.)

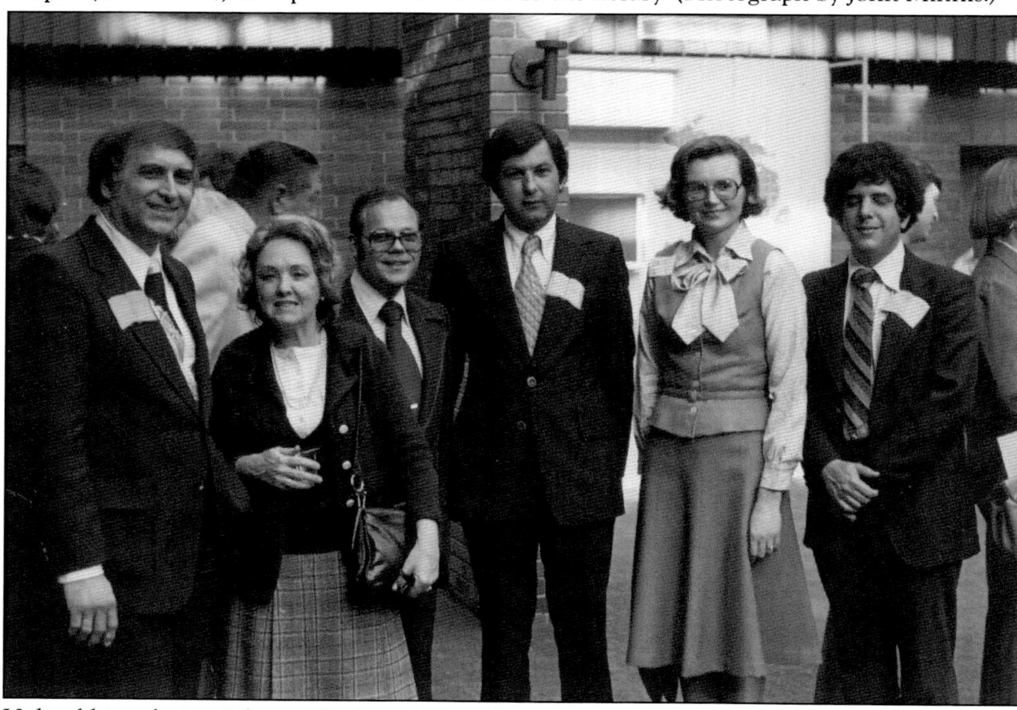
Hobnobbing during Library Week in 1979 in Lansing are, from left to right, Sen. Gil DiNello, East Detroit Library director Jane McGraw, Warren Library director Larry Davenport, Sen. Art Miller, Roseville Library director Rose Kollmorgen, and state representative Nick Ciaramitaro. Special events are held across the country in celebration of National Library Week.

Five

Roseville's Finest

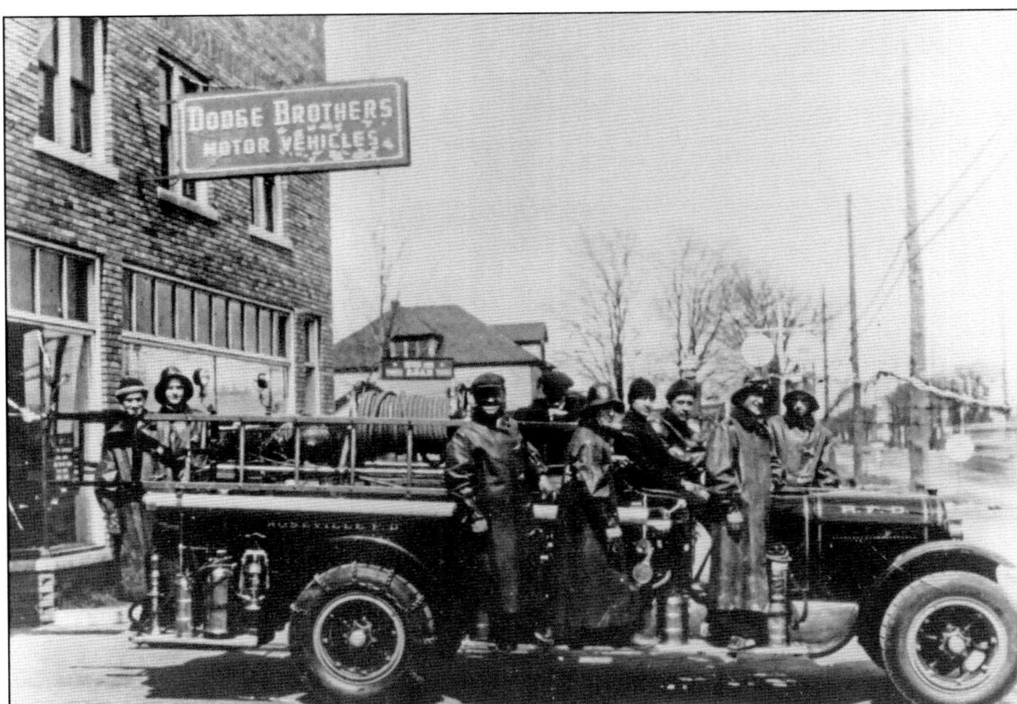

The Dodge Brothers dealership, owned by Arthur Jahn, was one of Roseville's earliest car dealers. The firefighters pictured here in 1926 with the department's first fire truck are, from left to right, Arthur Pickler, unidentified, Charles Pickler, William Noble, unidentified, Ed Pulaski, John Fessler, and two unidentified men. One month later, the department obtained a large Graham Brothers fire truck equipped with a Pirsch pump and chemical apparatus. The equipment was the finest of its day.

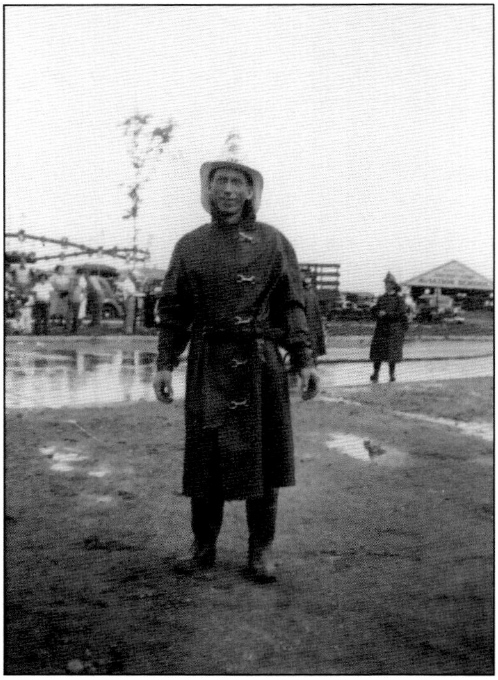

Fire chief Harold Flechsig is pictured here in 1937 on the grounds of Hartung Airport. The Flechsig family settled in Roseville in 1912 when Harold was just five years old. Interestingly, Roseville's first fire chief was Adolf "Jimmie" Hartung. For a brief time, Ed Pulaski served as fire chief, but Hartung, who served from 1926 to 1934, is generally recognized as Roseville's first fire chief.

The wedding of Pauline Kerby and Joseph Moritz (on top of the truck) took place in front of the home of fire chief Harold Flechsig and his wife, Kathleen (pictured foreground), on Park Street near Common Road. Justice of the peace Wally Nichols performed the ceremony. Also pictured on the back of the truck are John Moritz and young John Moritz, and, at the rear wheel, Kate Kerby.

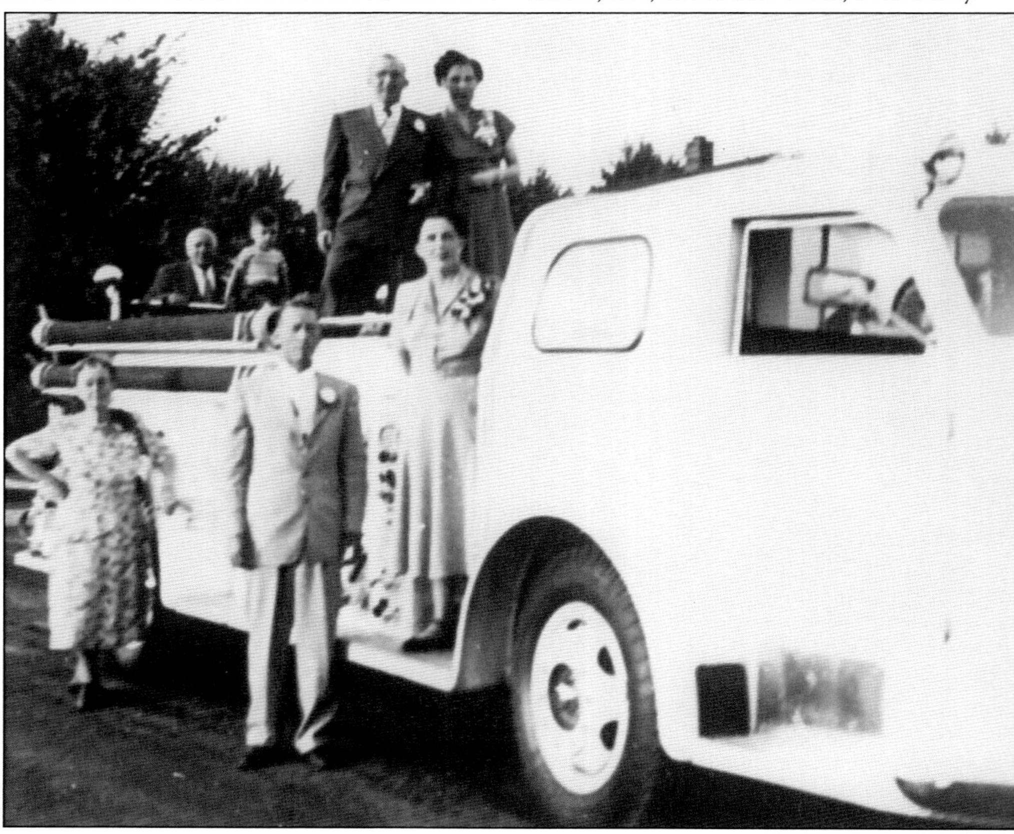

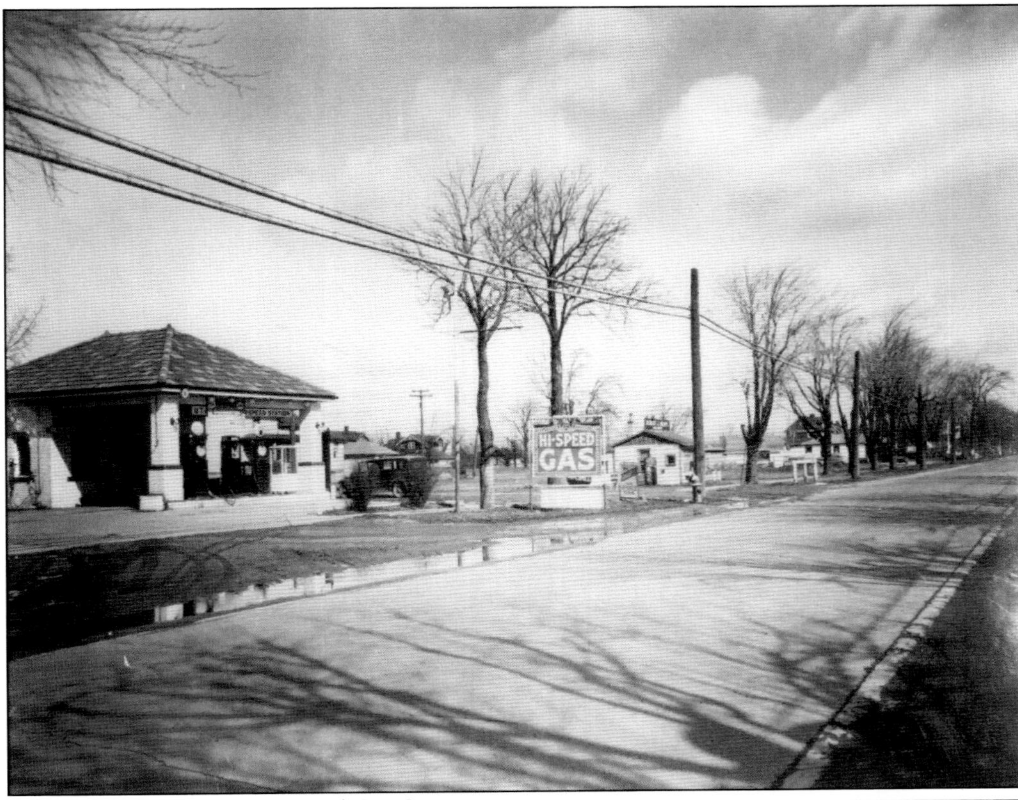

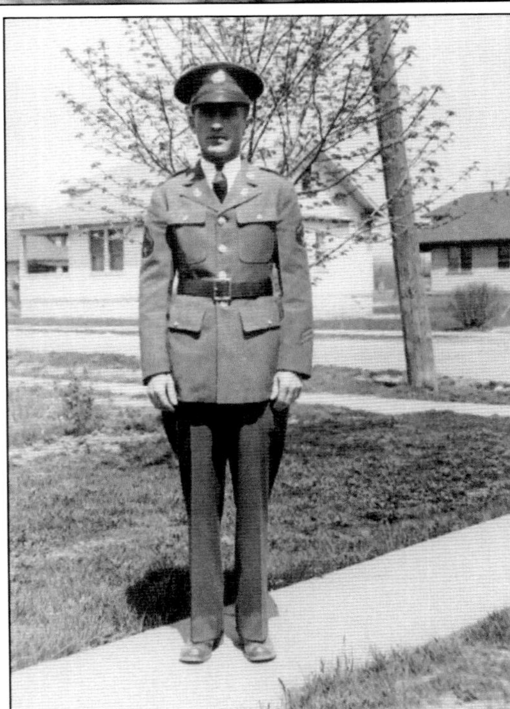

On June 15, 1937, the Hi-Speed Gas Station located on Gratiot Avenue at Kershaw Street was burglarized. Patrolman Lawrence Cooney, pictured at right, and patrolman William Oliver were shot by a juvenile suspect who was being apprehended for the crime. Oliver was the arresting officer. The suspect and a second juvenile suspect were handcuffed together and being placed into a patrol car when one of them grabbed Patrolman Oliver's service weapon and shot him. Patrolman Cooney responded to the scene, chased the suspects, and was also shot with Oliver's gun. Cooney drove himself to the police station, where he collapsed. He died later that day. Patrolman Oliver was taken to a local hospital by a passing milkman. Patrolman Oliver succumbed to his wounds on July 12, 1937. The suspect was arrested and sentenced to life in prison. Patrolman Cooney was the first of Roseville's finest to lose his life in the line of duty. He was survived by his wife and two sons.

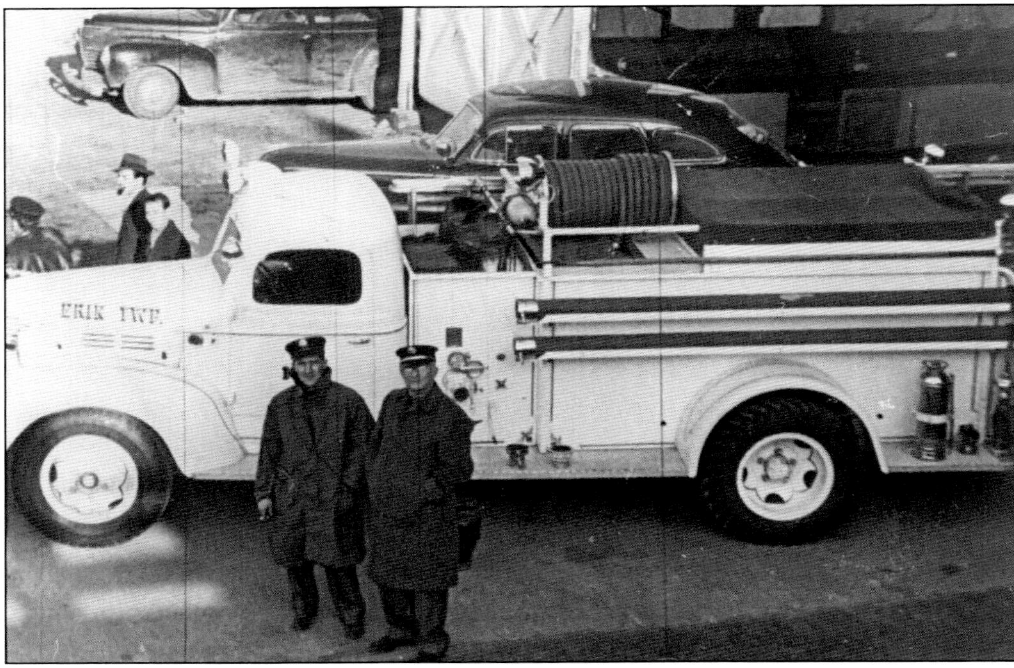

Above, fire officials Jimmy Mitchell (left) and Sylvester Barbret pose alongside their pumper truck. Below, in 1959, Roseville fire captain Joe Moritz supervises the filling of the pumper truck from a city fire hydrant. Notice the truck still reads "Erin Twp." on the hood. The village of Roseville was chartered in 1926, and that same year, the Roseville Fire and Police Departments were established. The village's first fire truck was a 320-gallon pumper. A second truck was purchased a month later from Graham Brothers, the largest independent truck builder at the time, and fitted with a Peter Pirsch Company pump, making it one of best fire rigs around.

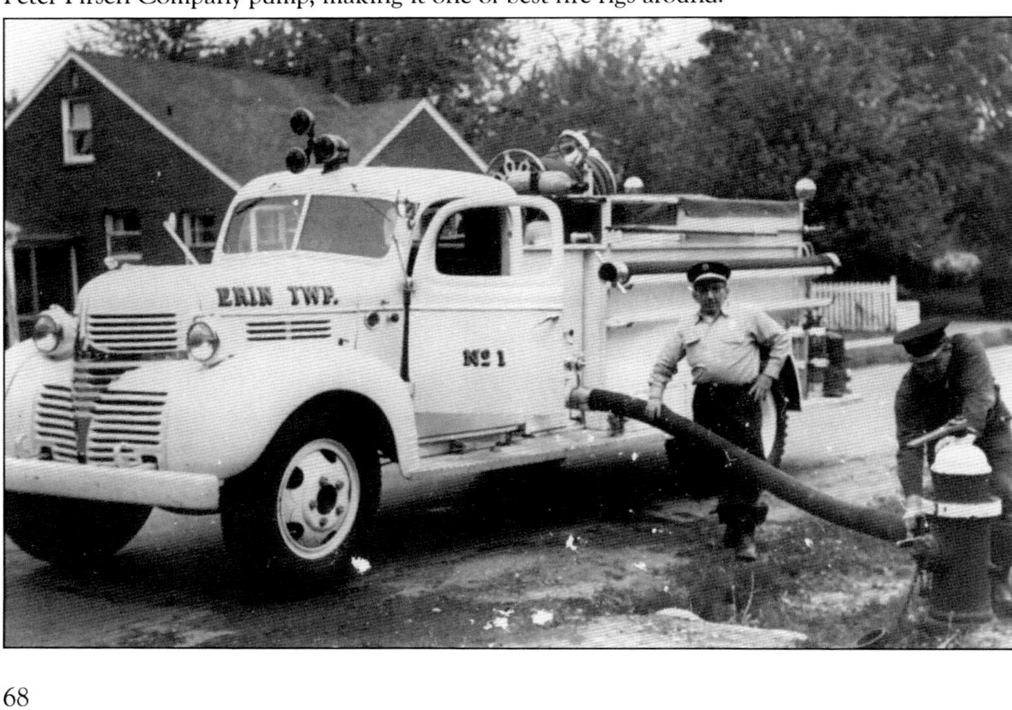

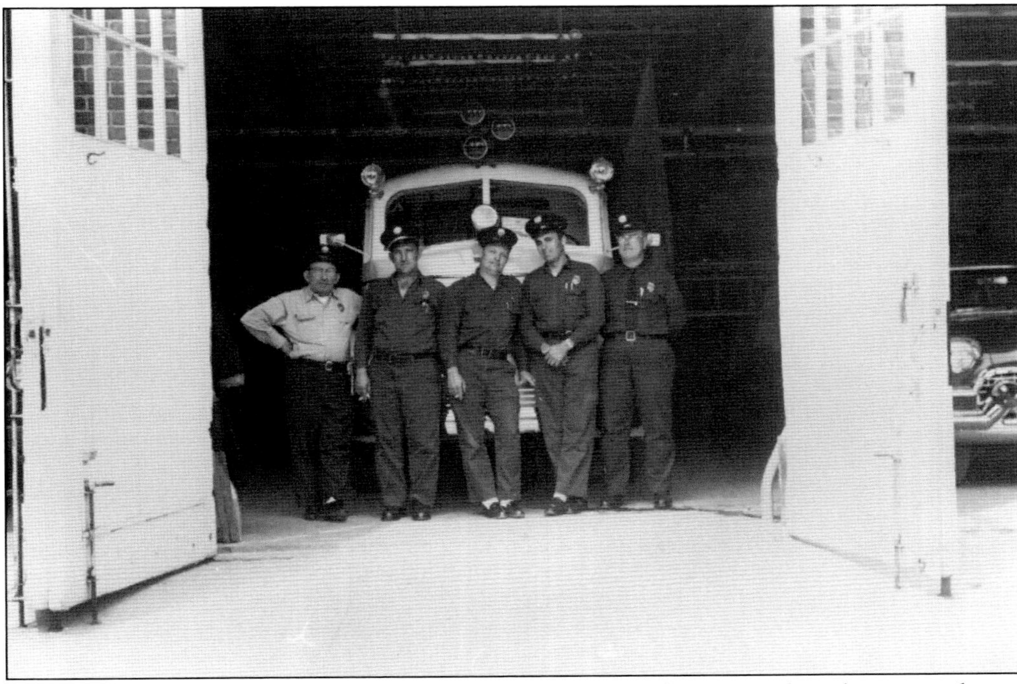

These two images, taken in a firehouse doorway on Meier Road, appear to have been staged some years apart. From left to right in both photographs are Capt. Joseph Moritz, Sgt. James Mitchell, Harold Helzer, Mike Muscat, and Owen Erdman. The firehouse was a lower structure attached to the rear of the grand Roseville Municipal Building on Gratiot Avenue, built in 1929. Moritz was one of two captains in the fire department. A newspaper article the year before described the Roseville Fire Department as consisting of a fire chief, assistant fire chief, two captains, two lieutenants, a first engineer, a second engineer, two assistant engineers, and nine firemen.

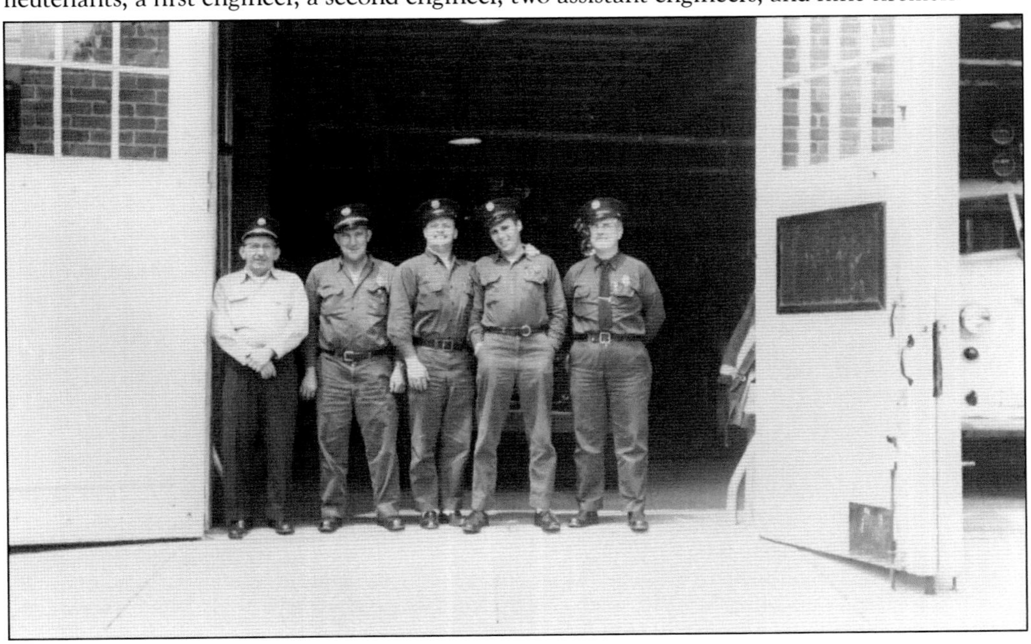

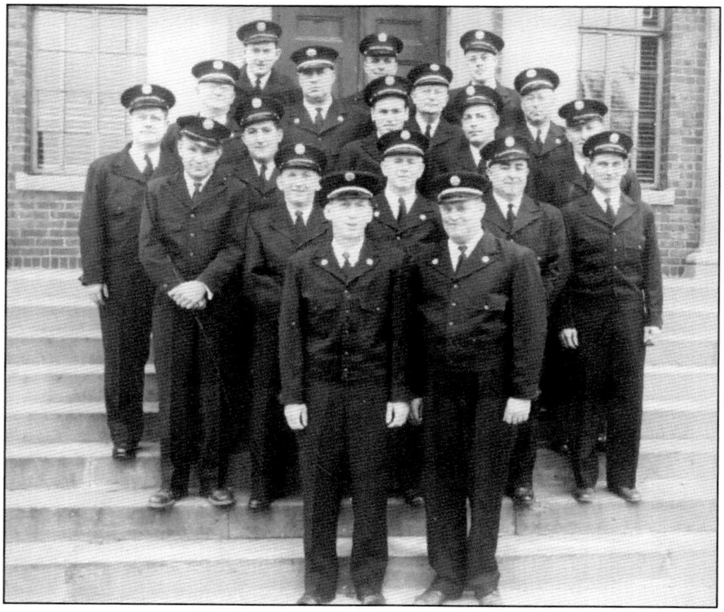

This group photograph of the Roseville Fire Department was taken in 1949 on the steps of the municipal building, located at Gratiot Avenue and Meier Road. Originally housed in Jahn's Garage, the fire department received its own firehouse when the new Roseville Municipal Building was constructed in 1929. The Jackson Coal and Lumber Company fire in 1946 and the Federal Department Store fire in 1978 were the two worst fires in Roseville history.

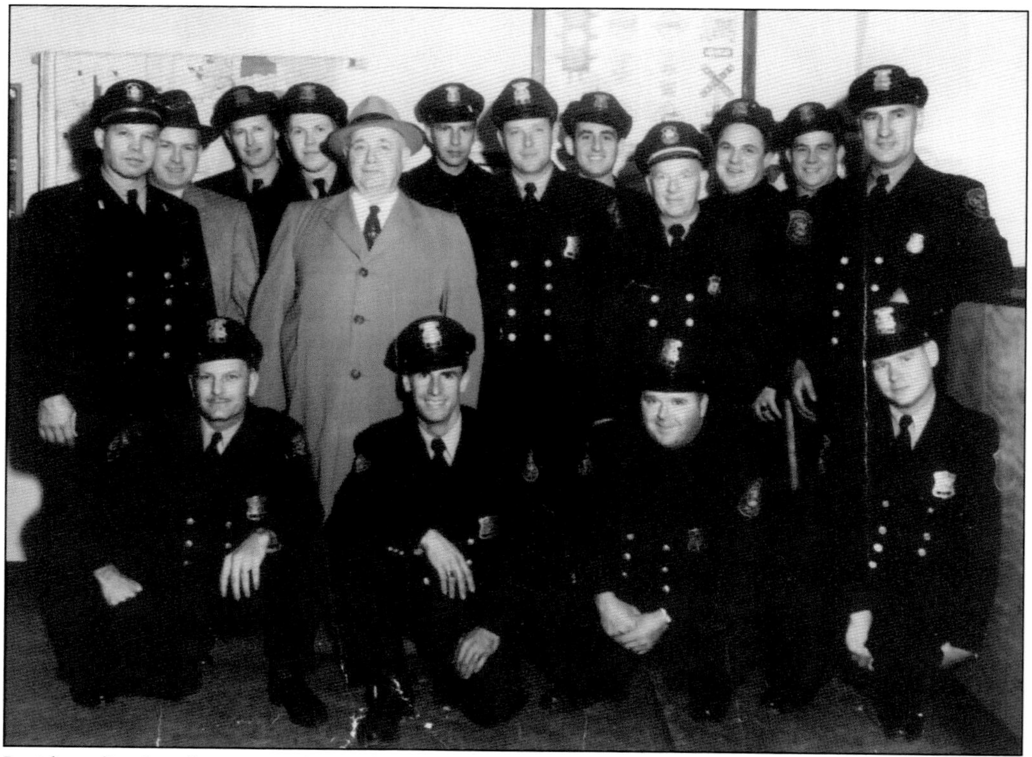

Inside police headquarters, the 1953–1954 Roseville police officers gather for their annual group photograph. From left to right are (first row) Robert Moers, Steve Vanlanot, Douglas Blight, and Ben Stern; (second row) Alvoy Depue, Maurice Pinsonneault, Thomas Robertson, James Murphy, Michael A. Miller, James Colby, Charles Moore, Anthony Scarsella, Walter Kimmerly, Ernie Thomas, Nelson Abbey, and Karl Schumann.

Roseville policemen pose on the steps of the Roseville Municipal Building at Gratiot Avenue and Meier Road in 1956. Pictured here are, from left to right, (first row) Ray Hartley and Alvoy Depue; (second row) John Perry, George Montgomery, and Lonnie Leitz; (third row) Nelson Abbey, Ray Kosciolek, and Jack Fairfield. Mike Miller (not pictured) was the police chief in 1956.

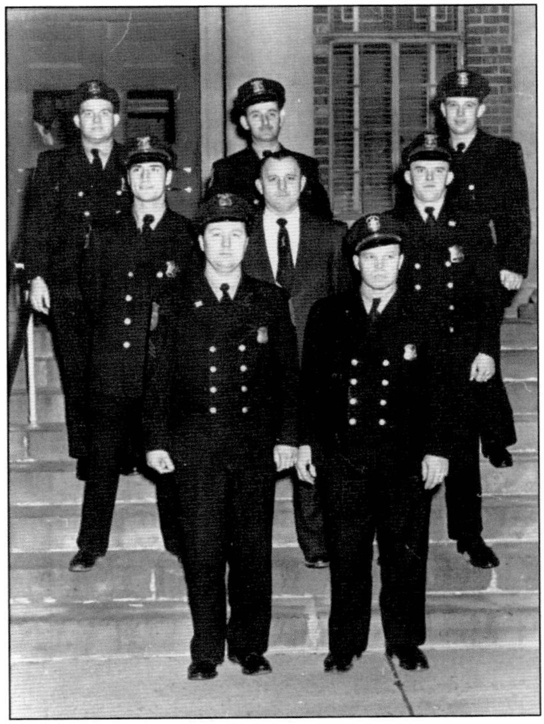

Roseville mayor Leonard Haggerty (right) presents a wristwatch to outgoing superintendent of police Robert Moers in keeping with a long-established tradition of honoring city employees on their retirement after extended municipal service. A 27-year veteran of the police department, Moers was named to the top command post in 1969. He closed out his police career on January 14, 1977.

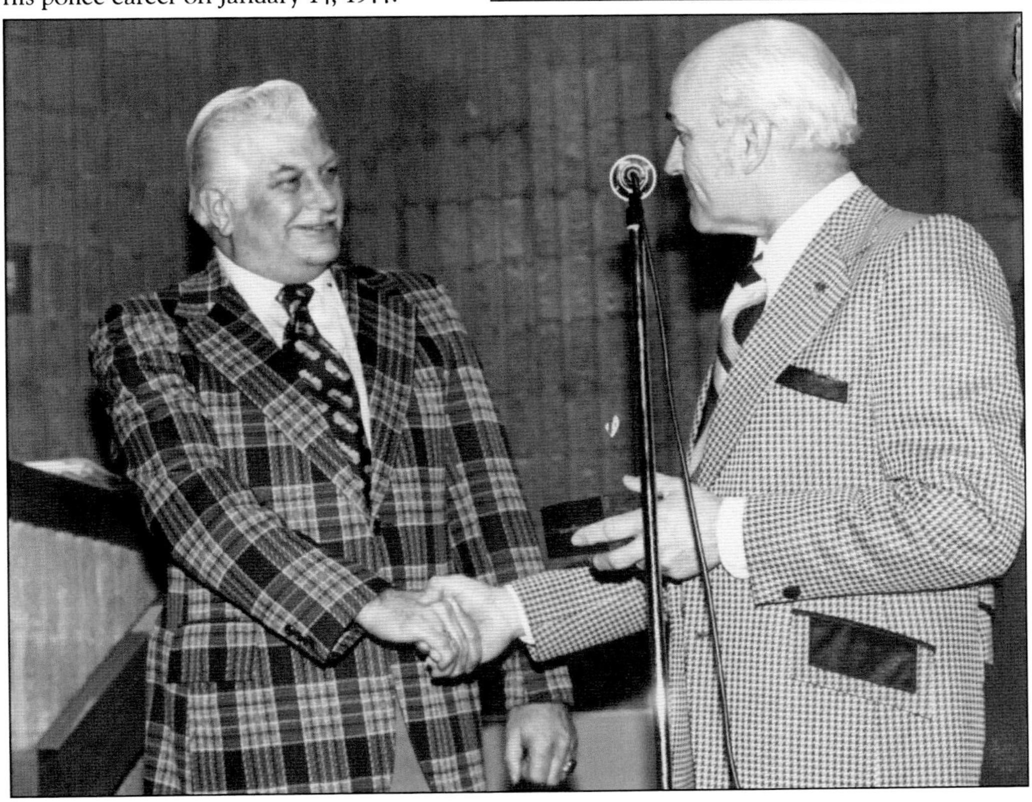

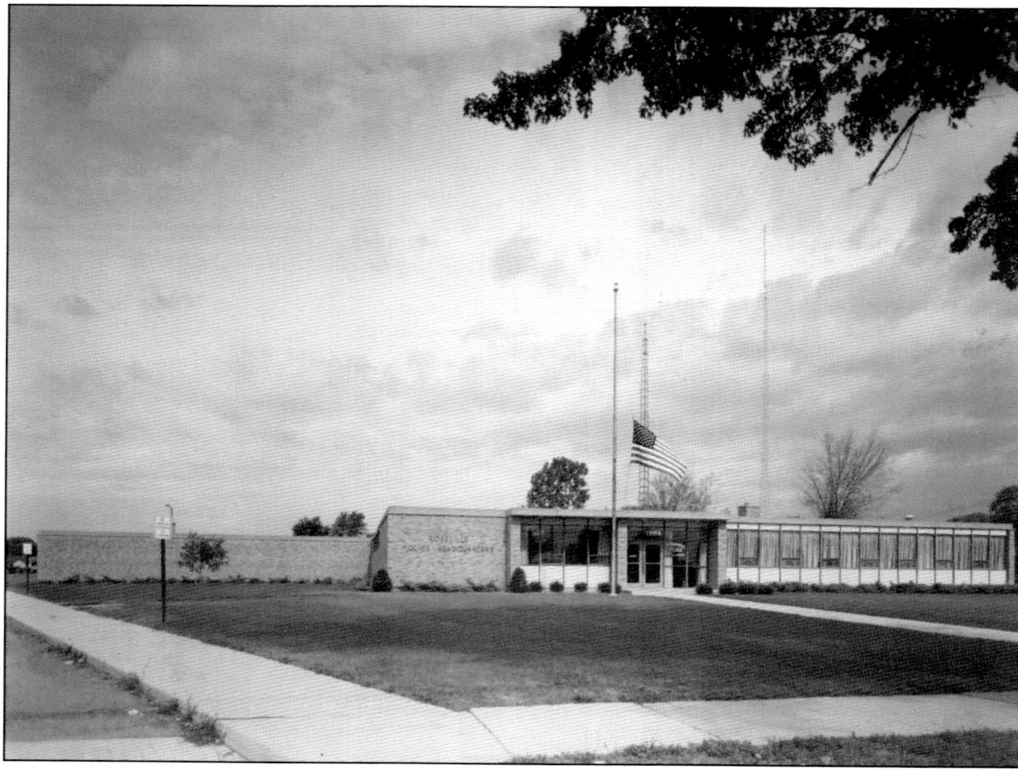

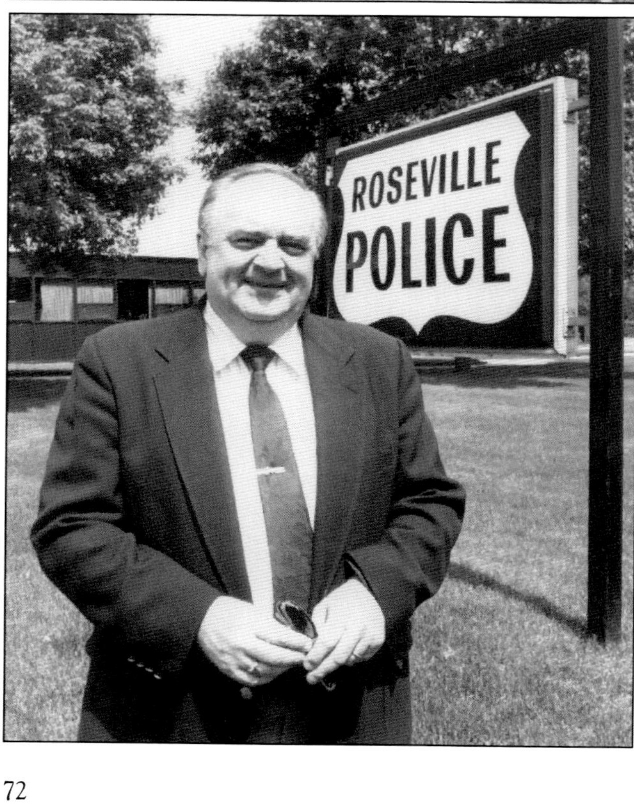

The police department was housed in the municipal building at Gratiot Avenue and Meier Road until the 1960s, when a separate station was constructed. This photograph was taken prior to the addition of the 39th District Court. The police station is located on Gratiot Avenue near Common Road in front of city hall, which was built in the 1970s.

Joseph Steenland, pictured in front of the Roseville Police Department building, began his career as a police officer in 1959. He served in various positions over a 33-year period, including commander of the detective bureau. He ended his career as an investigator with the Macomb County Prosecutor's Office, retiring in 2007.

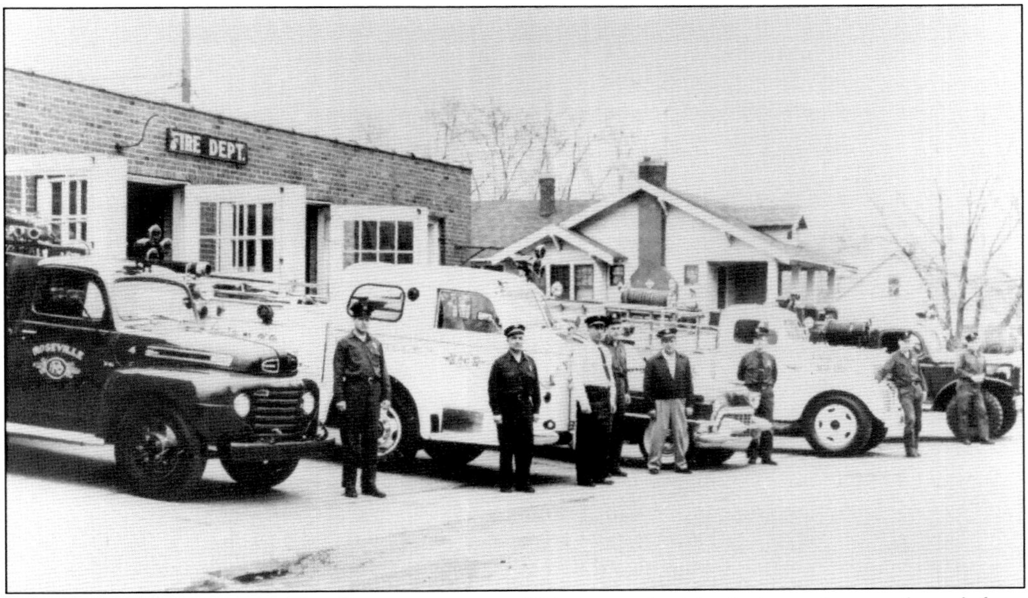

Members of the Roseville Fire Department in 1956 pictured with their trucks are, from left to right, Raymond Jensenius, John Pomante, Chief Harold Flechsig, Morley Ireland, James Mitchell, J. Owen Erdman, Cephas Taylor, and Frank Nicki. Flechsig would continue to serve as chief for another 11 years. Pomante and Ireland would both serve as fire chiefs in later years. Mitchell died in the line of duty in 1968.

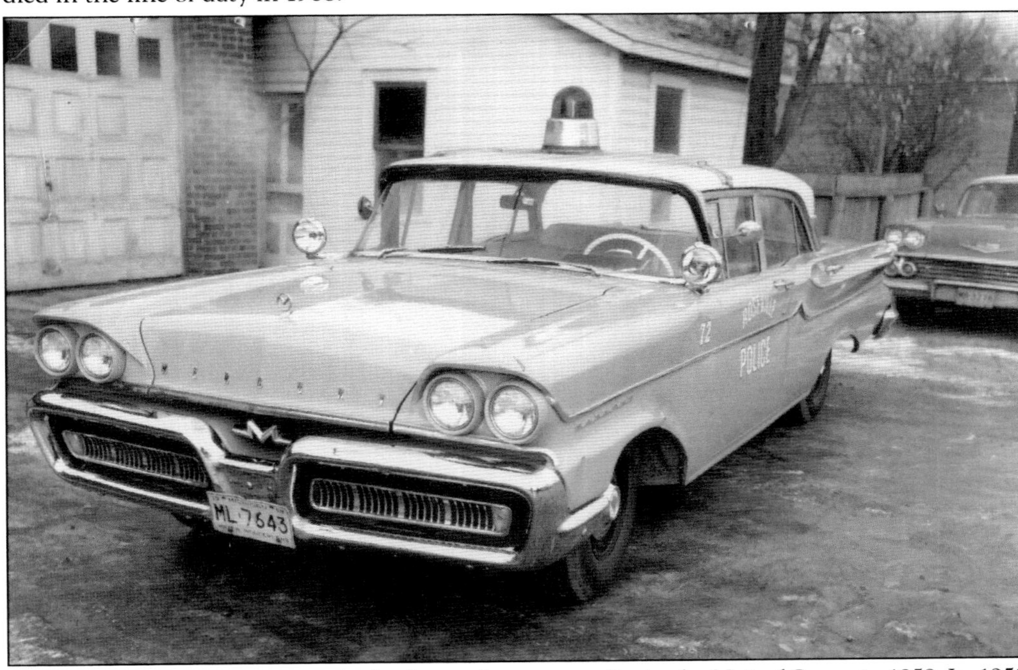

The Ford Motor Company was the leading police car supplier in the United States in 1958. Its 1958 Mercury police cruiser, pictured, came standard with a 312-horsepower V-8 engine; a 360-horsepower option was also available. In his book *Ford Police Cars, 1932–1997,* Edwin J. Sanow wrote, "This 4,100-pound cruiser easily met the requirements for state police and highway patrol use."

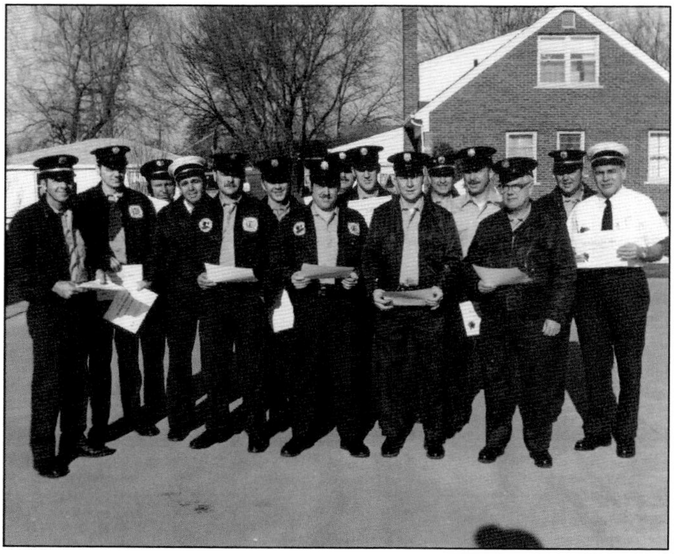

Roseville firefighters completing the Michigan State Firefighters Training Council's 60-hour training course were awarded certificates in June 1975. From left to right are (first row) Sgt. Paul Rener, Morley Ireland Jr., George Hickman, Elba Messer, and Owen Erdman; (second row) Roger Barczi, assistant chief Michael Muscat, Lyle Mueller, Thomas May, Ronald Flechsig, and assistant chief Morley Ireland Sr.; (third row) Lt. John Weisgerber, Michael Wurm, Sgt. Raymond Jensenius, and Sgt. Ralph Junga.

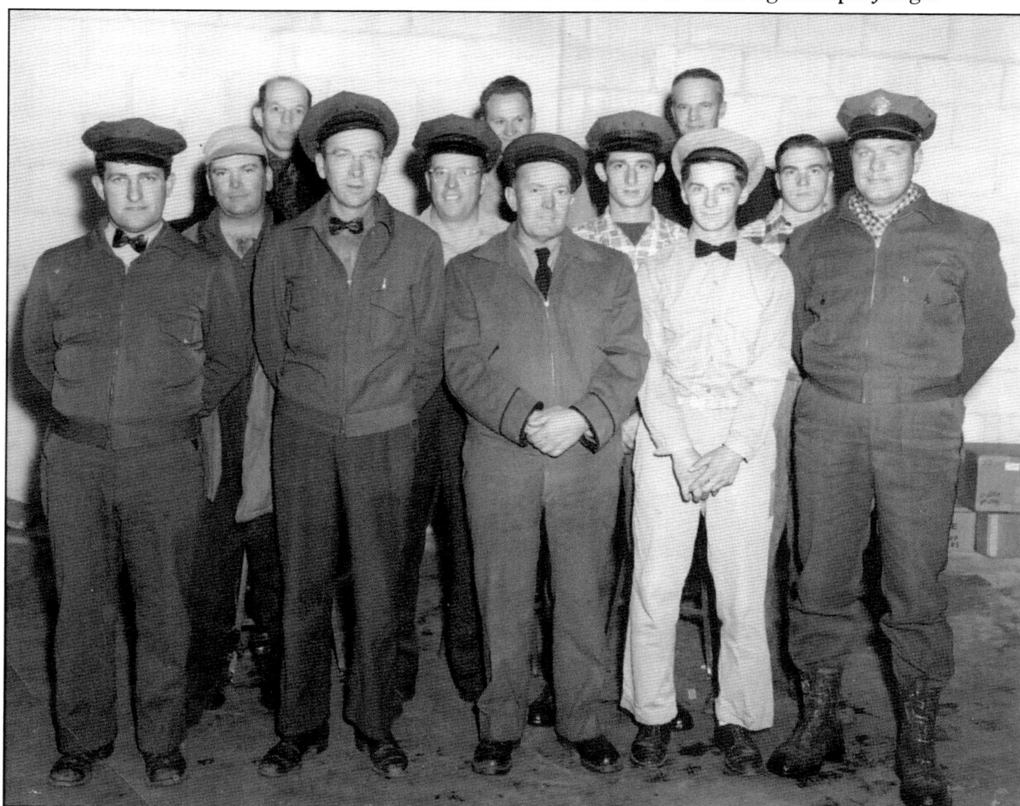

The well-known postal service motto, "Neither snow, nor rain, nor heat, nor gloom of night, stays these couriers from the swift completion of their appointed rounds," certainly applied to the 1954 Roseville postal carriers. From left to right are (first row) Jack Hilles, Bob Killawald, Mile Bravick, Don Schmidt, and Joe Riesterer; (second row) William MacMasters, Kenneth Longcore, Jack Diebold, and Earl Ureel; (third row) Mart Horst, George Walker, and Ellis MacDowell.

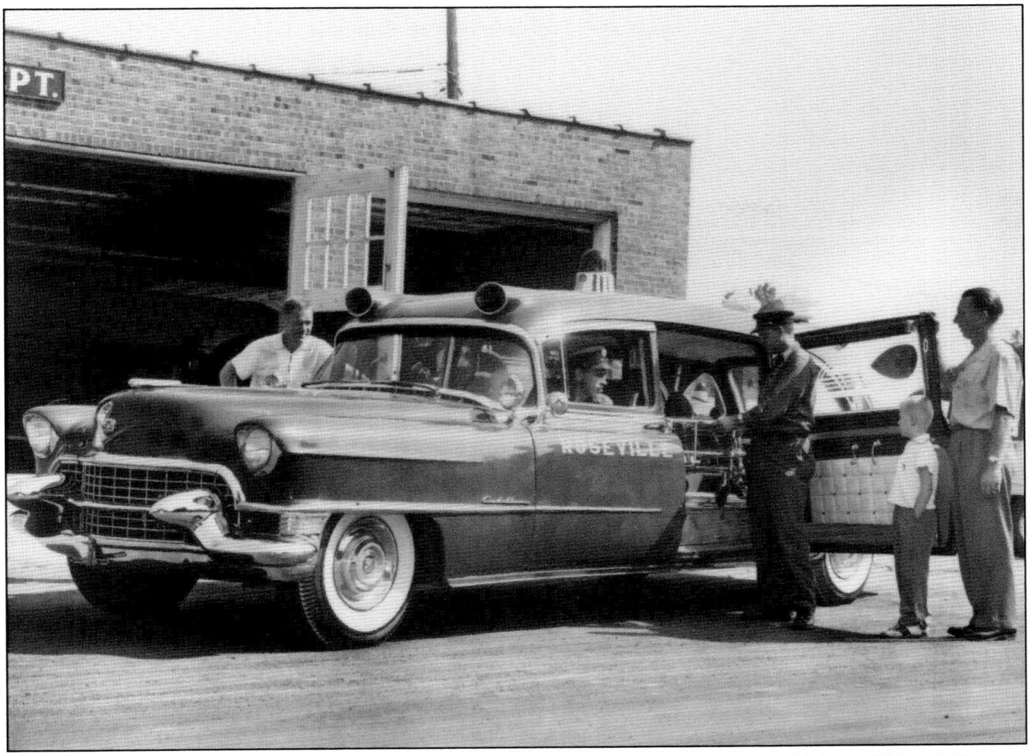

Nothing is too good for his Roseville residents. Village president Glen Alsip was on hand at the fire department for the delivery of a new ambulance—a Cadillac. The Ghostbusters' Ectomobile, Ecto-1, in the 1984 movie *Ghostbusters*, was a 1959 Cadillac Miller-Meteor ambulance. Miniature replicas of the vehicle were mass-produced as children's toys. In early 2013, Hot Wheels Elite released an Ecto-1A, as seen in *Ghostbusters II*.

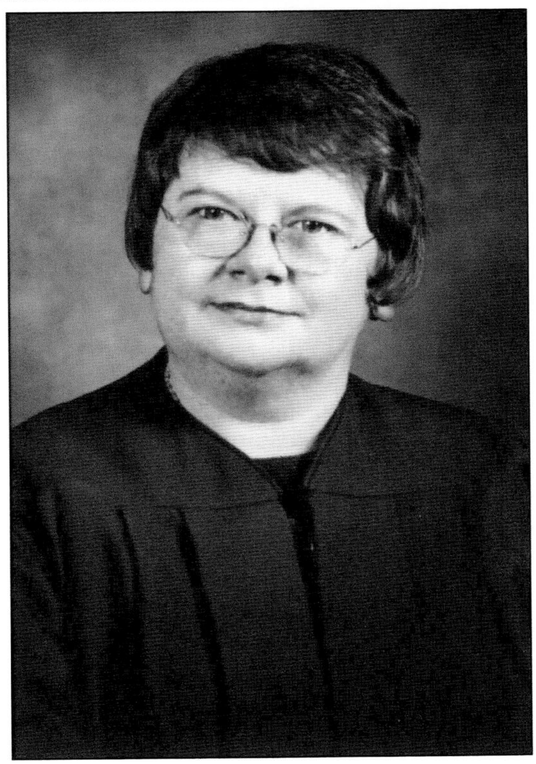

Mary E. McDevitt served as a judge for the 39th District Court in Roseville for 28 years, as municipal judge for 10 years, justice of the peace for Erin Township for more than a year, and as a juvenile court judge for Macomb County for two years. She has the honor of being the first female judge in Macomb County. She died in March 2007.

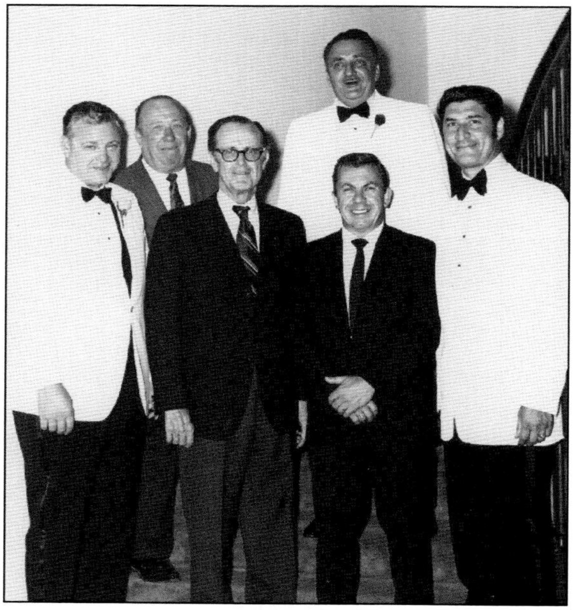

Roseville city government officials met with Sen. Phil Hart in 1969. Hart had previously served as Michigan's lieutenant governor from 1955 to 1959. He married Jane "Janey" Briggs Hart, the daughter of philanthropist and former owner of the Detroit Tigers Walter Briggs, in June 1943. From left to right are (first row) Mayor William McDonald, Senator Hart, and Councilmen John Gregg and John Perry; (second row) Councilmen Ed Spybrook and Lester DeClerk.

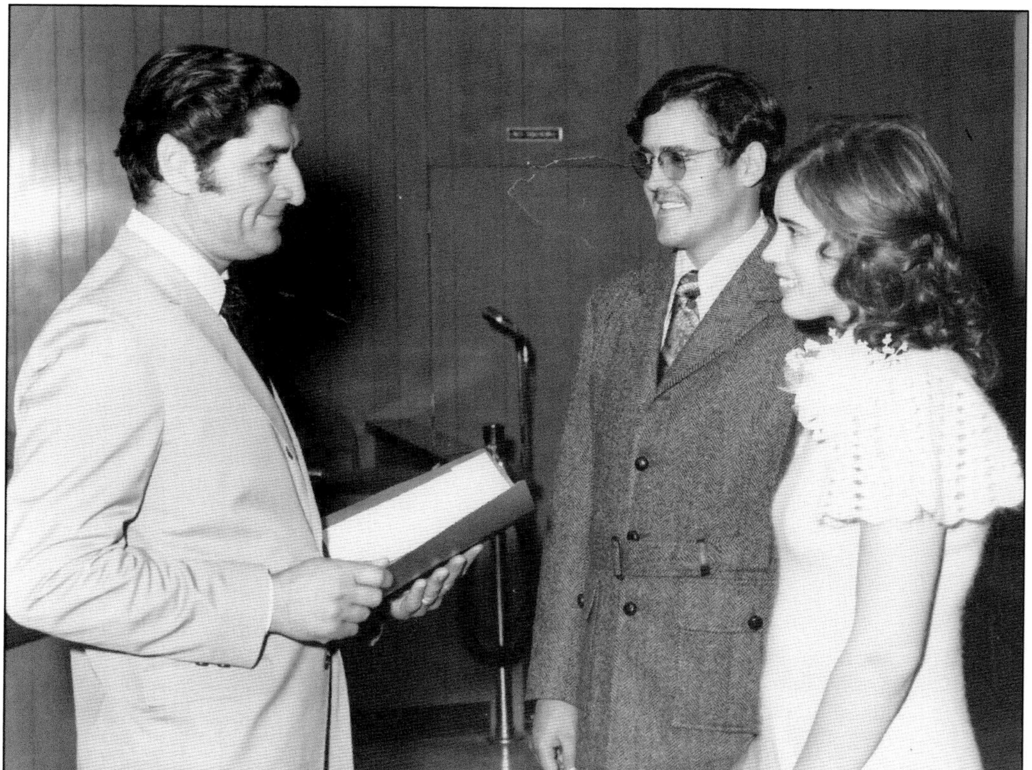

Mayor John Perry (left) officiated at a wedding ceremony for the first time under a new state law that permitted a mayor or mayor pro tem to perform a marriage rite in his or her community. Taking their vows in the city council chambers at city hall are Richard Perdue, of Ennis, Texas, and Vivian Lorimar, of Roseville. The marriage took place on September 8, 1972.

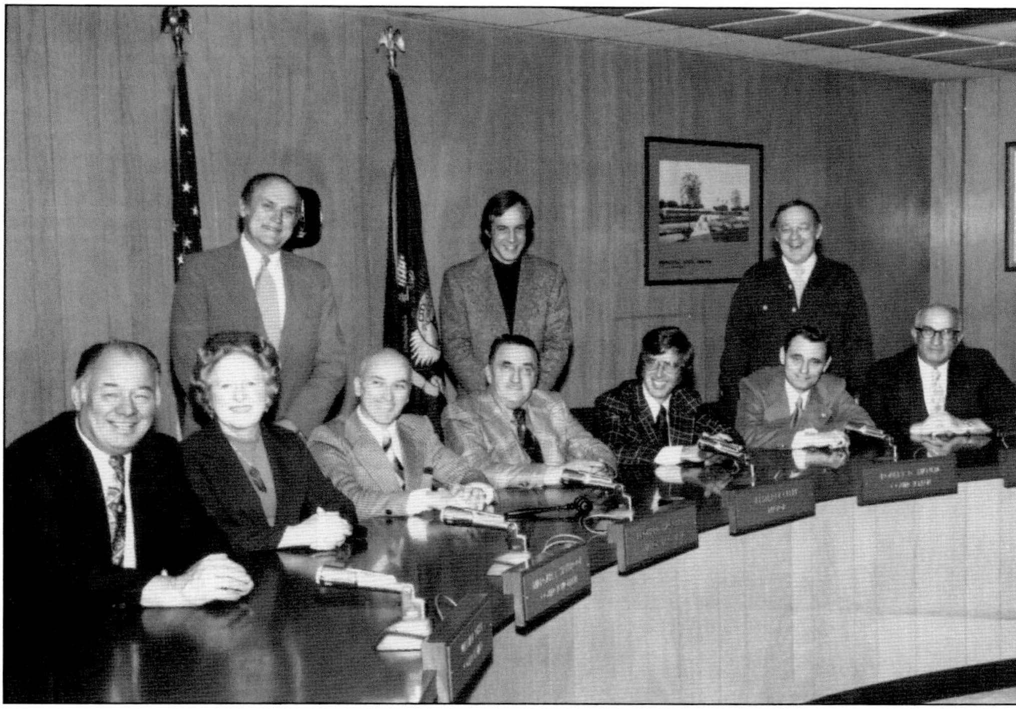

The city council enjoyed its new council chambers when it moved into its digs in 1974. Pictured here in the council chambers in 1975 are, from left to right, (first row) William Luski, Margaret Spybrook, Leonard Haggerty, Lester DeClerk, Robert Matuja, Billie Williams, and Richard Drager; (second row, standing) Joe McCloskey, Russell LaBarge, and Joe Savage.

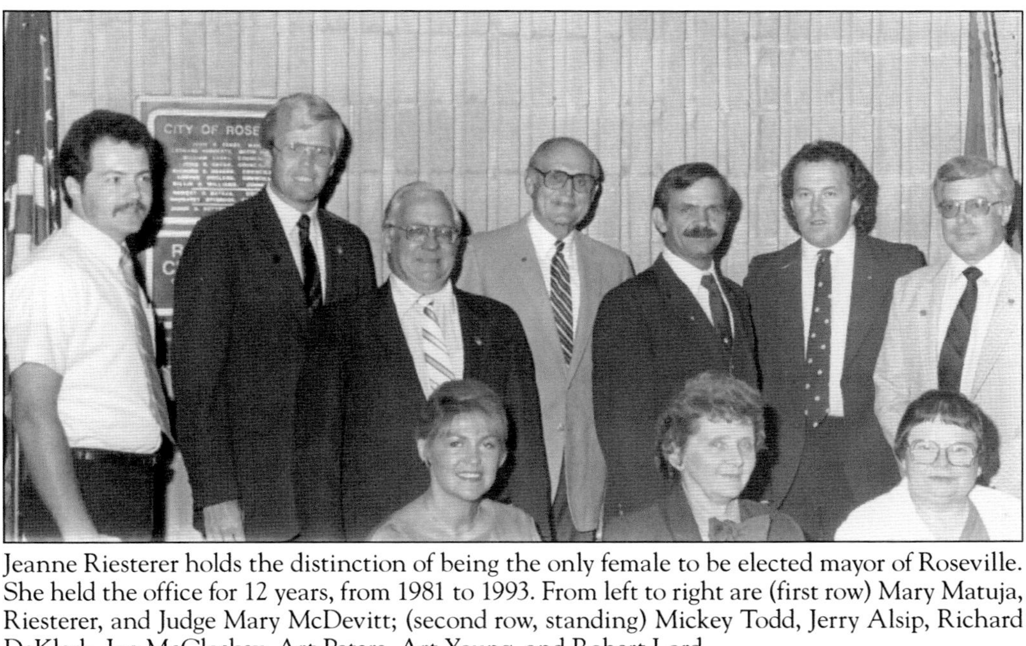

Jeanne Riesterer holds the distinction of being the only female to be elected mayor of Roseville. She held the office for 12 years, from 1981 to 1993. From left to right are (first row) Mary Matuja, Riesterer, and Judge Mary McDevitt; (second row, standing) Mickey Todd, Jerry Alsip, Richard DeKlerk, Joe McCloskey, Art Peters, Art Young, and Robert Lord.

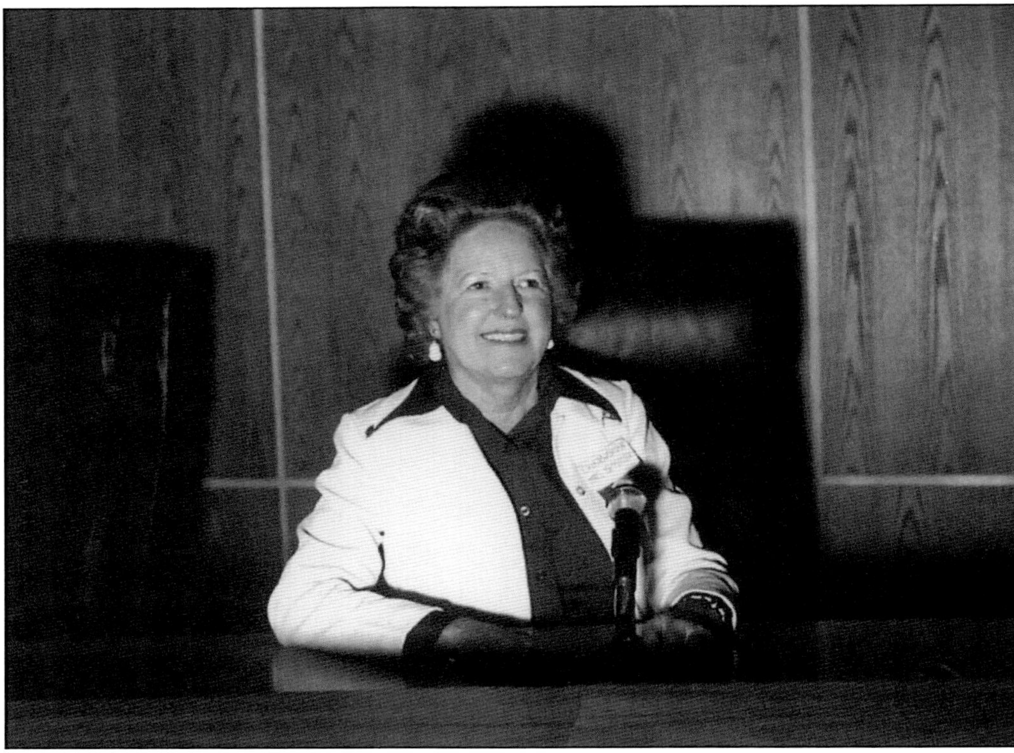

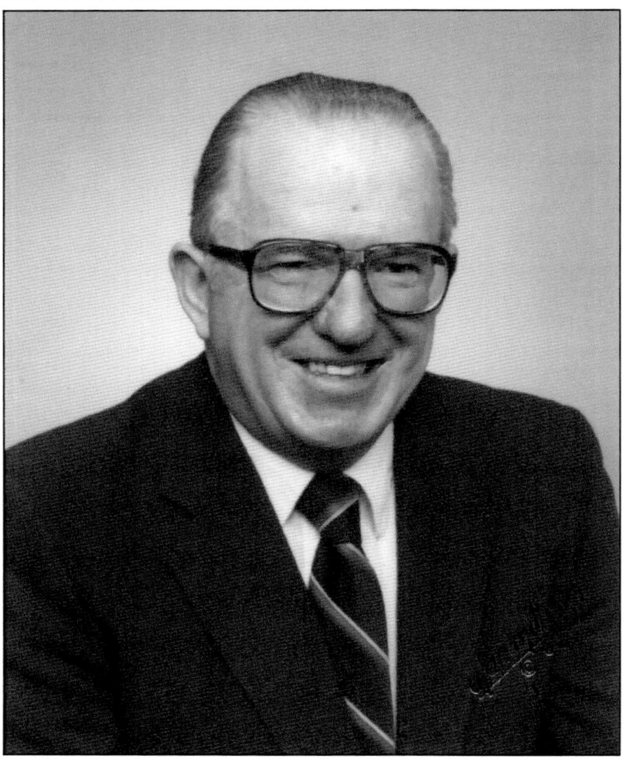

The Spybrook family has been a part of Roseville politics since 1954, when Edward Spybrook was elected to the post of village commissioner. He served on the city council from 1958 to 1972. After his death in 1972, his wife, Margaret, pictured above, ran for his seat on the council and was elected in 1973. She served until 1991. The couple's son Frank Spybrook, pictured at left, followed in their footsteps and was elected to fill his mother's seat in 1991. He served one term. Frank was also known as a local historian, helping to found the Roseville-Erin Historical Society and serving as secretary-treasurer in 1964. A third generation, grandson Bill Shoemaker, currently serves on the Roseville City Council.

Six

Cruisin' Gratiot and around Town

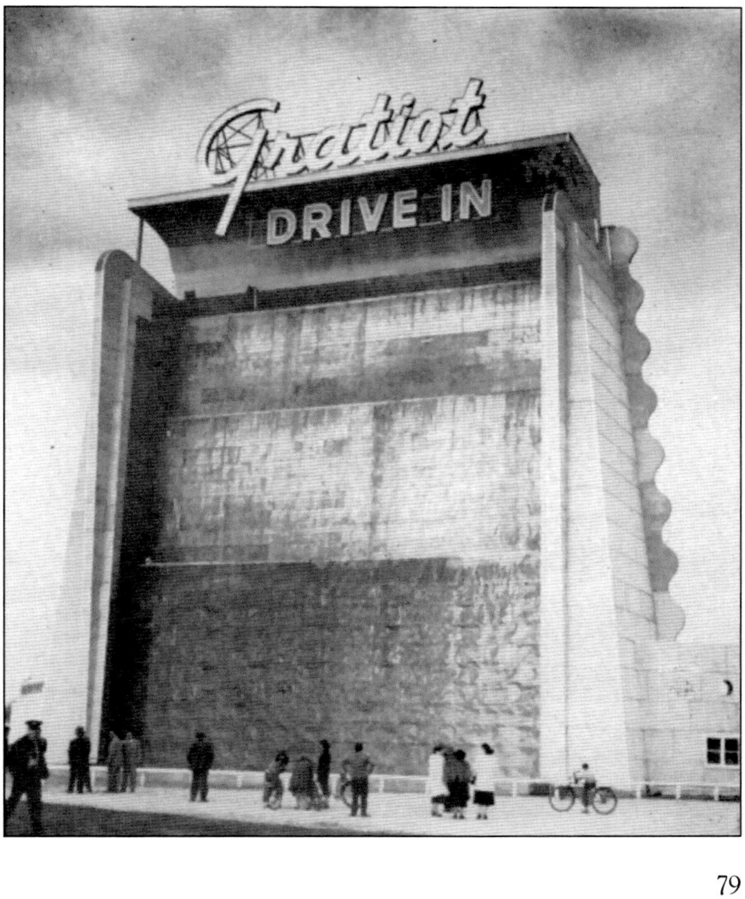

With its waterfall facade, the Gratiot Drive-In was a popular landmark—and destination—in Roseville. Harry Skrdla, author of Arcadia Publishing's *Michigan's Drive-In Theaters*, from the Images of America series, called the Gratiot "Detroit's most spectacular drive-in." The Gratiot Drive-In was one of only two waterfall theaters in the world, the other being in Camillus, New York. The water feature was turned off in the late 1950s. (Courtesy of Harry Skrdla.)

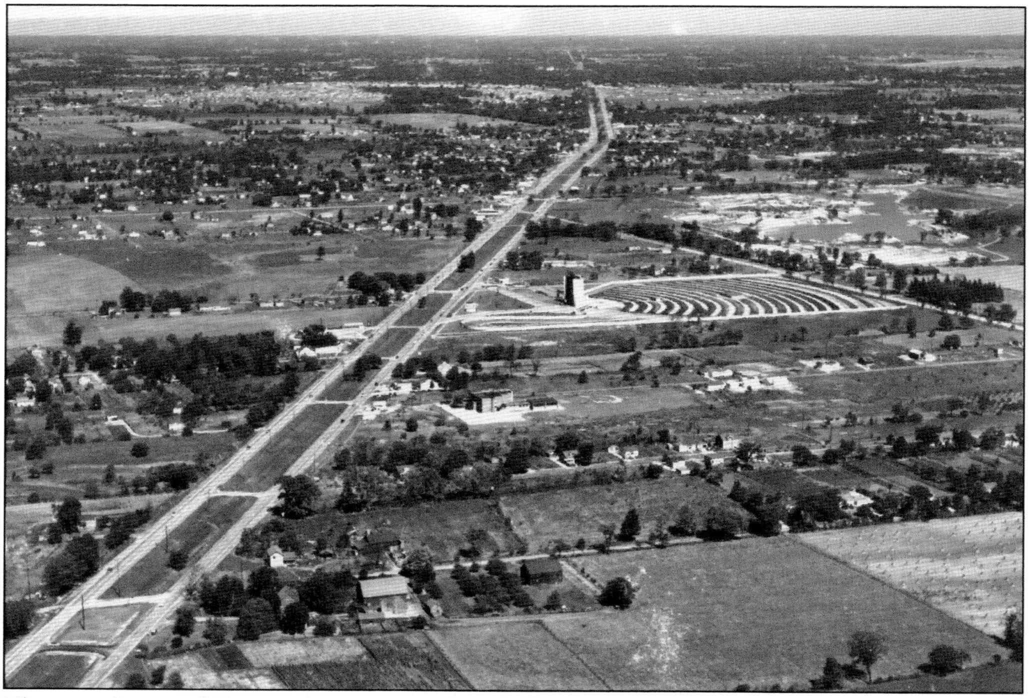

This aerial view of Gratiot Avenue in 1954 is looking north. The Gratiot Drive-In can be seen near the center right of the photograph with an empty lot and the projection building toward the center. Just northeast of the drive-in is the Marsack Sand and Gravel Pit. Greater Gratiot School can be seen in the center. The area at this time is still predominantly farmland.

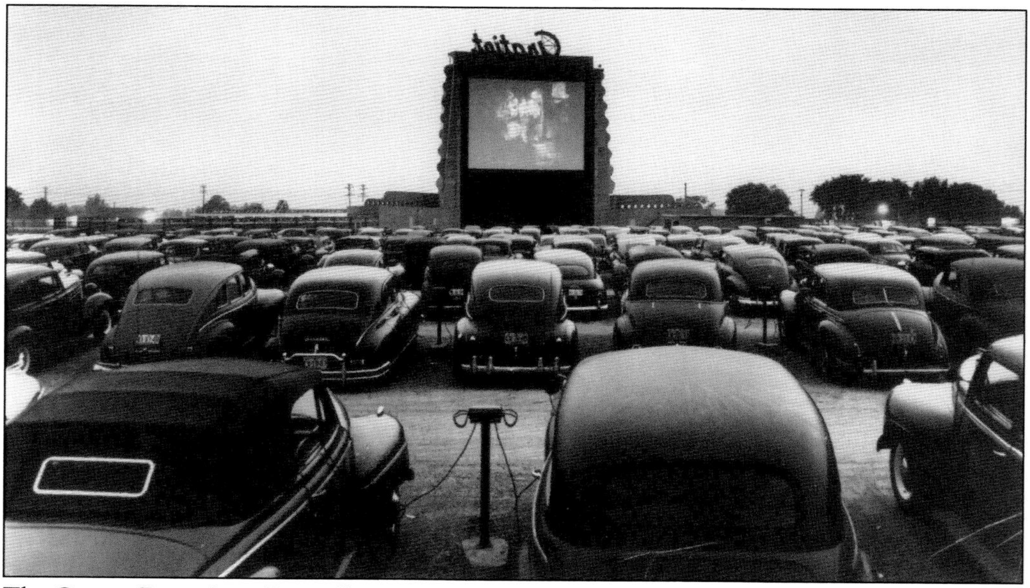

The Gratiot Drive-In in Roseville was an instant hit in the Motor City when it opened in 1948. The Gratiot could hold 1,056 cars in 17 rows, or ramps. The big screen tower also contained an apartment. The Gratiot's huge parking area was twinned, divided in two with two screens, in the late 1950s.

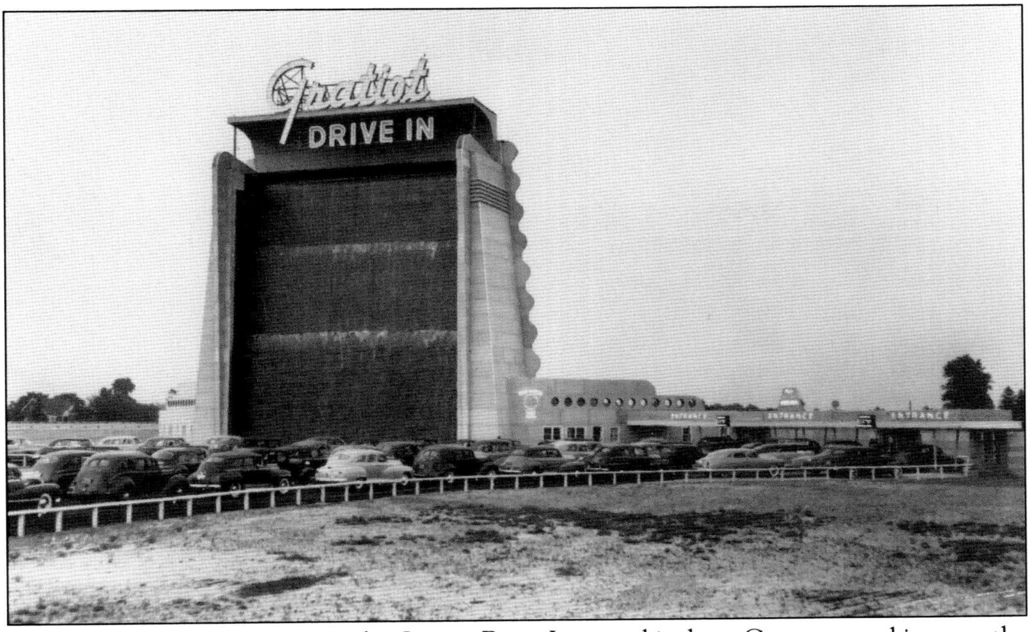

Even from opening day in 1948, the Gratiot Drive-In was a big draw. Cars streamed into see the latest western or musical and enjoy popcorn and pop from the brand-new concession stand. The Gratiot's playground area was fully equipped and even offered pony rides. In later years, a flea market operated during weekend daytime hours. The Gratiot Drive-In was demolished in 1984.

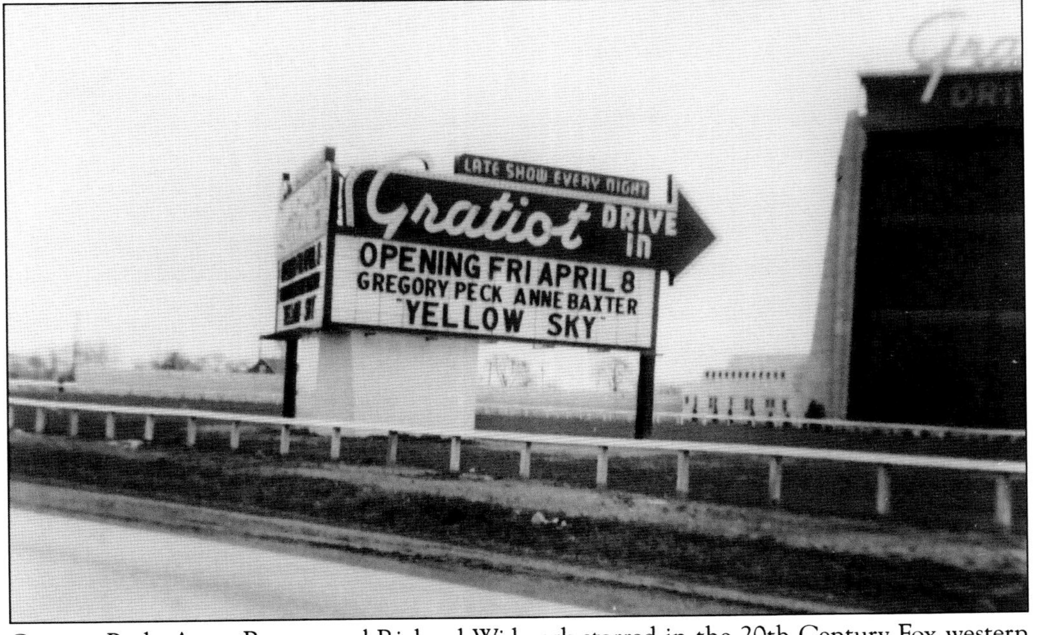

Gregory Peck, Anne Baxter, and Richard Widmark starred in the 20th Century Fox western *Yellow Sky*, released in December 1948, reaching the Gratiot Drive-In the following spring. The plot revolves around a grandfather and his granddaughter, played by Baxter, a gold mine, a gang led by Peck's character, and a romantic interest between Baxter and Peck's characters—typical western fare for the time.

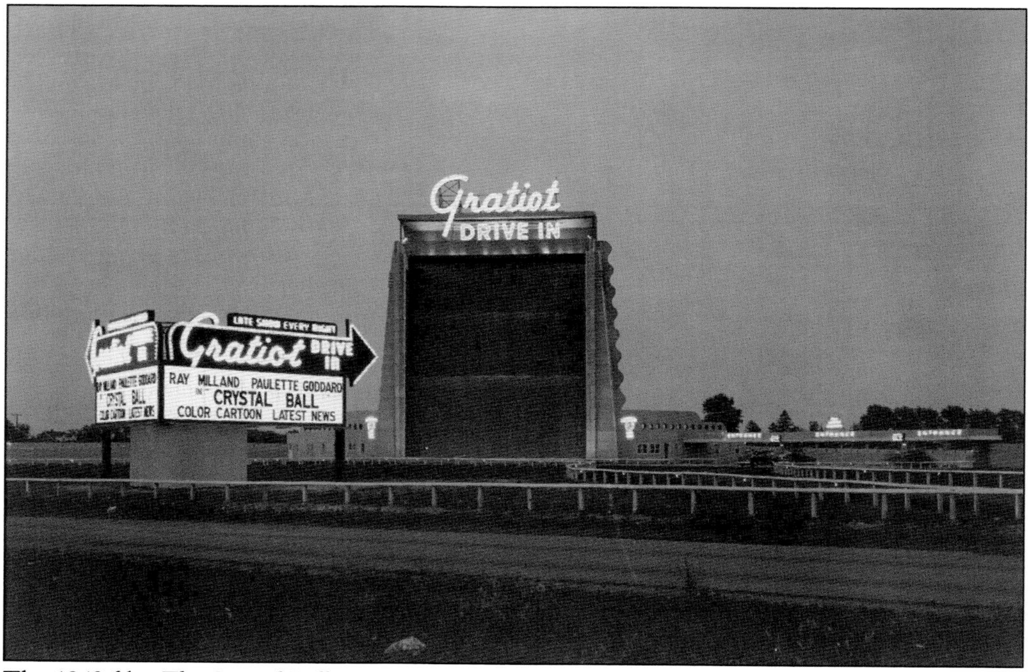

The 1943 film *The Crystal Ball*, starring Ray Milland and Paulette Goddard, was showing at the Gratiot Drive-In when this image was captured. Goddard plays the role of a fake psychic being found out, while Milland plays the wealthy lawyer driving around in an odd micro car. The story line is bland but made tolerable by the star cast and a supporting role by William Bendix as Milland's valet. (Courtesy of Harry Skrdla.)

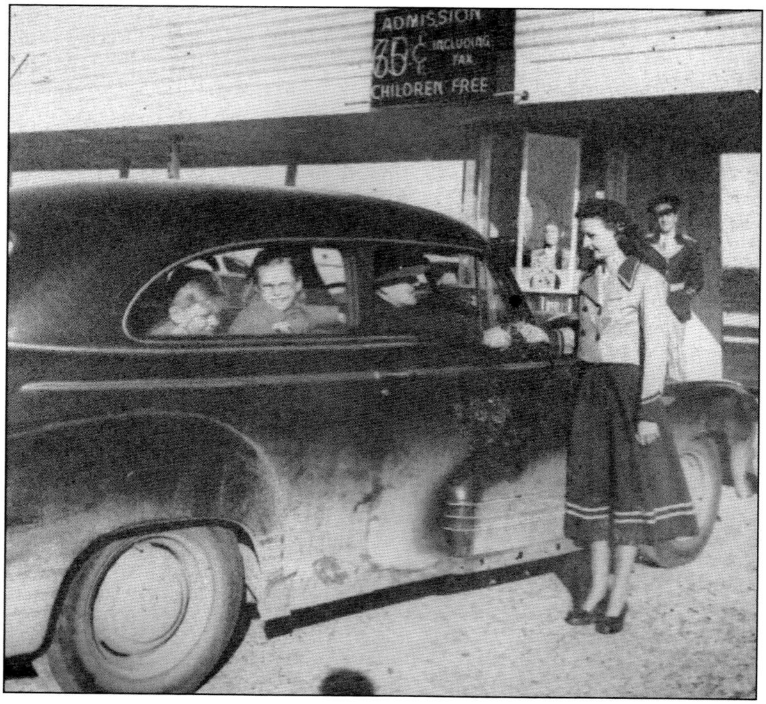

Going to the Gratiot Drive-In was quite a treat for the kids. Drive-in ticket takers dressed the part and welcomed families by the carload. Unlike most drive-in theaters, according to author Harry Skrdla, the Gratiot had attendants working outside the two booths to greet cars and sell tickets in all six lanes entering the theater. (Courtesy of Harry Skrdla.)

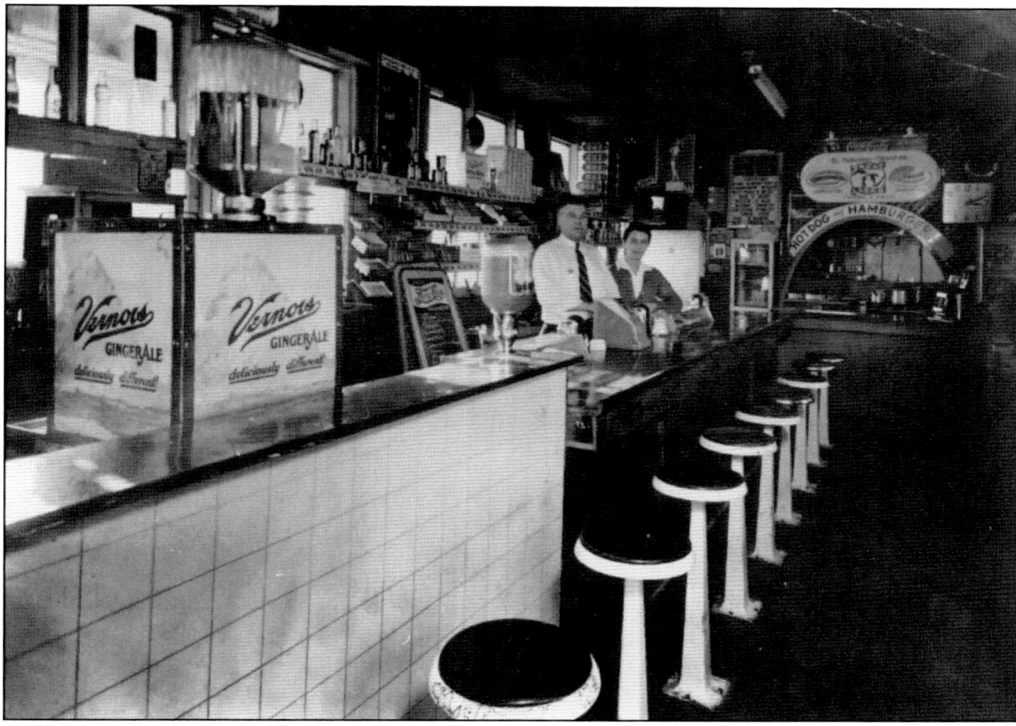

Frank's Place was located on 14 Mile Road near Little Mack Avenue. The back room of the diner was often used to show movies. Note the Vernor's Ginger Ale soda fountain. Vernor's began in Detroit in 1866 and is the oldest remaining ginger-ale brand in the United States. Vernors, as it is now called, is now owned by the Dr. Pepper Snapple Group and no longer bottled in Detroit.

Wimpy's Drive-In was located on Gratiot Avenue at Florian Street. Across the street was Frenchy's Auto Parts. The popular drive-in eatery was owned by the Denton family. With the boom in Las Vegas in the 1950s, the family sold the restaurant and moved west, where one of the family members had plans to become a dealer at the Sands Casino, according to a former employee of the drive-in.

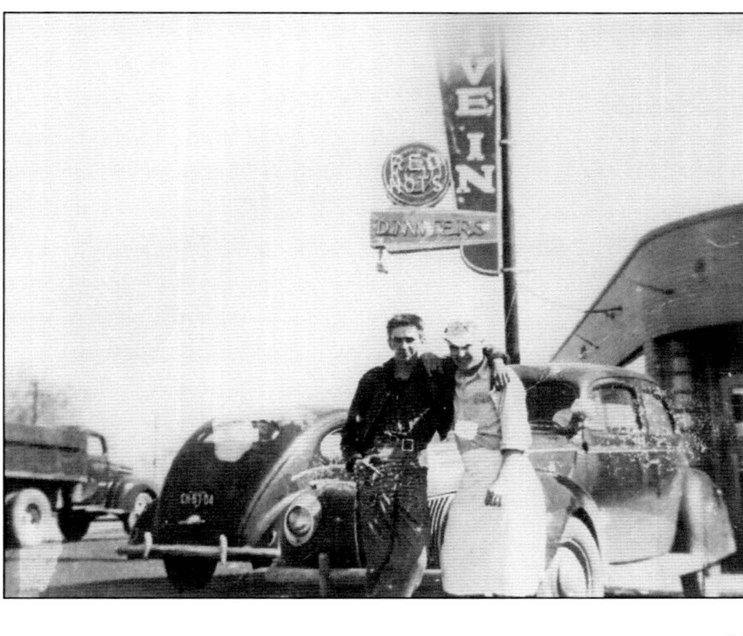

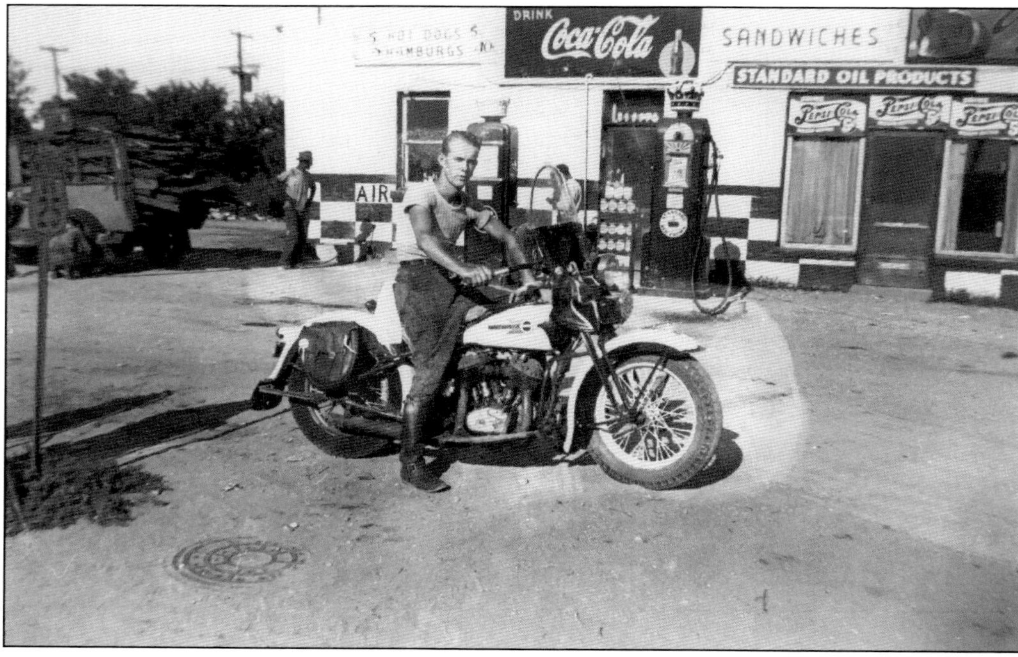

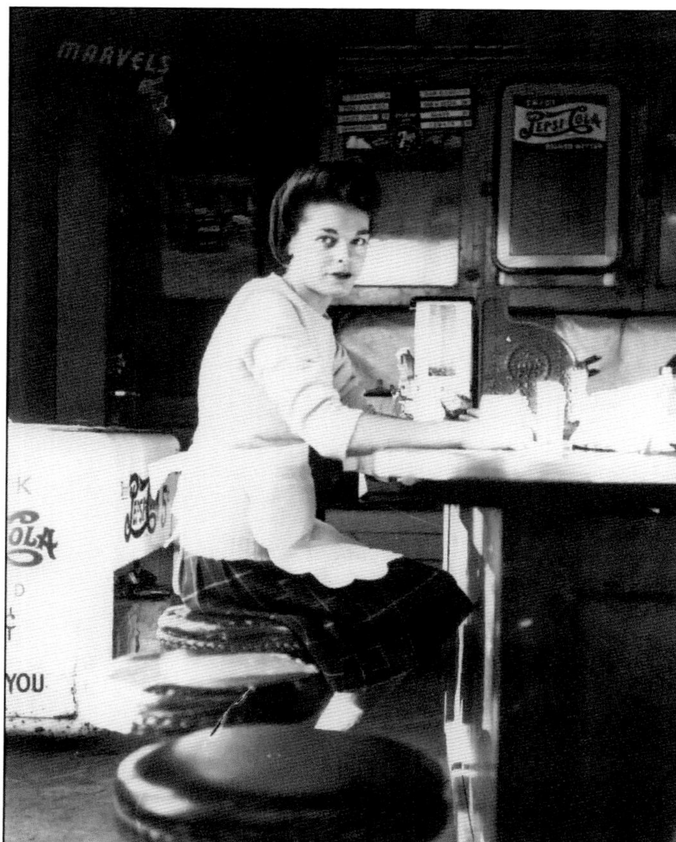

Mom & Pop's Gas Station and Restaurant, owned by Ray and Florence Taylor, was located on the northeast corner of Gratiot Avenue and 11 Mile Road. The gas station was one of Standard Oil's Red Crown stations. Jack Taylor (above), son of the owners, enjoys the day on his Harley-Davidson. Florence Taylor (at left) takes a rest at the counter inside the restaurant. Red Crown was a gasoline blend developed by Standard Oil. Later, the stations selling the blend were known as "Red Crown" stations. Red Crown also developed aviation fuel that was likely sold at Roseville's airfield. A BP station is at that corner today.

While the serviceman posing for this 1942 photograph outside Mom & Pop's Gas Station and Restaurant at 11 Mile Road and Gratiot Avenue is unidentified, it could easily be one of the Taylor boys. Raymond Taylor, oldest son of Ray and Florence, enlisted in the Army in 1941, followed almost immediately by his brother Walter that same year. Jack Taylor enlisted in 1942.

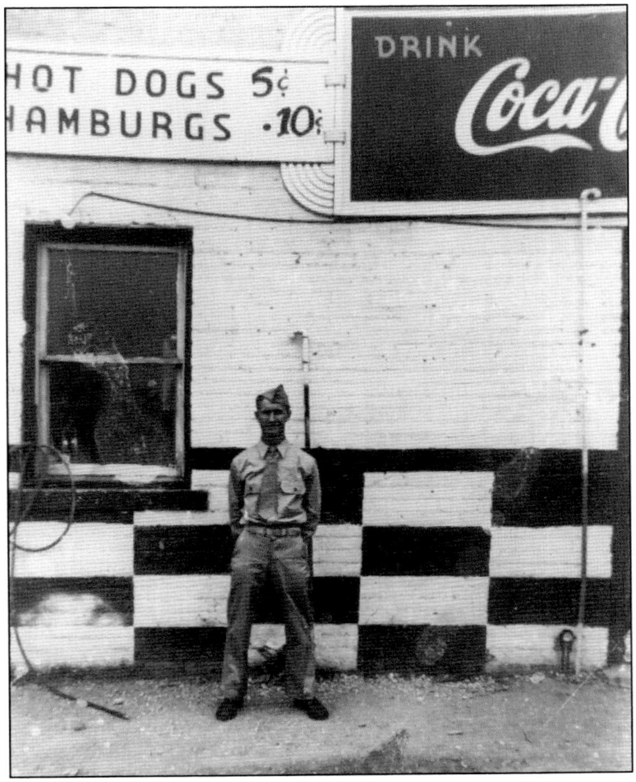

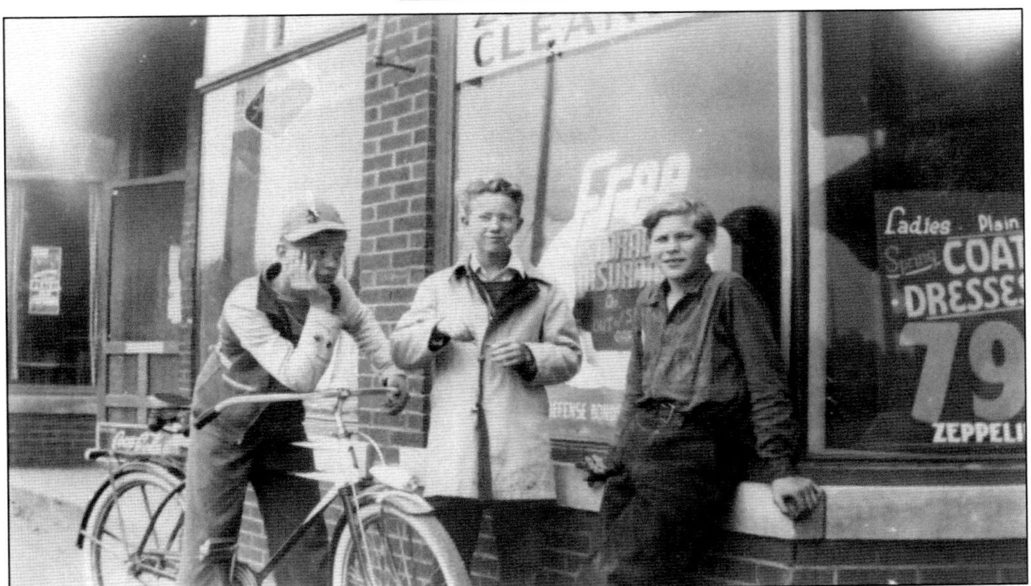

Neighborhood friends gather in front of Zeppelin Cleaners on 11 Mile Road, east of Gratiot Avenue, in 1944. From left to right are Benny Blauser, Kenny Taylor, and Bill Schultz. Defense bonds are offered in the window. These were later marketed as war bonds. Eight different sales drives were conducted, raising some $185.7 billion. Records indicate that both Blauser and Schultz enlisted in the Army in early 1946.

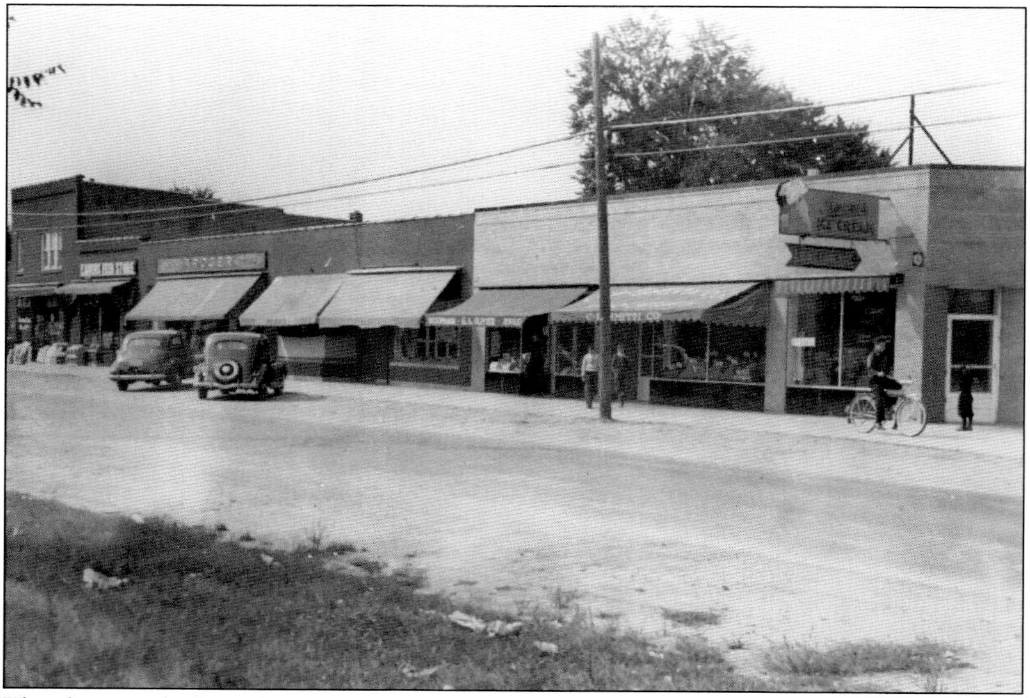

The photograph above depicts the block of businesses on Gratiot Avenue, between Martin Road and Elizabeth Street (just south of Utica Road), taken a few years before the photograph below. Notice Lauer's Feed Store remains in the two-story building and the addition of Lauer's Beer Store on the north end in the newer photograph. Kroger also remains in its location next to Lauer's. The Barnes Ice Cream store later became a popular hangout for Roseville teens, known to most as Dorlis Mae's Dairy Bar. This block in the Utica Junction area of the city still houses many retail establishments, including a longtime business, the Roseville Clock Shop.

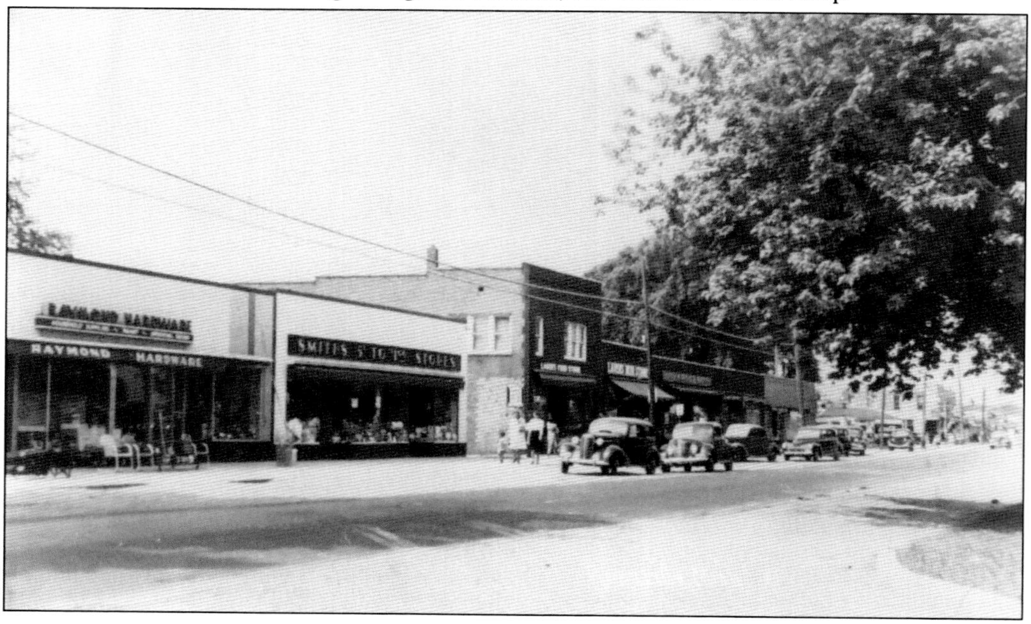

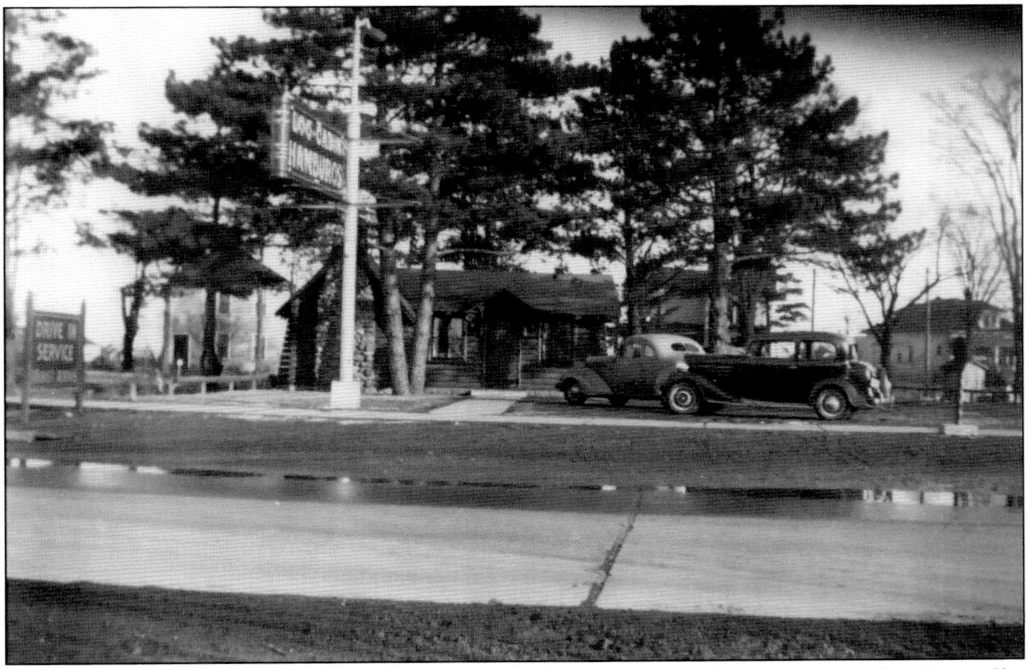

Arjay's Log Cabin Restaurant, seen in 1937, was a favorite among the young crowd in Roseville. The name Arjay's was dropped when ownership was changed sometime in the late 1940s or early 1950s. The restaurant was located at 11 Mile Road and Gratiot Avenue and removed during the construction of the I-696 expressway.

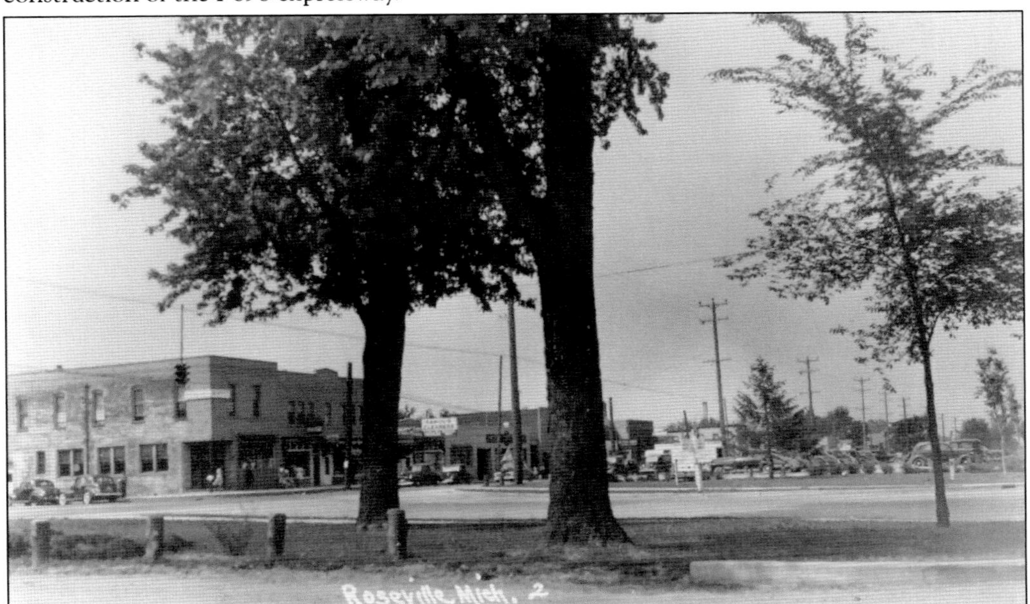

Looking north from Utica at the west side of Gratiot Avenue, this view of the Junction in the early 1940s shows, from left to right, the Roseville Bank (later a beauty shop), Suburban Drugs, Roseville Bakery, Quality Meat Market (owned and operated by John and Anna Hardiewich), A&P Grocery Store, Rolly's Grocery (owned and operated by Roland Thornton), and Famous Cleaners.

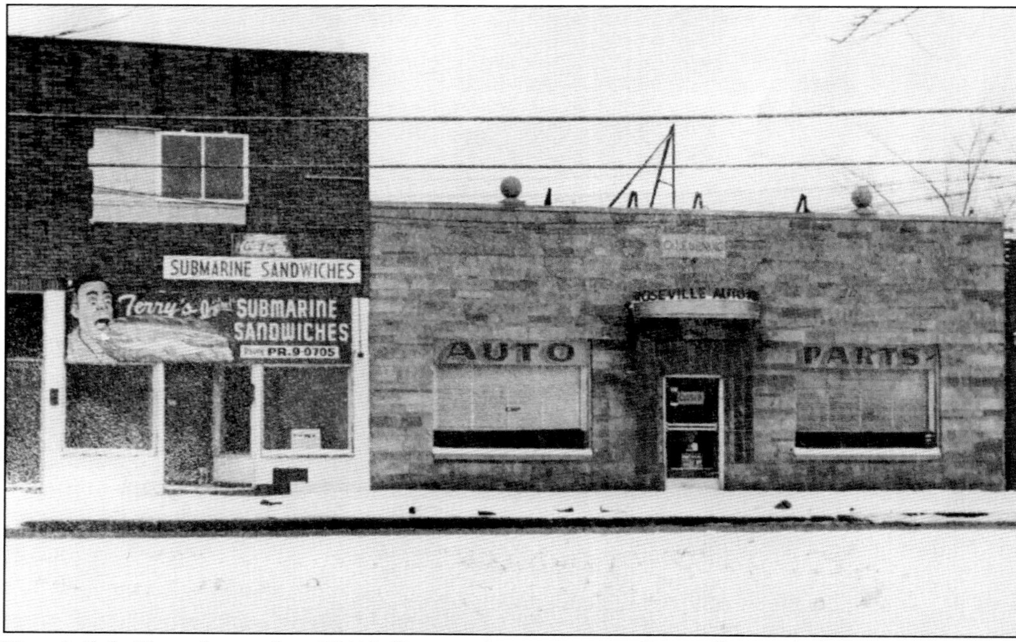

Terry's Sub Shop, located at 27419 Gratiot Avenue, was a Roseville staple known for its huge submarine sandwiches wrapped in wax paper. The popular sub shop was owned by John Jacobini and named for his son Terry. It opened in Roseville in 1957 and relocated to a standalone building on 15 Mile Road in Clinton Township sometime in 1976. It is now under new ownership. John Jacobini died in 2006.

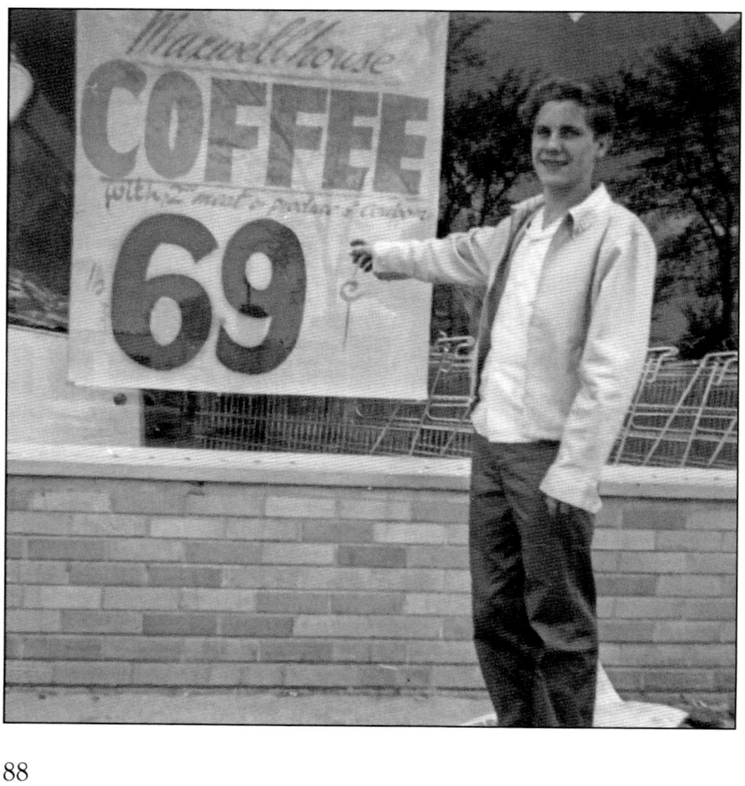

Frank's Super Market was located at 28705 Gratiot Avenue, just south of 12 Mile Road. Stock boy Johnny Garnett displays his loyalty by pointing out the good price for Maxwell House coffee. This photograph was taken in 1958. Frank's was owned by the Rudowski family. (Courtesy of Dorothy McRill.)

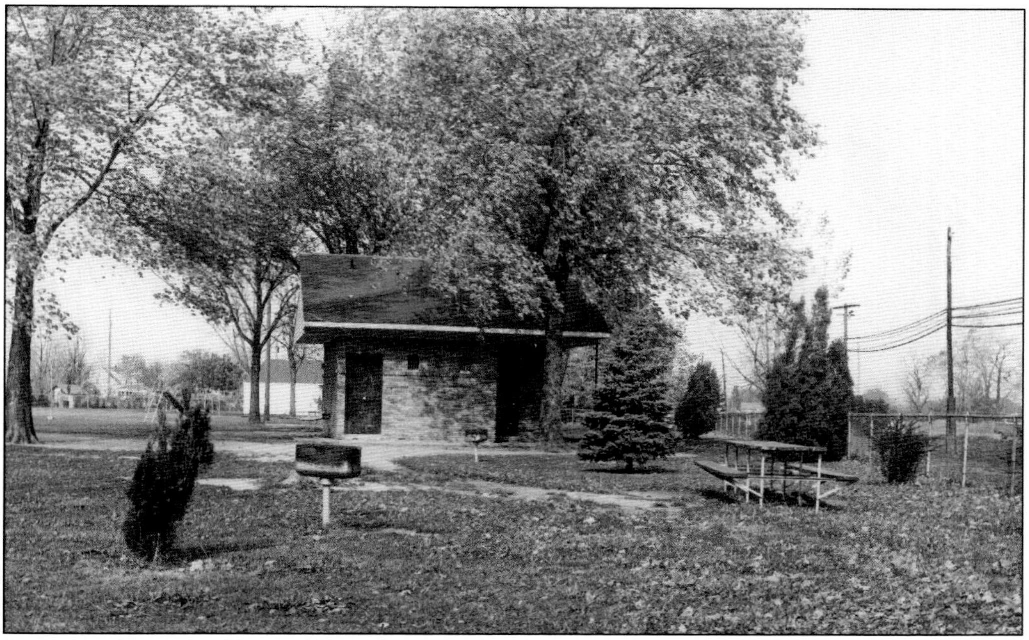

Rotary Park is one of Roseville's eight parks (not counting the recreation center). There are two other service club parks in Roseville: Kiwanis Park on Martin Road and Lion's Park on Wellington Street. Rotary Park at Utica Road and Eastland Street has a baseball diamond, tennis courts, restrooms, updated playground equipment, and a heavily used covered pavilion. Other Roseville parks include Dooley, Huron, Macomb Gardens, Packard, and Veteran's Memorial.

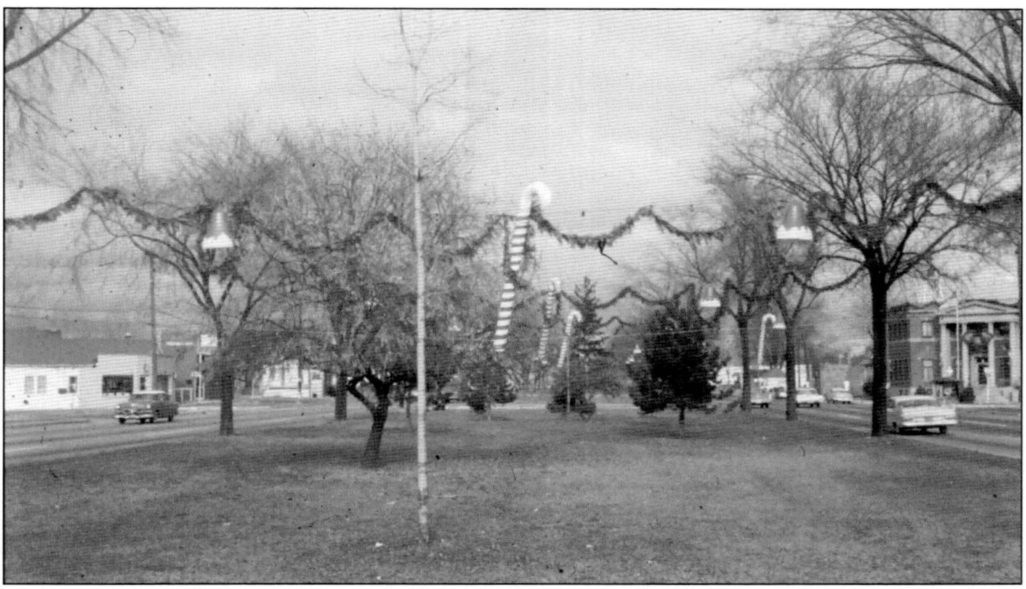

The City of Roseville Department of Public Works has always gone all out to decorate the city for the holidays. And where do cities go for holiday decorations? The Bronner's Christmas Wonderland store in Frankenmuth, of course. Billed as the largest Christmas store in the world, Bronner's was founded in 1945 by Wally Bronner and is visited by over two million people a year. (Courtesy of Bronner's Christmas Wonderland.)

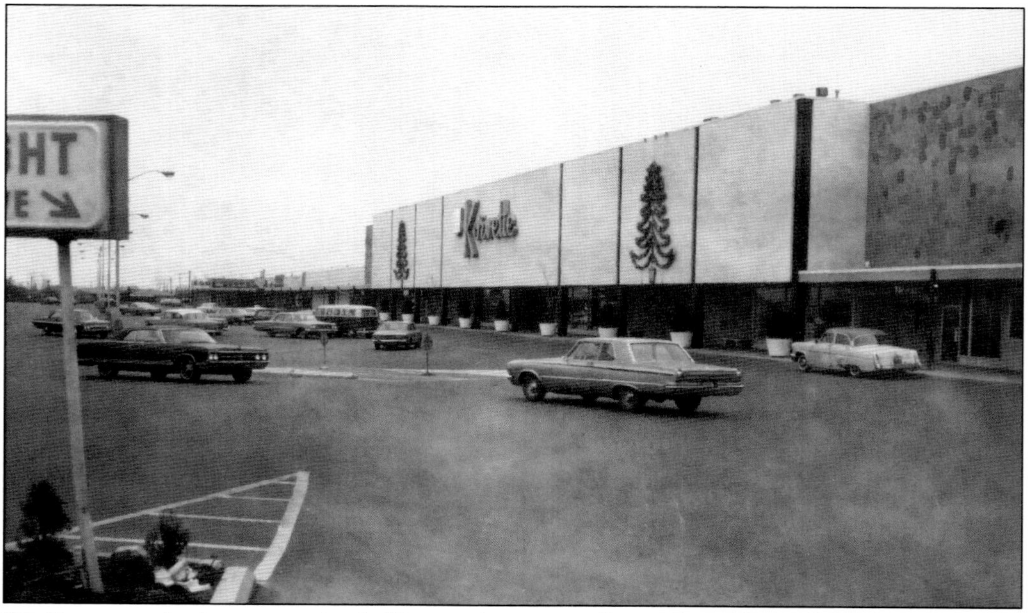

E.J. Korvette, also known as simply Korvette's, came to Roseville in the early 1960s. Located at 12 Mile Road and Gratiot Avenue opposite the Top Hat restaurant, Korvette's became a popular department store among Roseville residents. The retailer fell on hard times in the late 1970s. E.J. Korvette entered bankruptcy in 1980. Roseville Towne Center currently occupies this location and hosts a Walmart, Dollar Tree, and CVS Pharmacy, among others.

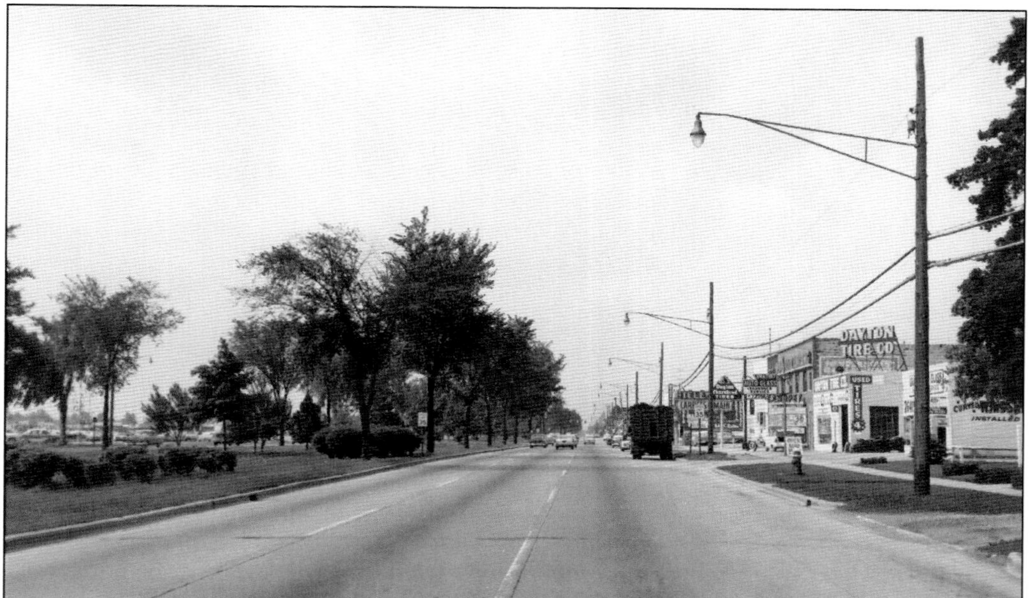

This early-1960s view is looking south down Gratiot Avenue across from the Eastgate Shopping Center. The commercial district looks little different today. This stretch of Gratiot in the late 1950s and early 1960s was home to Brockmann Funeral Home, Dayton Tire Company, Courtesy Cab, and Guiseppe's Pizzeria, just to name a few. Some of the businesses along that stretch in 2015 include Christopher Ross Funeral Home, Corky's, Mr. Windshield, and Oceans and Seas.

Metro Detroit has long been the bowling capital of the world. In the late 1970s, there were some 300,000 members of the Metro Detroit US Bowling Congress. Continental Lanes was opened by local jazz musician Eddie Pawl as a side investment and operated for 50 years before being razed in 2014. An astute businessman as well as accomplished musician, Pawl owned other entertainment venues, including Thunderbowl Bowling Lanes, Sunny Acres Golf Course, and Lido's on the Lake. Pawl died in 2013 at the age of 85. Other bowling alleys in Roseville over the years included Roseville Recreation, Topper Lanes, Joe's (DeCarlo's) Bowling Alley (still operating as Apollo Bowling Center), Liberty Bowl, and Rose Bowl. Richard McRill (below), of Roseville, was in top form while bowling for many years on men's leagues at popular Continental Lanes in Roseville. (Both courtesy of Dorothy McRill.)

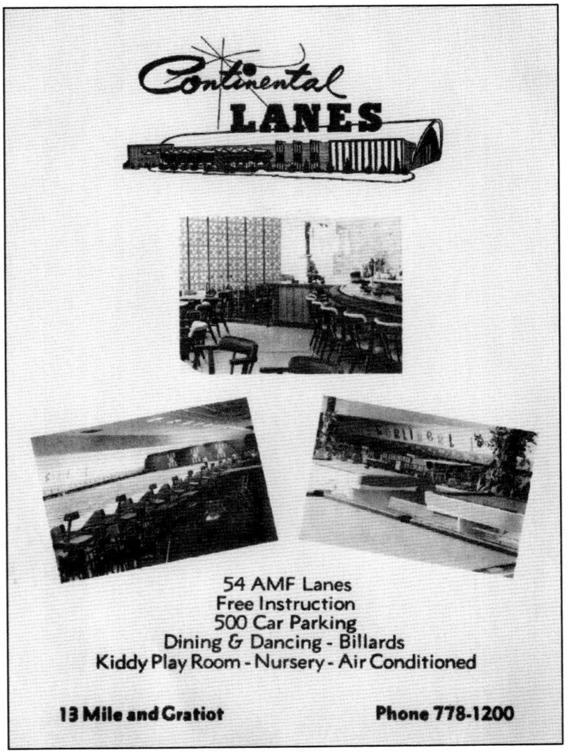

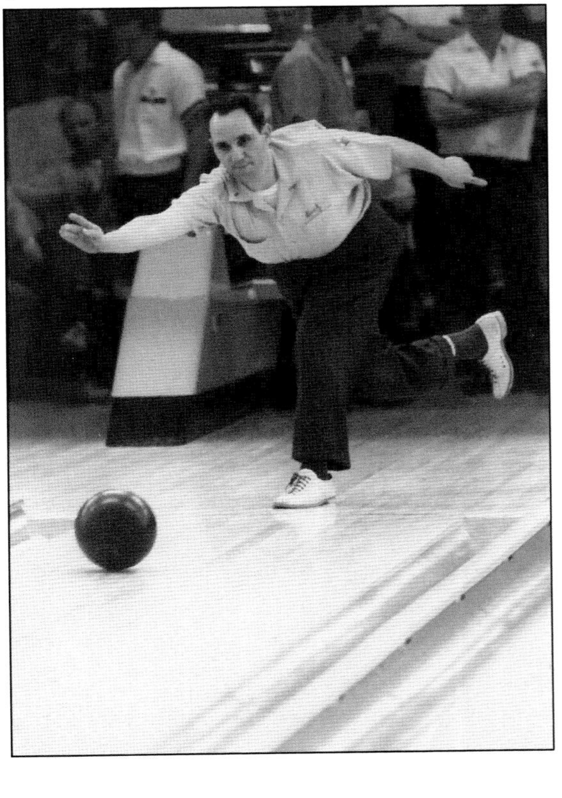

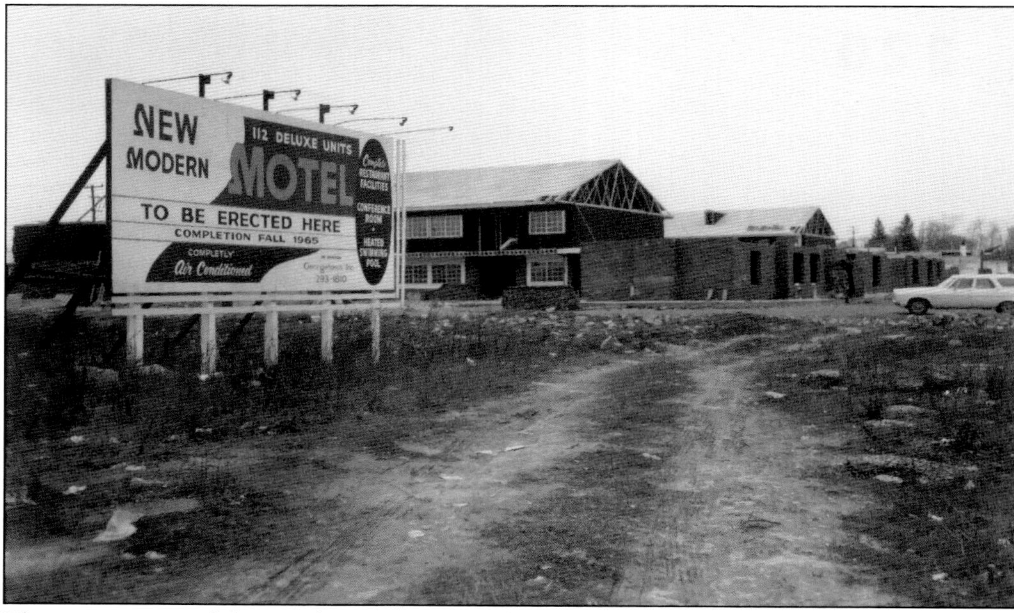

The construction of the swanky Georgian Inn (above) with 112 air-conditioned deluxe units was a big deal in Roseville in 1965. By the early 1970s, the Georgian Inn, with its Georgian brick and elegant appointments (below), was already a destination for upscale travelers. The development included a banquet center, conference center, restaurant, lounge, and heated outdoor pool. It has been through several remodels and owners, most recently going from a Best Western to a Days Inn property. Days Inn hotels are now part of the Wyndham Hotel Group. Its location just off I-94 makes Roseville a perfect location for hotels and restaurants.

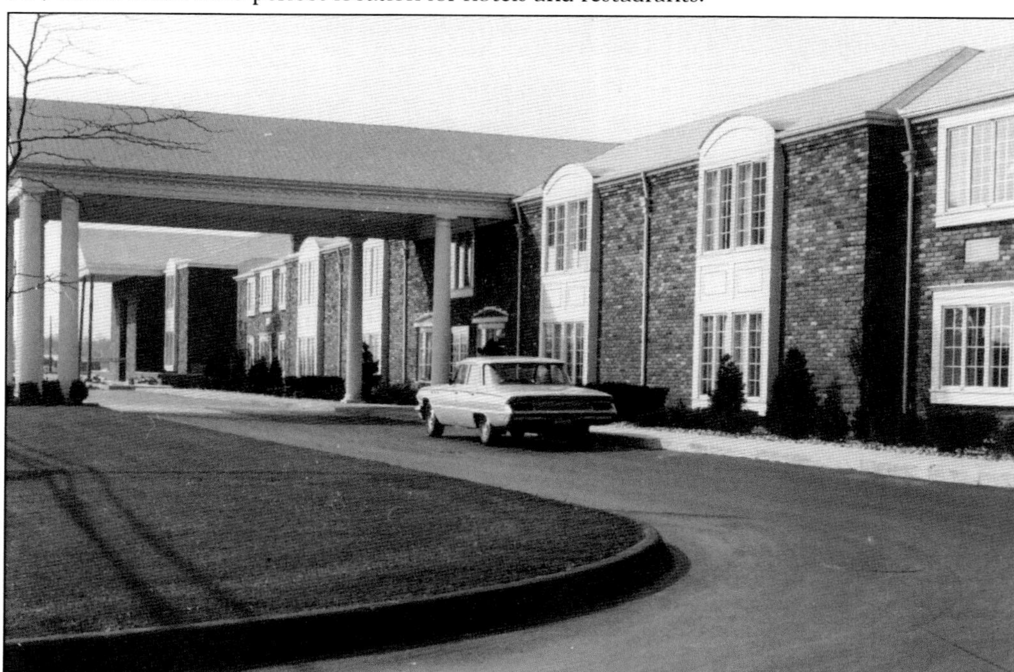

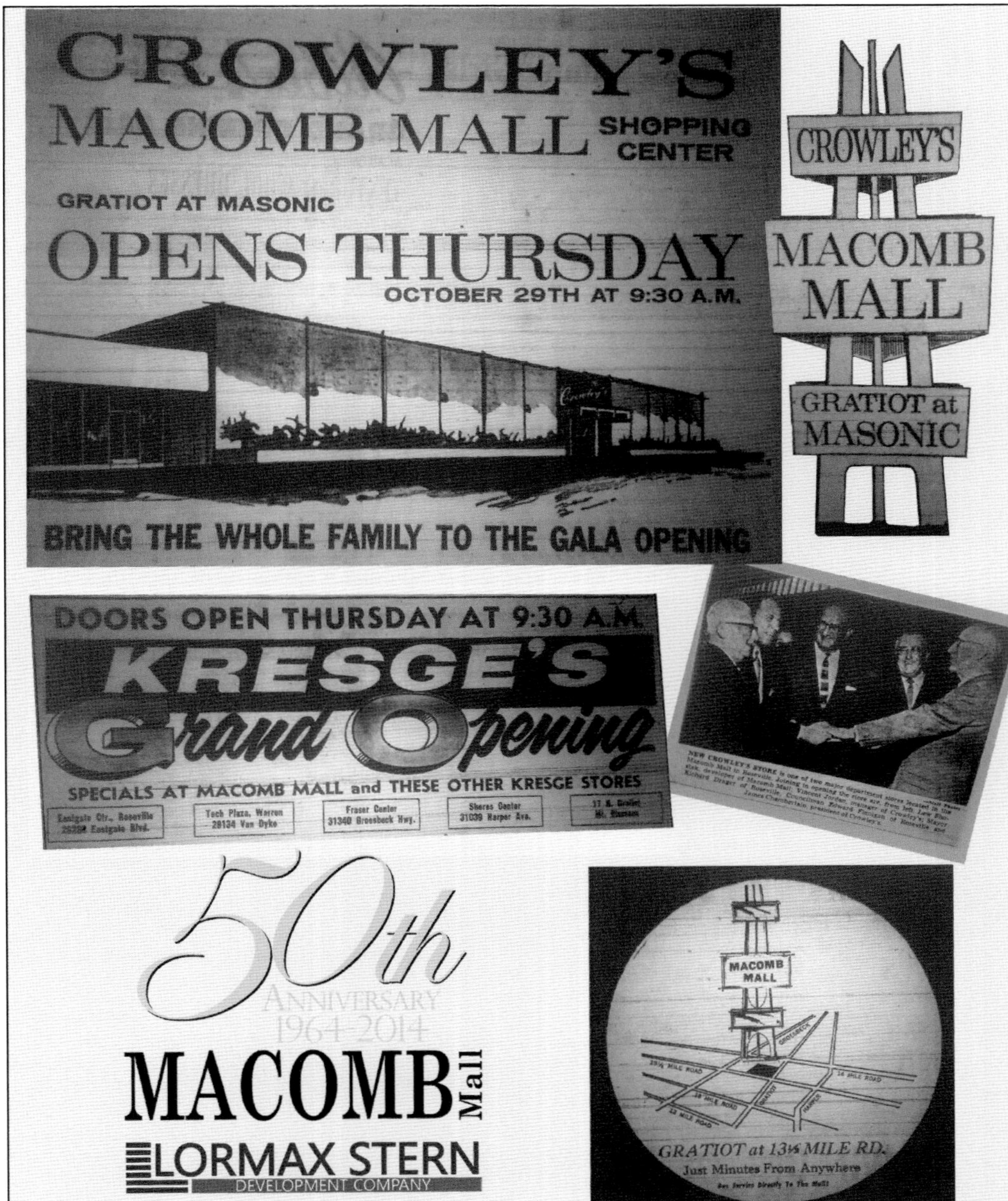

Macomb Mall, one of the earliest in the country, opened with great fanfare on October 29, 1964. Its anchor stores included Crowley's, Sears, and Kresge. The mall was developed by Schostack Brothers of Detroit. The mall was expanded in 1985 when a Main Street store was added. The store was converted to Kohl's in 1989. A larger renovation took place in 1999 when Old Navy was added, and Crowley's, which had filed for bankruptcy, was sold to Value City. The Schostack Brothers continued to manage the property until selling it in 2004. Ownership changed hands a couple of times before Lormax Stern Development purchased Macomb Mall in 2013. In 2014, its new owner, Lormax Stern Development Company, celebrated the mall's 50th anniversary again with great fanfare and the announced opening of Dick's, the sporting-goods giant, where Crowley's once stood. (Courtesy of Macomb Mall.)

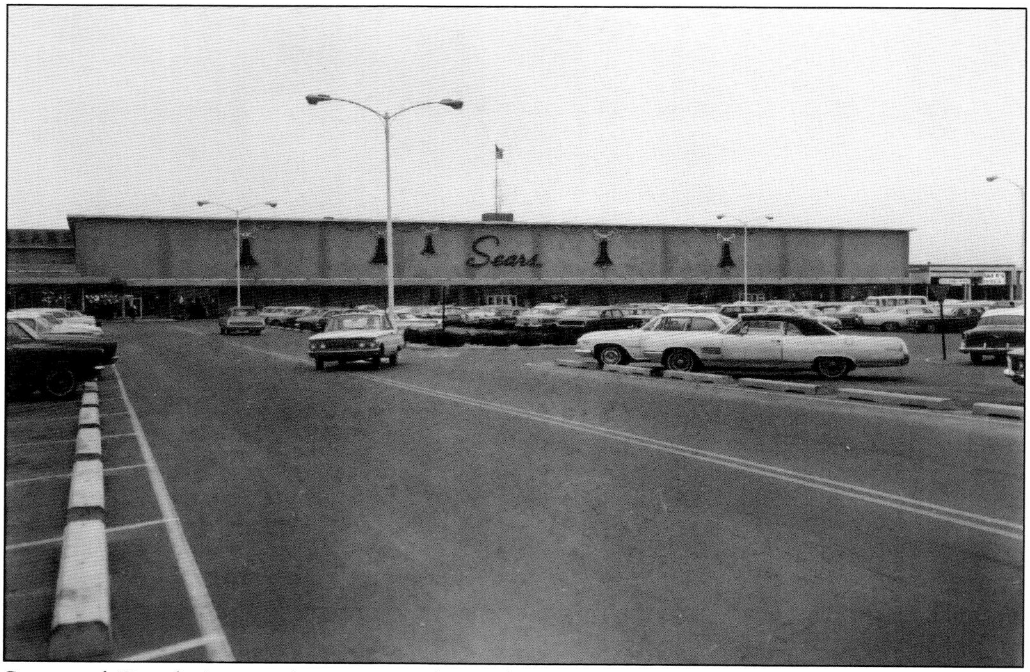

Sears and Crowley's were the major anchors when Macomb Mall opened in 1964; Sears is still there. Today, Sears and Kmart are held under the same holding company. Generally referred to as Crowley's, Crowley Milner and Company was a department-store chain founded in Detroit in 1909. After several years of financial difficulties, the company ceased operations in 1999, and its assets were sold. Packer's was one of the many food chains in Roseville at the time. The Packer's store is now occupied by Party City, and a Babies 'R' Us store has been added at the far north end.

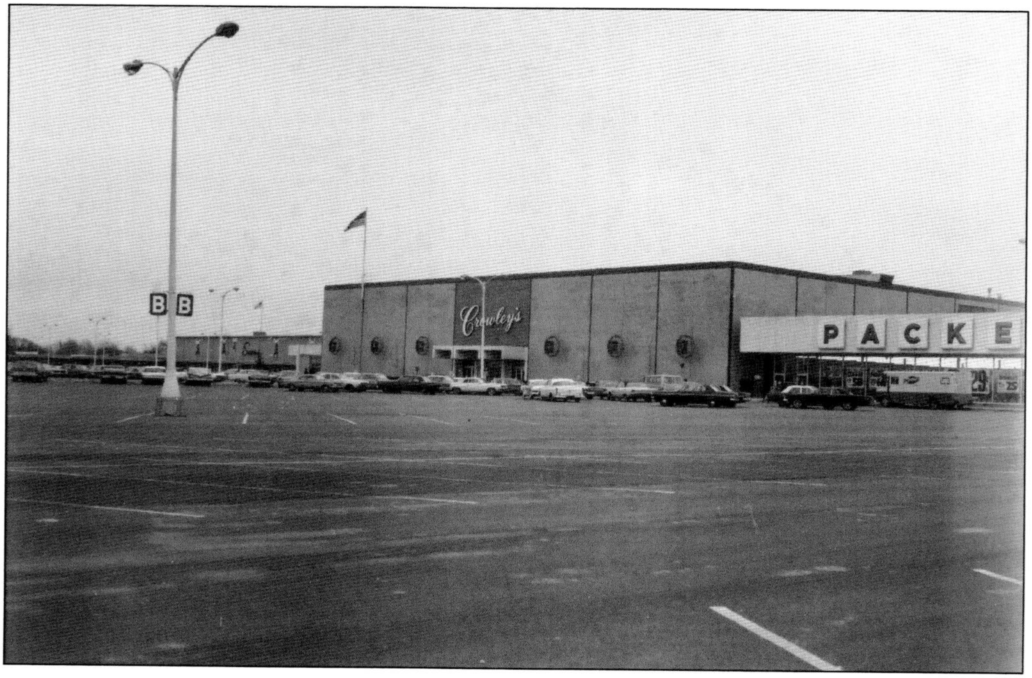

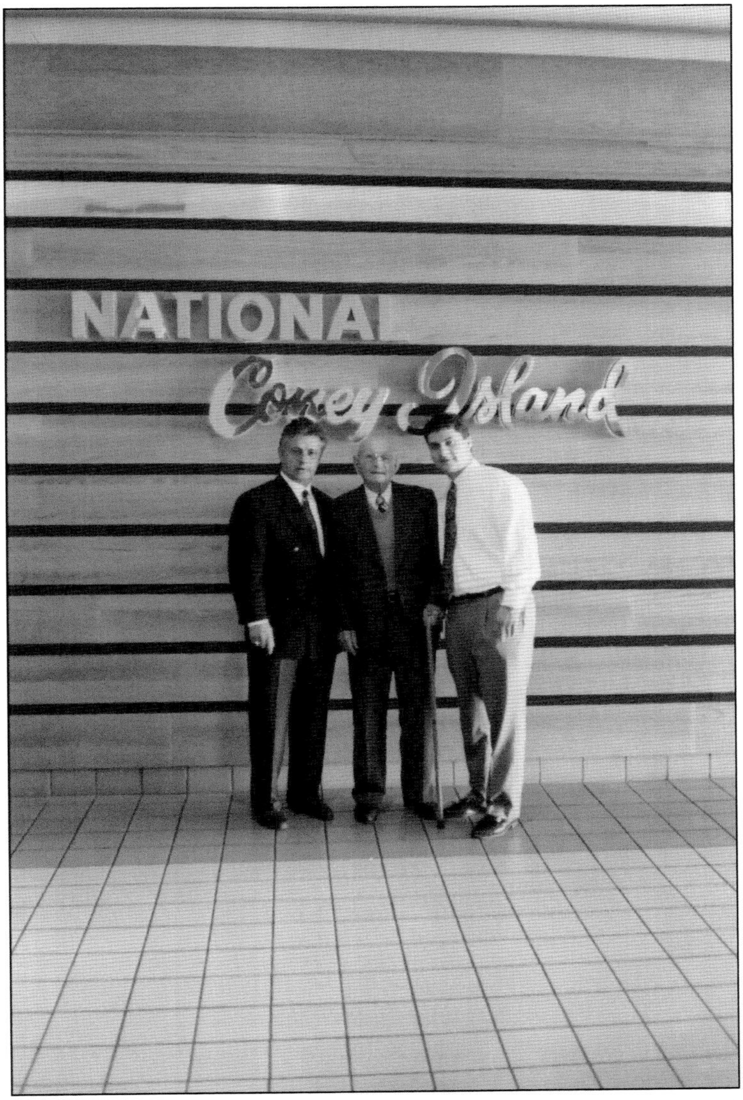

When Macomb Mall opened, one of the new tenants was James Giftos. In 1965, in a narrow unit inside the mall, Giftos started a small restaurant serving Coney dogs, hamburgers, and fries. The little store would become the first among the National Coney Island group of 20 restaurants. Pictured at right in 1987, outside their expanded location at Macomb Mall, are founder James Giftos (left); son Tom Giftos Jr. (right), current president of National Coney Island, Inc.; and the founder's father, Tom Giftos. James Giftos and his father have since passed away. Below is the original menu board from the Macomb Mall diner. (Both courtesy of National Coney Island.)

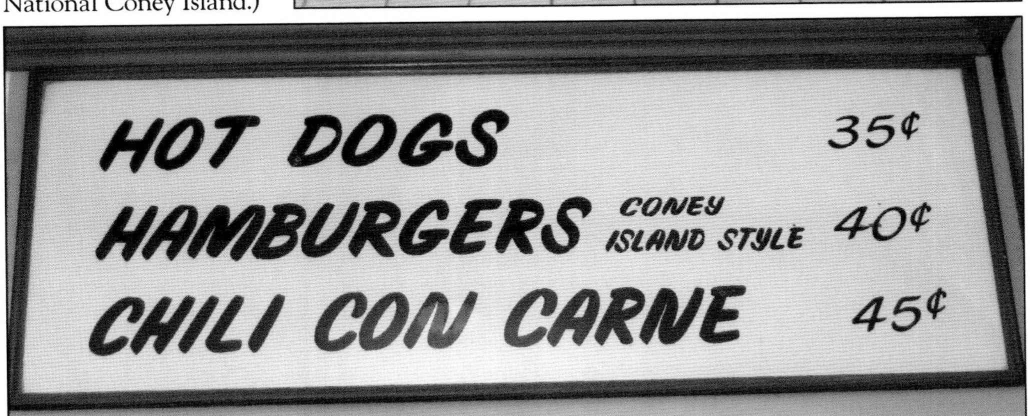

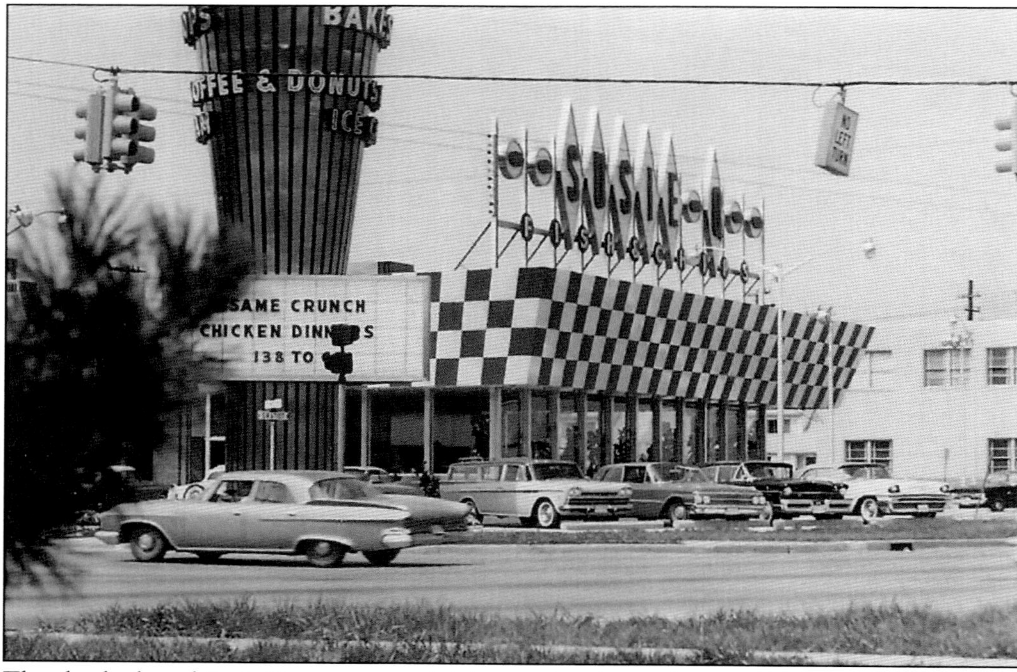

The checkerboard Susie Q restaurant, with its rotating sign at the corner of Gratiot Avenue and 11 Mile Road, was a popular meeting place for teenagers and Gratiot Avenue cruisers in the 1950s and 1960s. This photograph was taken by Albert Gerbel, grandfather of Terry Koss, who posted it on the Susie Q Facebook page and later reposted on the "I Grew Up in Roseville" Facebook page. (Courtesy of Terry Koss.)

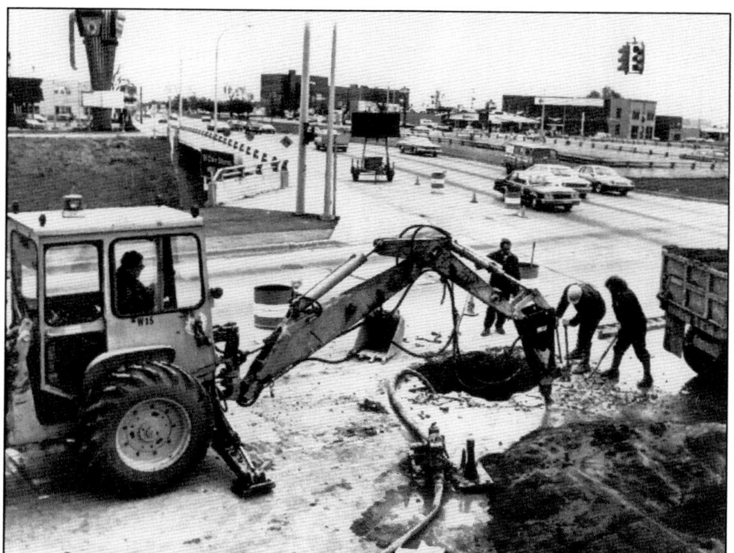

Some years later, Arthur Treacher's, the fish-and-chips chain, took over the restaurant space; however, after the I-696 freeway went through, the restaurant and sign (in the background of the construction photograph below) fell into serious disrepair. After restoration of the sign by its new owner, National Coney Island, the sign again rotates happily to Gratiot Avenue cruisers' (and I-696 motorists') delight.

A ribbon cutting was held for the February 1, 1967, opening of the final 5.5-mile final stretch of I-94 between Vernier Road in Harper Woods and Masonic Boulevard in St. Clair Shores. I-94 makes up half of Roseville's eastern city limits. Begun in 1963, the Macomb County segment of the 275-mile Michigan portion of I-94 is named after James G. O'Hara, the US Representative for Roseville from 1959 to 1977.

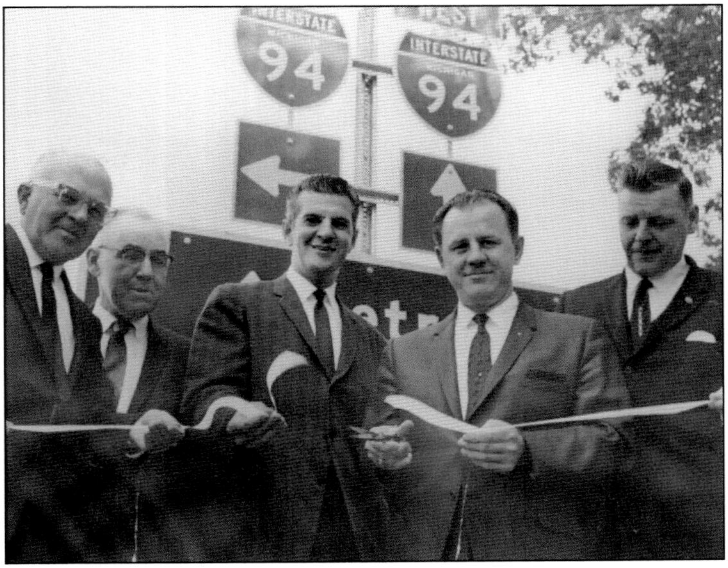

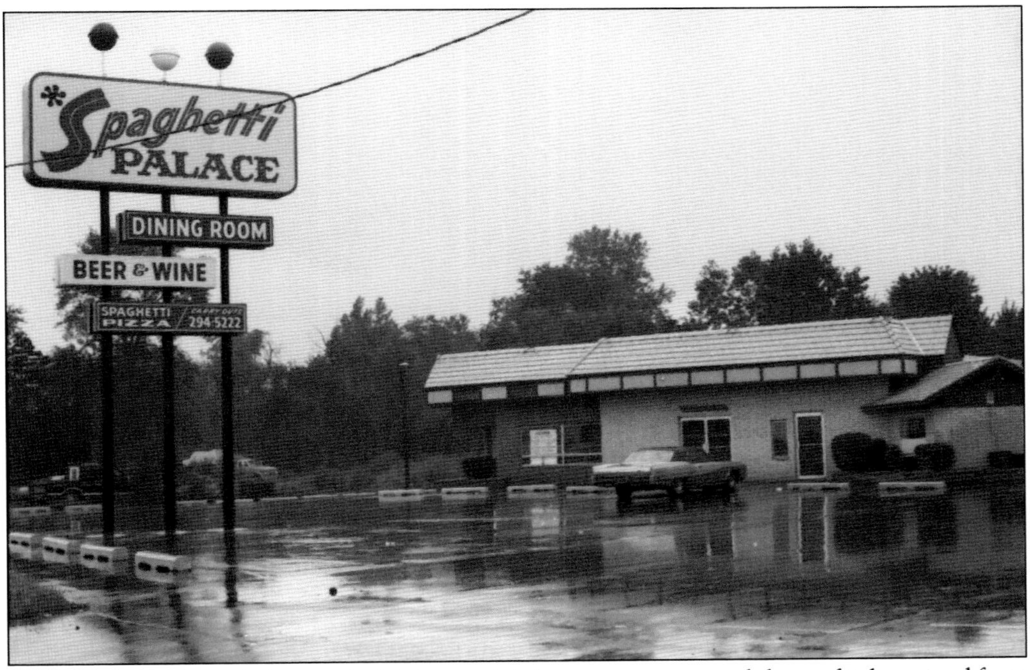

Anthony "Tony" Zerilli, known for his Detroit Mafia connections, used the profits he gained from the sale of the Hazel Park Raceway to open the Spaghetti Palace Restaurant on Gratiot Avenue in 1968. Tony worked at the Detroit Italian American Bakery in Roseville during his teenage years. The Spaghetti Palace became the Zerilli headquarters and was a staple in Roseville until its closing in the early 1990s.

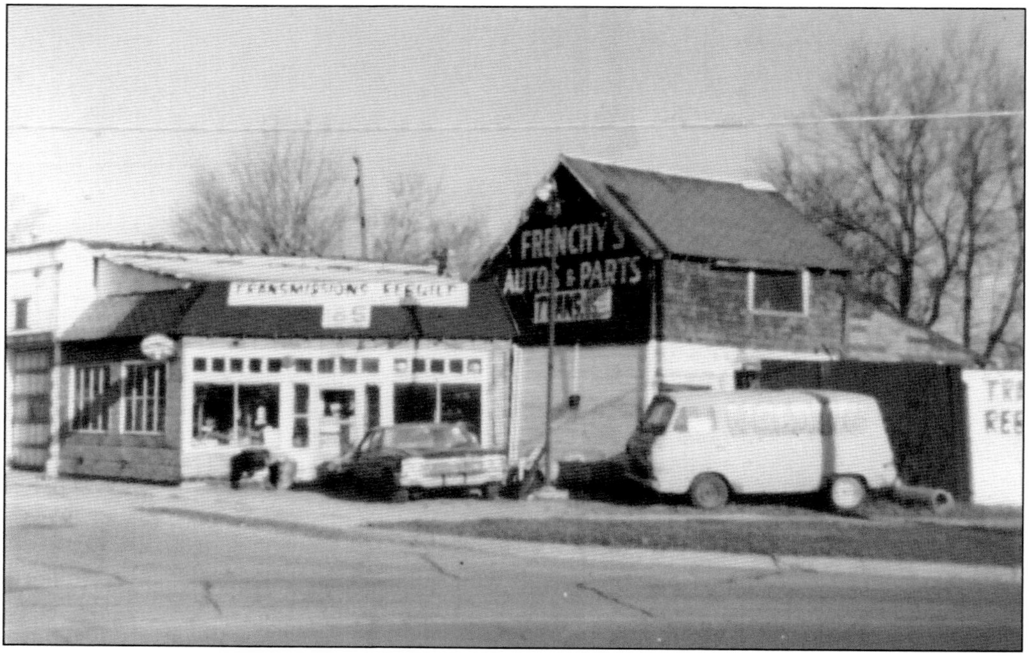

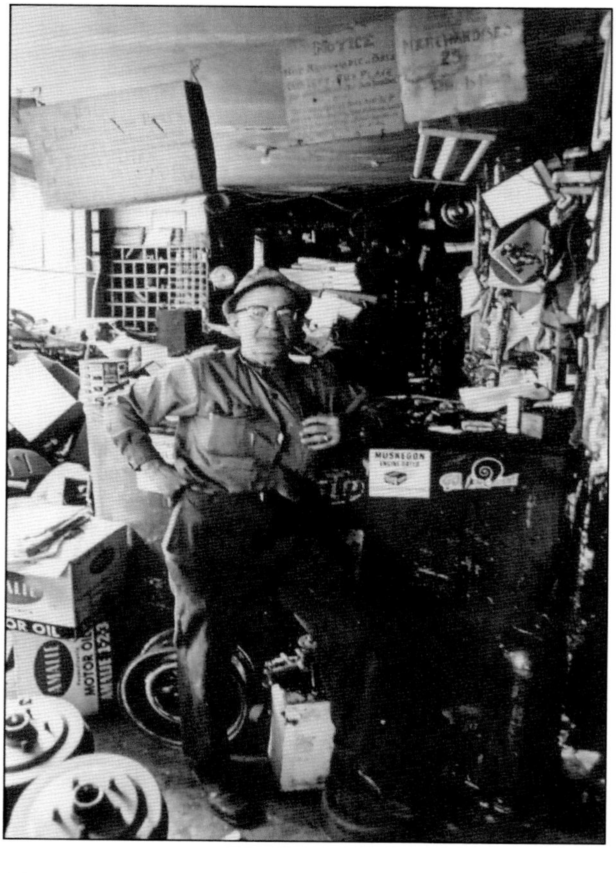

During World War II, new cars and parts were scarce, so everyone in Roseville and beyond went to Frenchy's Auto Parts on Gratiot Avenue at Florian Street, where he and his wife, Anna, filled their two-acre former farmland with old cars and parts. Dumitru "Frenchy" Simionescu (at left) was born in Romania and moved to Roseville in 1925. He died in 1985 at the age of 95. He married Anna in 1944. They recovered and rebuilt from a devastating 1949 fire. The family lived in a home on Florian, near the auto parts store. Anna ran the business until she passed away in 2002. (Courtesy of the Simionescu family.)

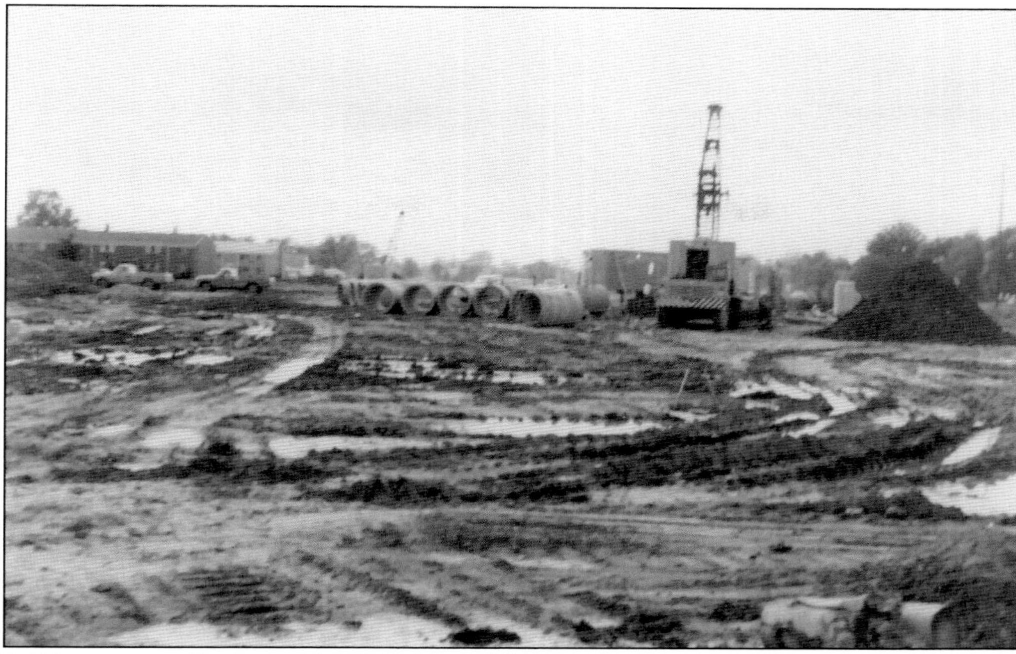

I-696 was originally proposed as I-98, part of the Interstate Highway System enacted in 1956; however, that designation was rejected. Construction for I-696 began in 1961. The Roseville segment and interchange with I-94 was opened in January 1979. Photographs of the construction taking place between Belleair and Collingwood Streets are from 1972. Many homes and businesses were moved or demolished to make room for the freeway through Roseville. The original Erin Township Hall, Trinity United Methodist Church, and the Odd Fellows Hall were a few of the casualties. Many homes relocated to vacant lots in Roseville, such as on Park Street where children, now adults, recall the recurring shout, "A house is coming! A house is coming!"

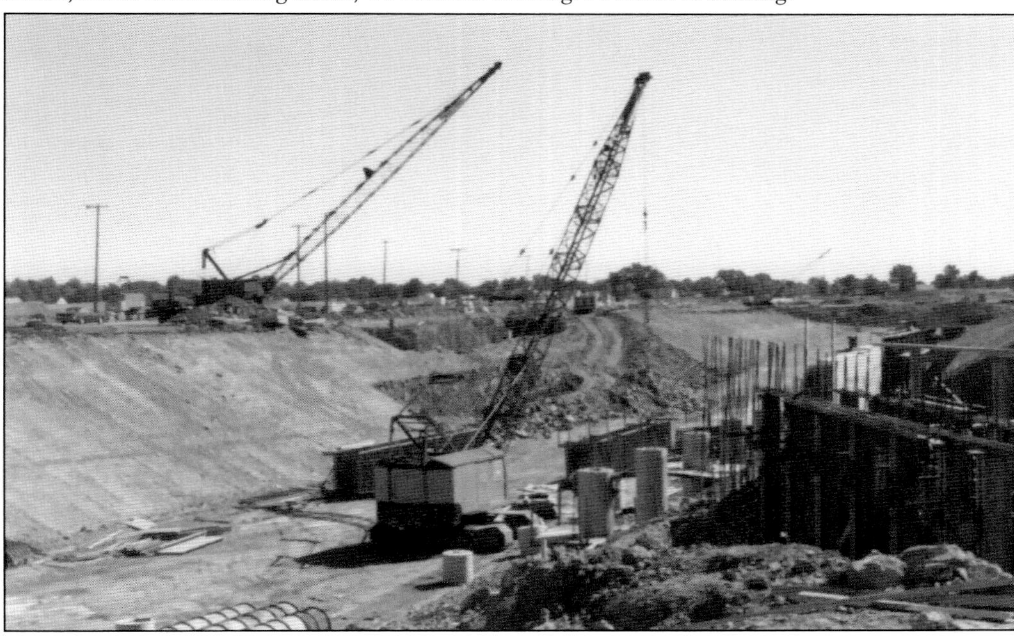

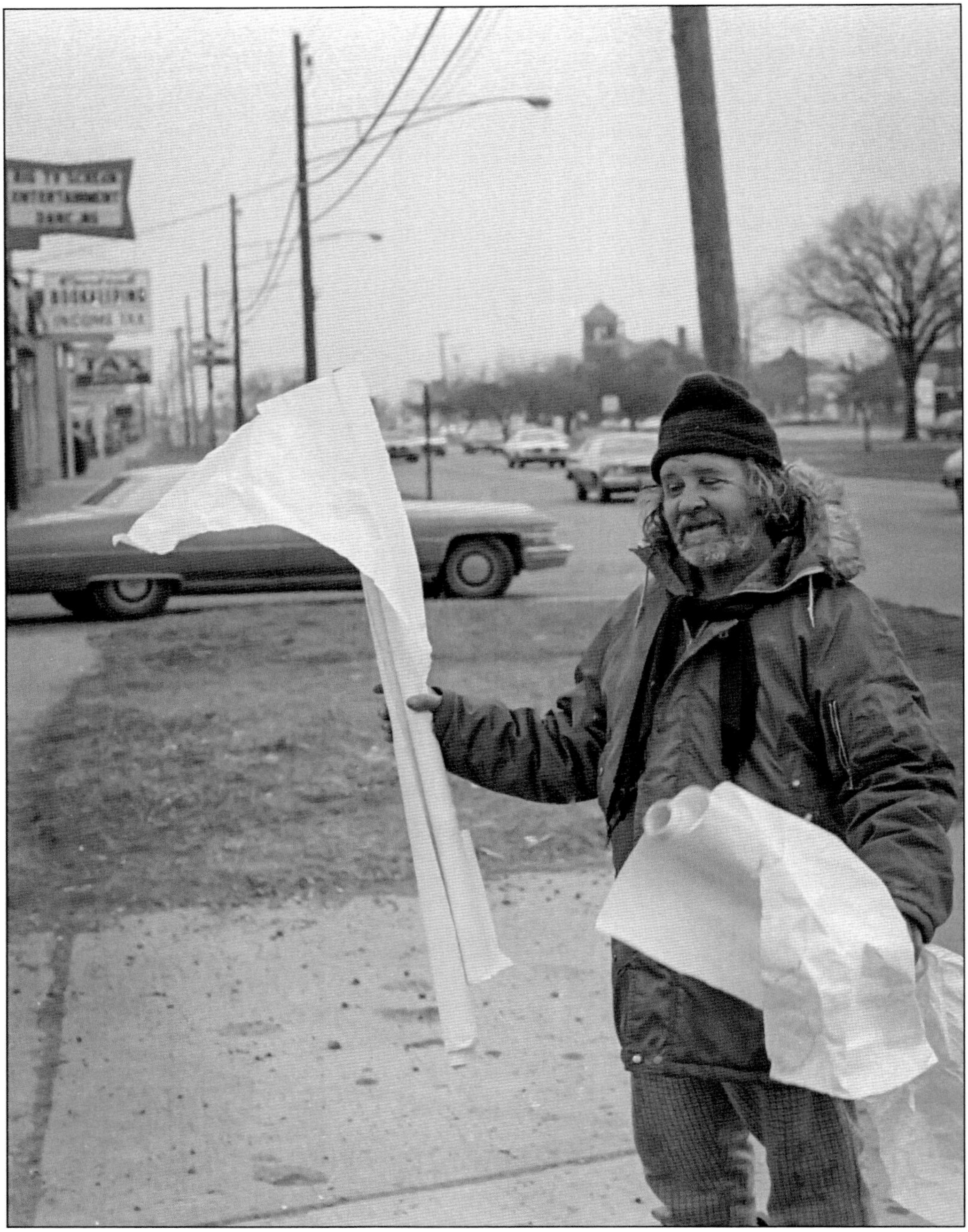

Ed Choley, affectionately known to Roseville residents as "Mr. Gratiot," is pictured here on Gratiot Avenue just south of Martin Road. Choley grew up in Roseville and served his country in World War II, returning home with what is known today as posttraumatic stress disorder. A talented artist, he drew caricatures and cartoon characters, giving them to children outside the library. He collected hubcaps, earning him the nickname of "Hubcap" as well as Mr. Gratiot. He often talked to "Joe," an imaginary friend, while he walked the streets of Roseville. Choley died in 1981 at the age of 59. (Courtesy of Bill Spengler.)

Seven

Around the Neighborhood

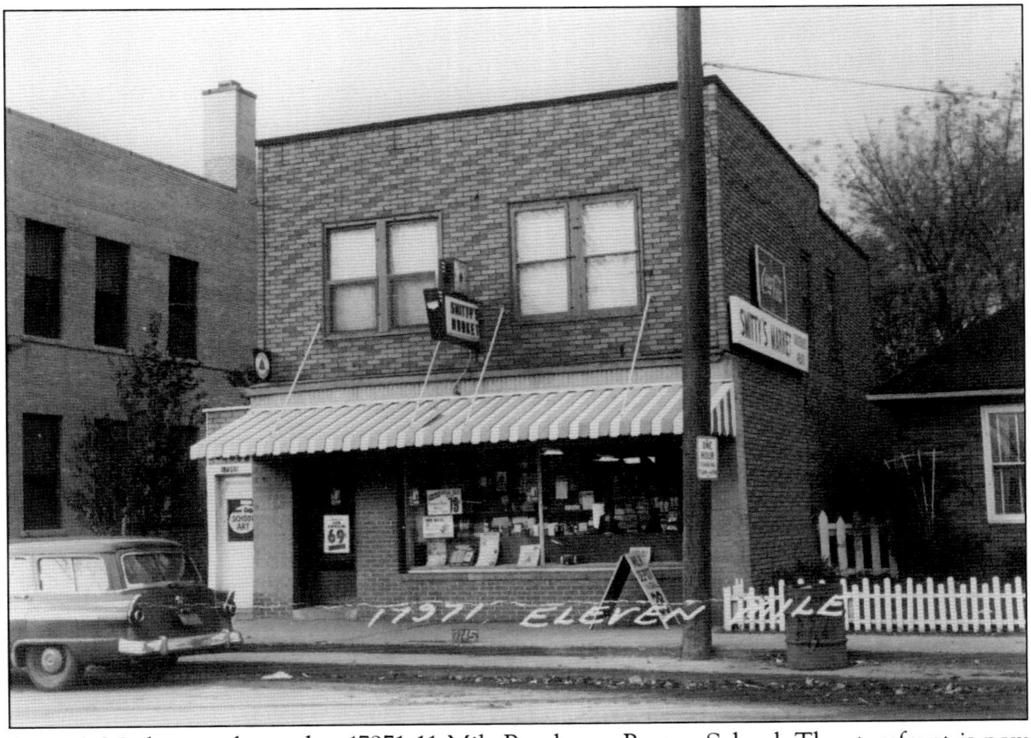

Smitty's Market was located at 17971 11 Mile Road near Burton School. The storefront is now occupied by the Hell's Our Home Detroit M/C, the founding chapter of Hell's Our Home Motorcycle Club. Hell's Our Home M/C was founded in 1949. The club regularly hosts benefit spaghetti dinners and barbecues and aids other members and families in need.

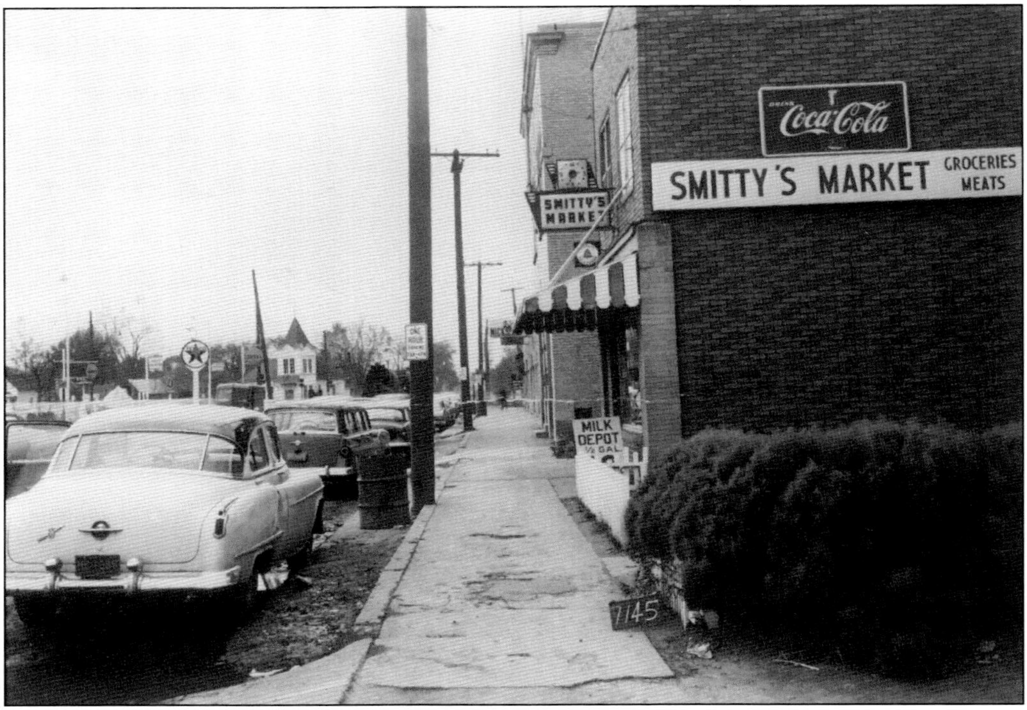

Smitty's Market, on 11 Mile Road east of Gratiot Avenue, carried everything from soup to nuts and was typical of the many mom-and-pop neighborhood stores in Roseville in 1940. Note the ubiquitous Coca-Cola advertisement above, as well as the Michigan Bell Public Telephone sign. Smitty's also advertised "Milk Depot ½ GAL." Although the price cannot be made out, half a gallon of milk in 1960 cost 52¢. Below, Bob Smith chats with unidentified customers. Note the advertisement for Lux soap. In 1885, Englishmen William and James Lever hired a chemist to develop a "self-foaming" soap made of palm oil instead of tallow. Lever Brothers became England's largest company at the time and virtually cornered the soap market. In 1930, Lever Brothers merged with a Dutch company to form Unilever, arguably the first modern multinational company.

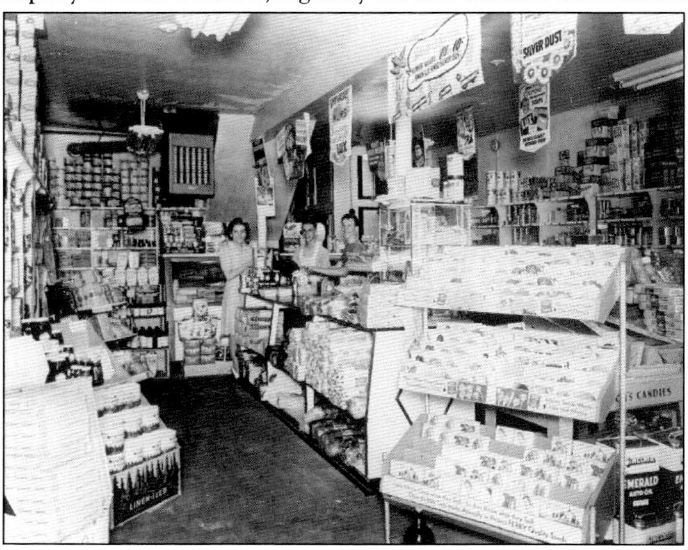

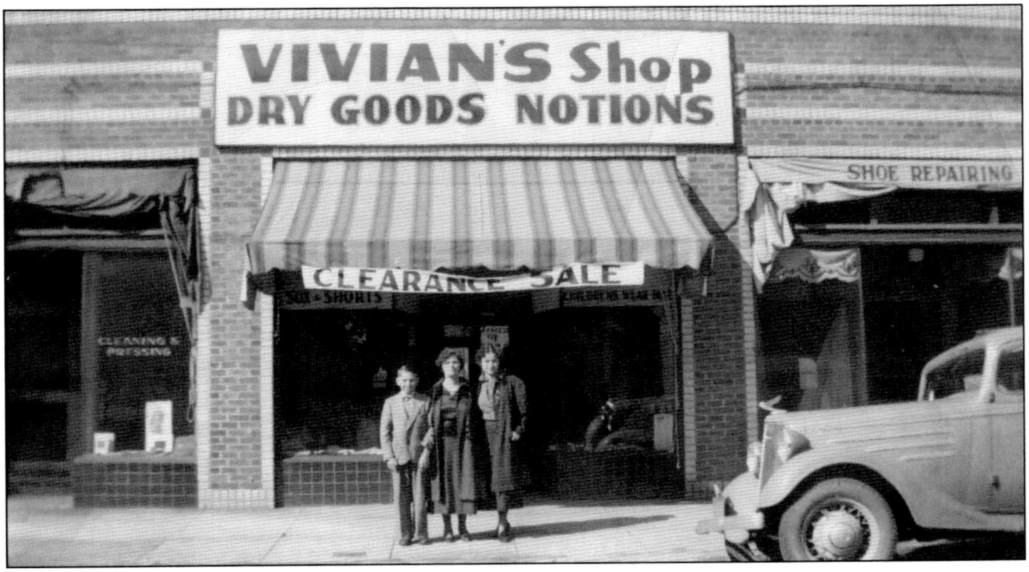

Seen above in 1934 outside their dry goods store on 11 Mile Road, just east of Gratiot Avenue near where the old Red Cross building and Hell's Our Home motorcycle club are today, are Jennie (center) and Grace Vivian with Harold Tolley. In the United Kingdom, Canada, and Australia, the term "dry goods" is used to refer to dry food. In the United States, dry goods are products such as textiles, ready-to-wear clothing, and sundries, excluding items carried by hardware and grocery stores. Below, Grace Vivian (left) poses with her many neighborhood friends, including Glen Alsip (second from left, in knickers), who would grow up to become Roseville village president. (Both courtesy of Pat Chownyk.)

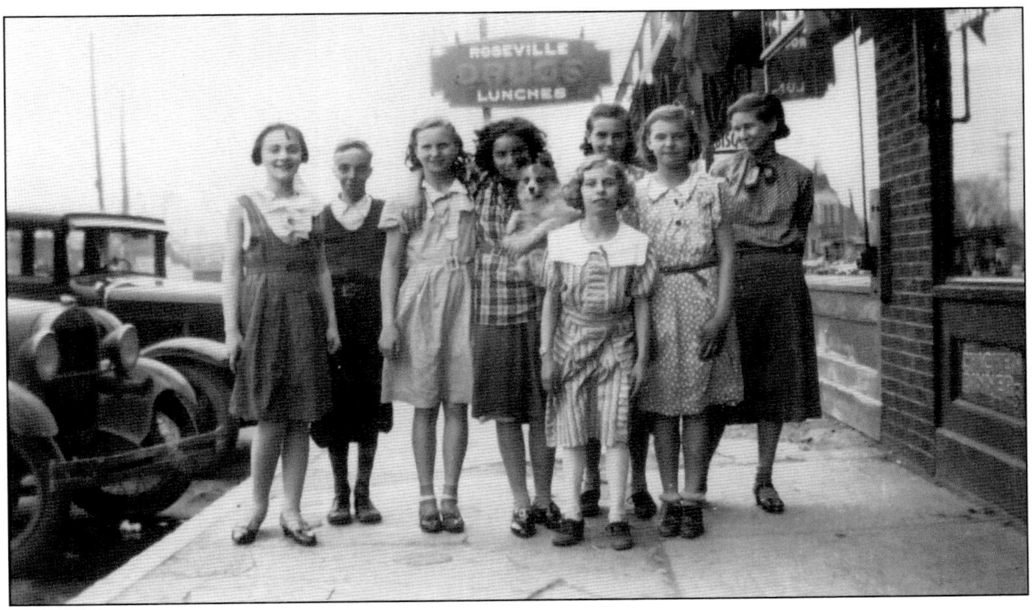

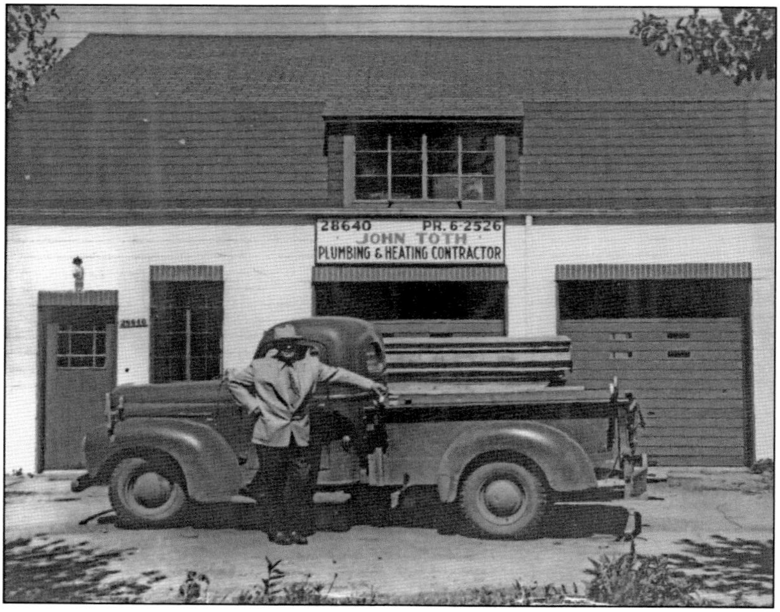

John Toth poses outside his plumbing and heating business at 28640 Utica Road; note the phone number, PR-6-2526. Longtime Roseville residents readily recall that "PR" stood for "Prescott" (7-7) on the phone dial. Telephone exchanges were phased out for an all-numeric system by the 1960s. Gregory J Auto Sales is located at that address today.

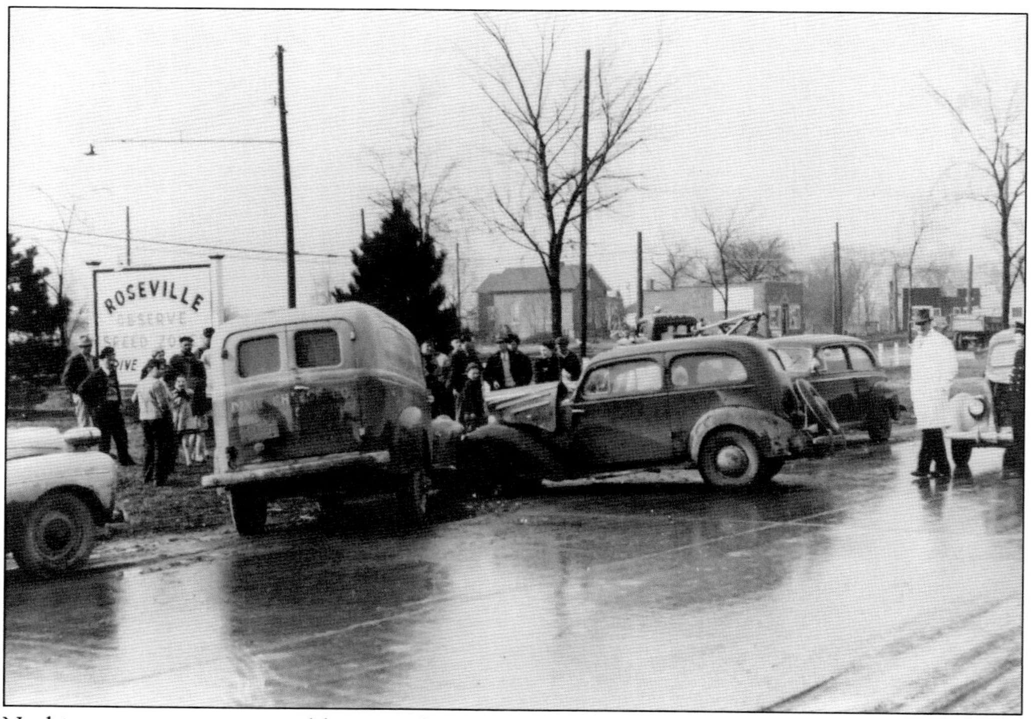

Nothing attracts spectators like a good truck-car crash. In 1947, while southbound traffic was detoured to the northbound side of Gratiot Avenue north of 10 Mile Road, Herman Haselhuhn's car was struck by a Dixie Cheese Company delivery van. Note the police car on the left with the fender-mounted siren. The Roseville sign in the back admonishes, "Observe Speed Zones."

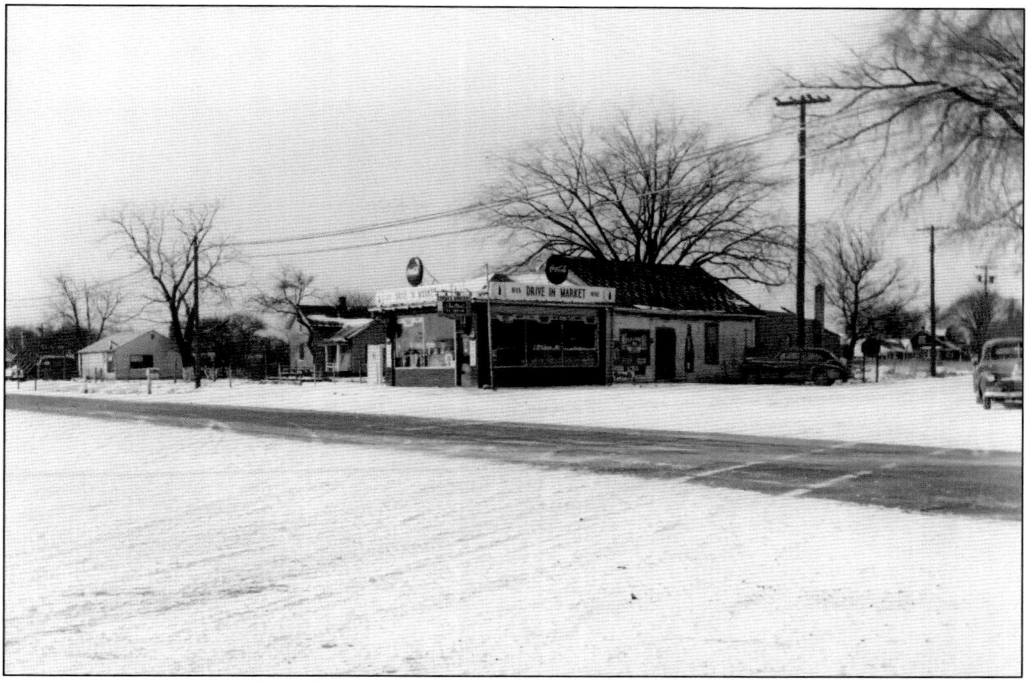

Zombo's Market, located on the southwest corner of Gratiot Avenue and Masonic Boulevard, was typical of the small neighborhood markets in the 1940s and 1950s. The photograph above was taken in 1940 and the one below in 1950. The location was later home to Zombo's Bar, where Ray Cavasos and John Logghe recall the 25¢ drafts. After Zombo's, it became Frantone's Bar from 1985 until closing in the 1990s. The building next door was used as a hardware store and for a brief time as a banquet hall. Today, the Vitamin Shoppe, Starbucks, and Subway are now on the corner opposite Macomb Mall.

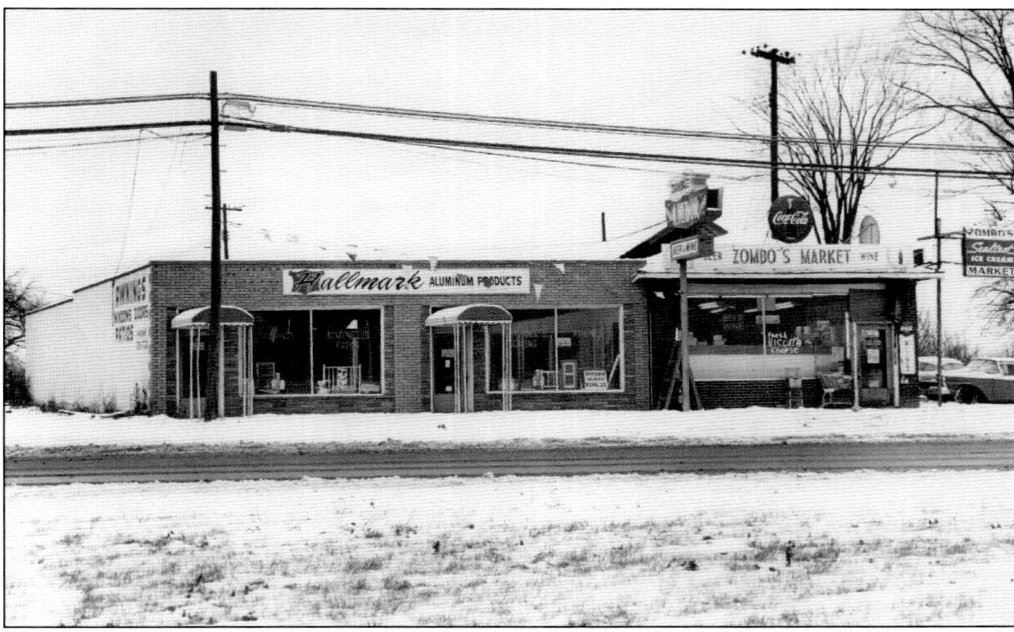

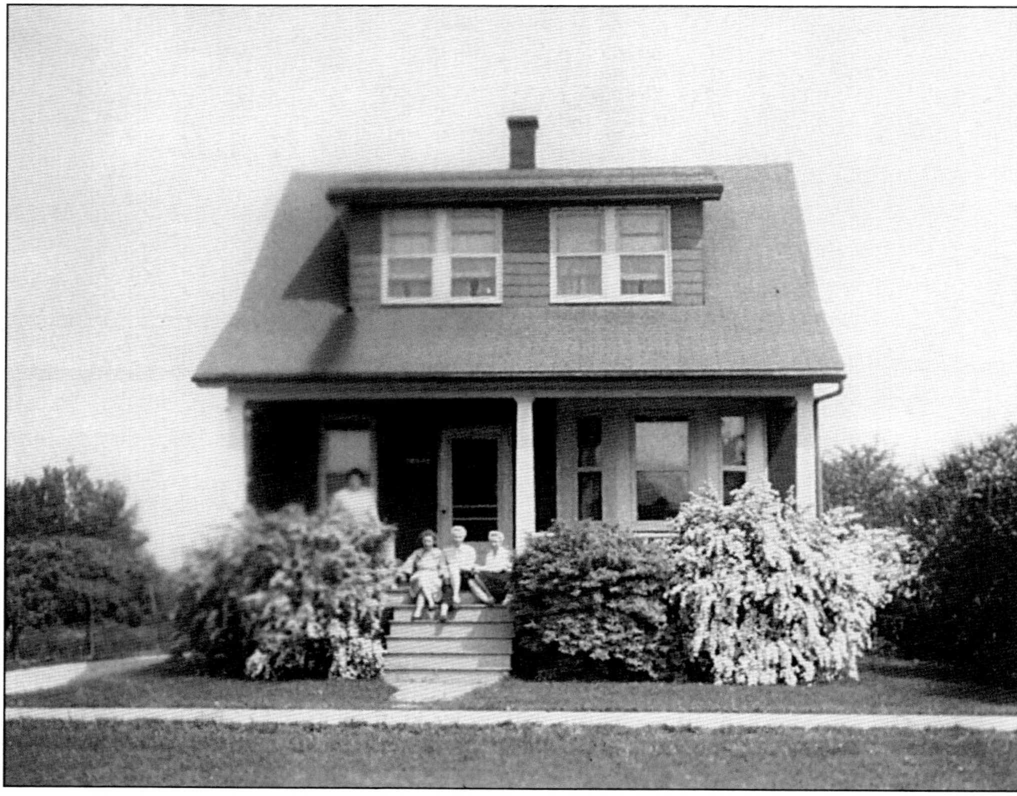

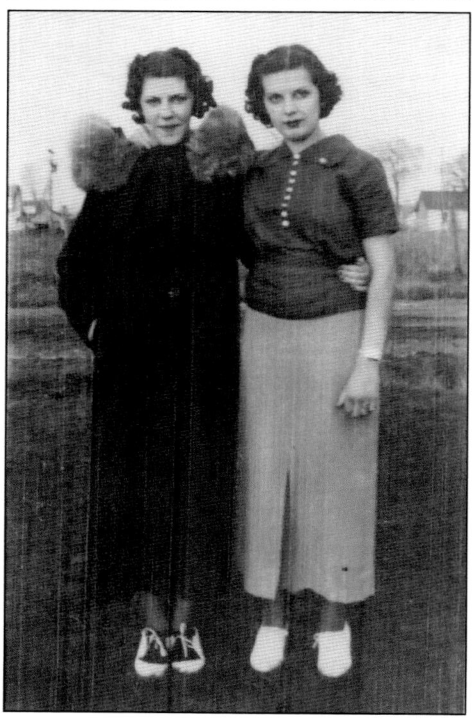

The three LeFevre girls—from left to right Dorothy Noellert, Shirley Primeau, and Charlotte Meldrum—opened a flower shop, Lu-An-Dor's, in this home on Gratiot Avenue. Primeau, "Lulu," as she was known to her many friends and family, died on December 28, 2010, following a brave battle with breast cancer. After the flower shop closed, the building was vacant for some time. A psychic now occupies the space.

Sisters Helen (left) and Dorothy Lumley pose for a photograph outside the family home at 27367 Maple Street. John Herbert Lumley built the house in 1922 with the help of his brother and men that worked at the Jackson Lumber Company. The family was known for their Election Day parties. Lumley would make elderberry wine, and the politicians would come to the home for their victory party. (Courtesy of Janice Carter.)

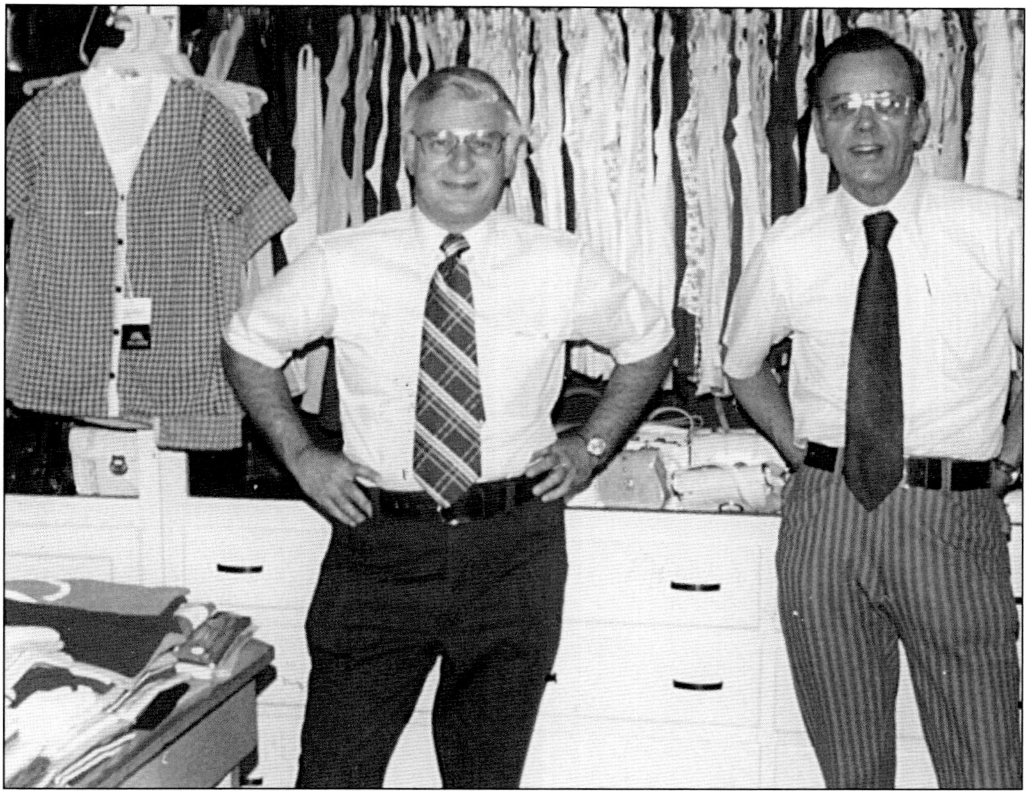

In 1928, brothers Samuel and Harry Lipsitt opened Roseville Department Store in the Roseville Theatre building, where it remained until it closed in 1989. Customers were often greeted by name; personal service was a priority. All one had to do was name it, and they would find it—in every color and pattern. It remained family operated by Samuel's son Harvey (left), pictured here with longtime employee Harry Versele inside the store.

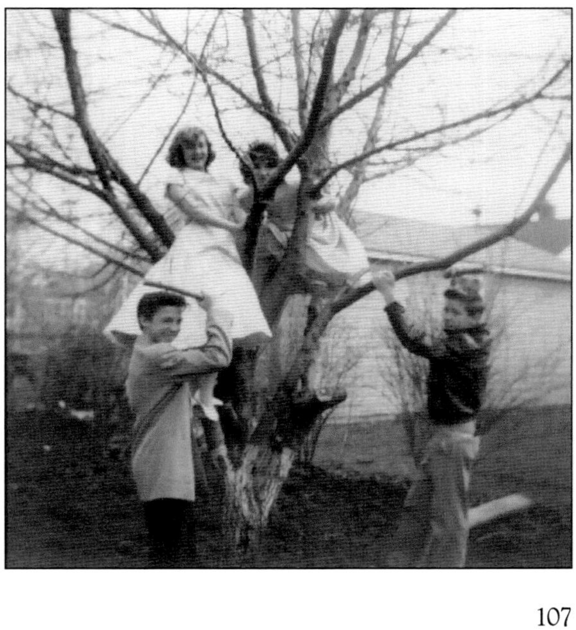

From left to right, Eddie Garnett Donna Atkinson, Sue McRill, and Johnny Garnett spend Easter Sunday in 1958 in the McRill family's side yard on Felician Street. It is not clear if the boys chased the girls up the tree or if the girls were just showing off their climbing abilities. The Atkinsons lived on Waverly Street and the Garnetts on Eastland Street, east of Gratiot Avenue. (Courtesy of Dorothy McRill.)

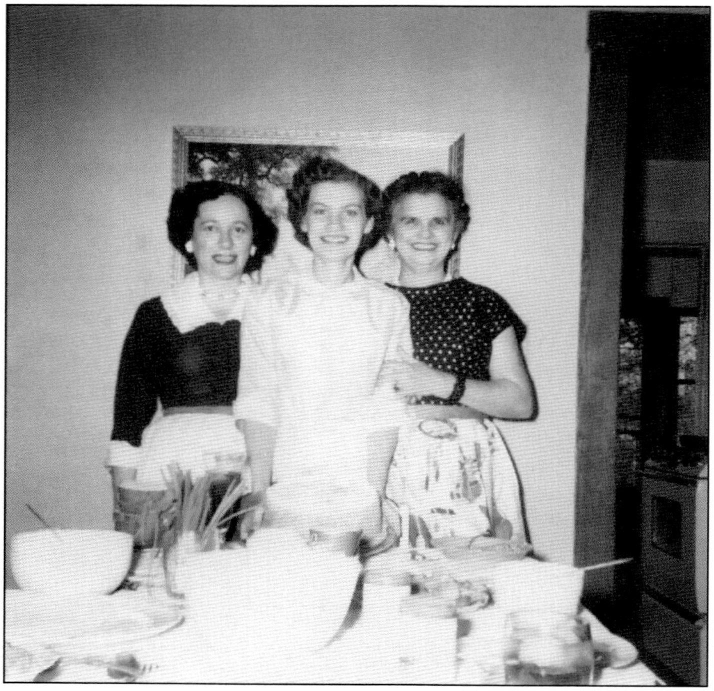

On Mother's Day in 1958, three mothers— from left to right, Evelyn McRill, Dorothy McRill, and Mary Garnett (author Terry Minnis's paternal grandmother, mother, and maternal grandmother, respectively)—celebrate their day at the home of Raymond and Evelyn McRill on Felician Street in Roseville. The women also cooked the beautiful meal before them. (Courtesy of Dorothy McRill.)

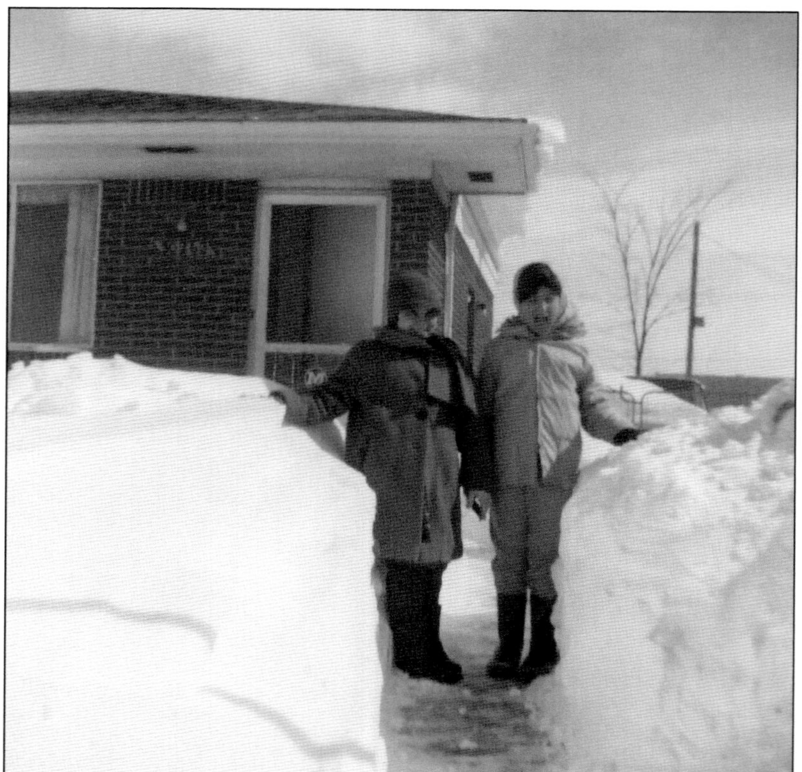

School closings for snow days were very infrequent in the 1960s. Best friends Terry McRill (left) and Claudia Bartalino enjoy a day off from Alumni Memorial Elementary after a snowstorm in early 1965. The roads were impassible for a couple of days, and the neighbors gathered sleds, took grocery orders, and walked to the corner store for supplies. (Courtesy of Dorothy McRill.)

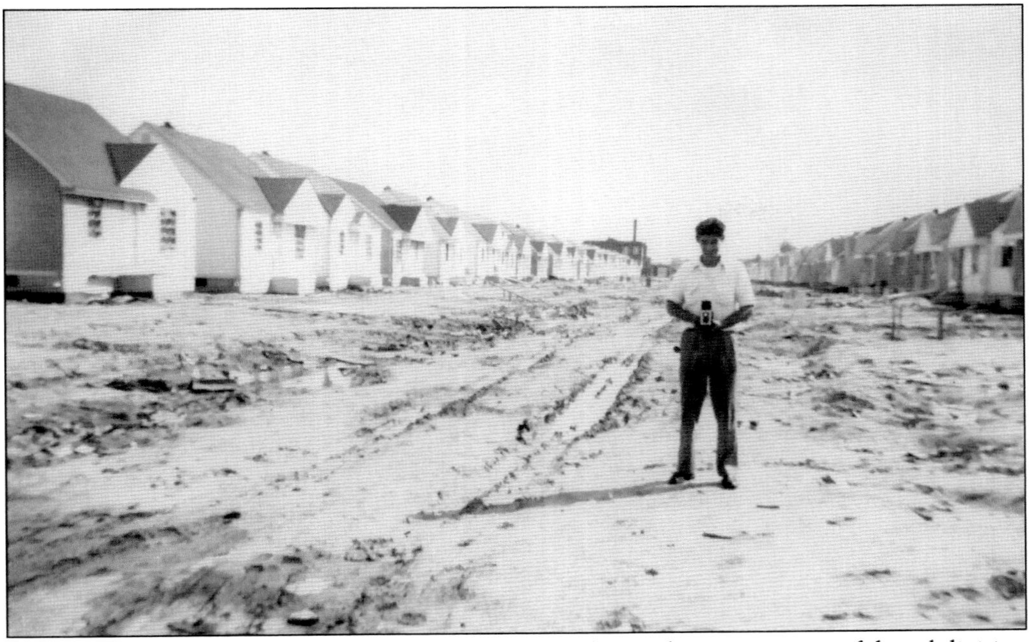

John Gaffigan stands in the middle of Quinkert Street during the construction of the subdivision near Common and Utica Roads. The bungalow-style homes were built in the 1950s, covering several blocks. This view is from Common Road looking south; Eastland High School can be seen in the distance. (Courtesy of M. Gaffigan.)

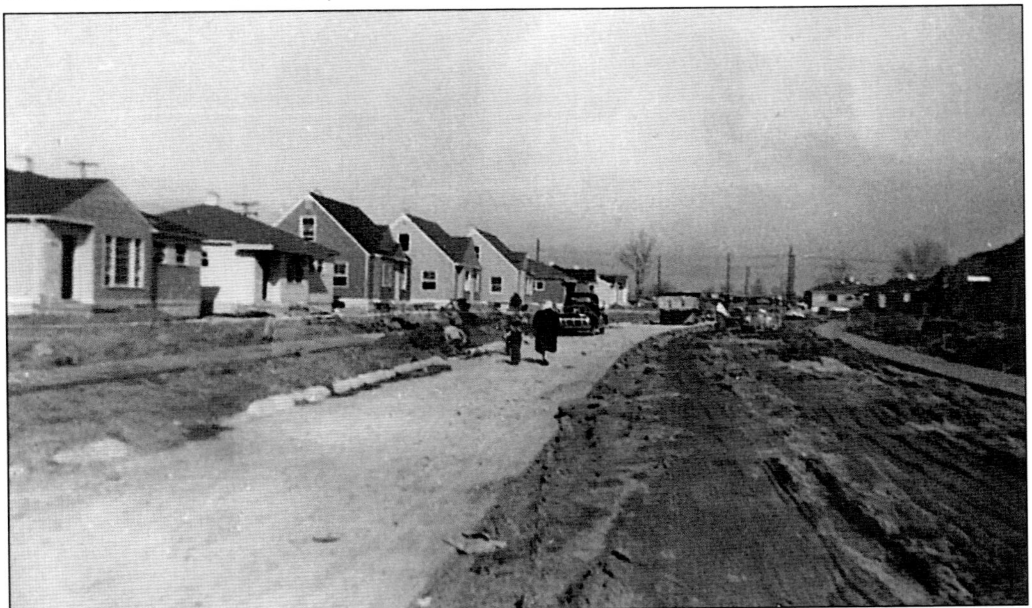

Nelson Park Subdivision, north of 12 Mile Road, west of Utica Road, was typical of the many homes built in the mid-1950s in Roseville. This photograph was taken on Commonwealth Street looking north. The bungalow on the left, just north of the white ranch, is where authors John and Terry Minnis lived for 30 years following their wedding in 1976. The Brincats were their neighbors to the north. (Courtesy of Diana Brincat.)

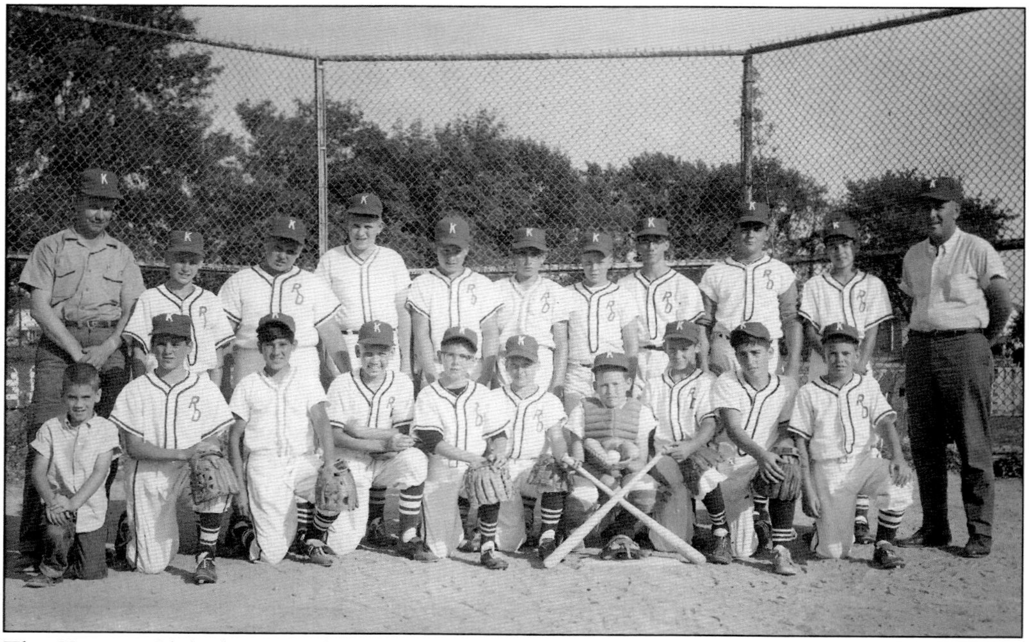

This Kiwanis Club championship team included future major leaguer Ernie Whitt. Pictured here are, from left to right, (first row) Mike Hollowell, Jerry Jiovani, Mike Venditto, Mike Hojna, Bob Sansara, Jean Raiche, Ernie Whitt, Dave Glass, Bruce Knight, and Pat Cooley; (second row) coach E. Whitt, Terry Horn, Paul Haratyk, Ron King, Greg Dennis, Will Aman, Lou Greenway, Jim Barry, Joe Bartalino, Lou Cervone, and manager Mike Hollowell. (Courtesy of Joseph Bartalino.)

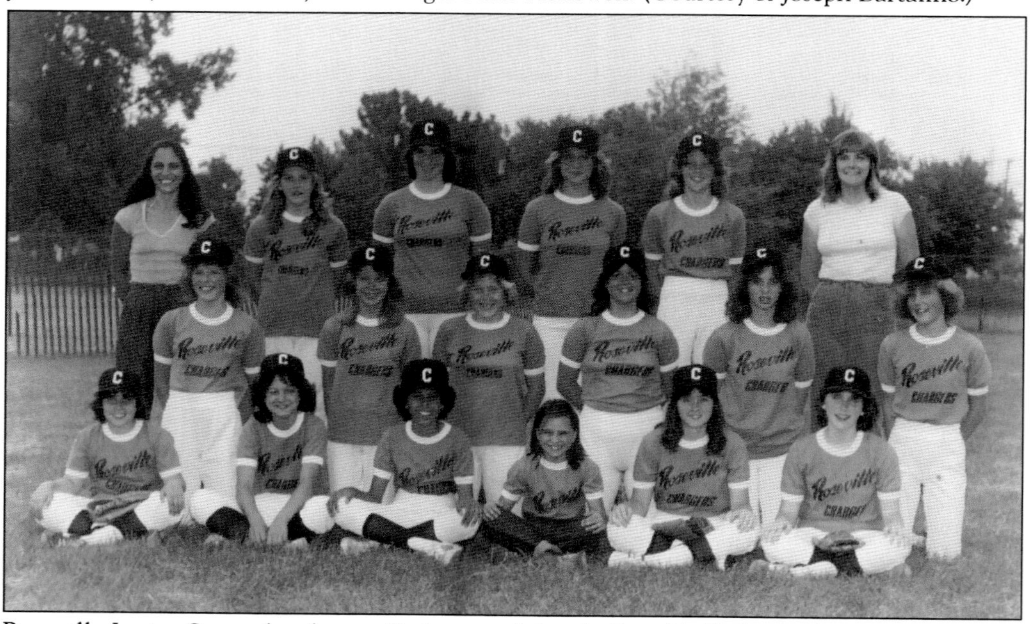

Roseville Junior Sports has been offering youth baseball, softball, football, and cheerleading programs for kids ages 5 to 14 since 1956. The organization is run by 100-percent volunteer help. The 1978 Roseville Chargers girls' softball team, with good friends Kris McRill (front row, far right) and Donna Silver (second row, far right), is pictured here. (Courtesy of Dorothy McRill.)

Eight

Rose Parade and Queen for a Day

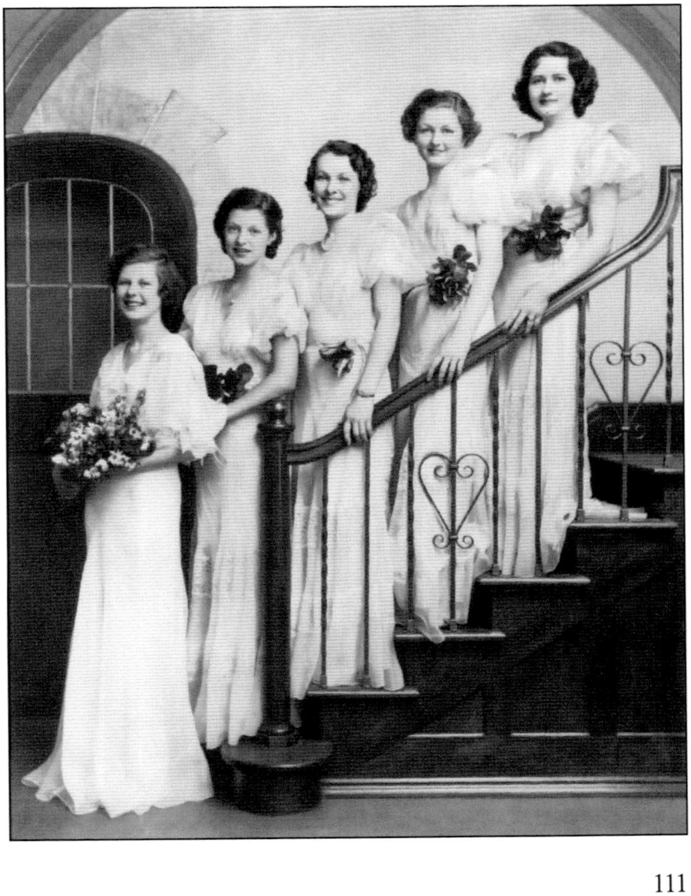

Roseville began crowning its Rose Queen in 1936. Gertrude Parscenski (in front with her court) holds the honor of Roseville's first Rose Queen. She was just 16 years old at the time. Crowning the queen was always a highlight of the Rose Festival. The festivals were held from 1936 until the onset of World War II. The contest for Miss Roseville (Rose Queen) was sponsored through various organizations in the city. Other previous winners include Marion Okes (1946), Joan Niedzielski (1959), Donice Rhodes (1965), and Brenda Smith (1975).

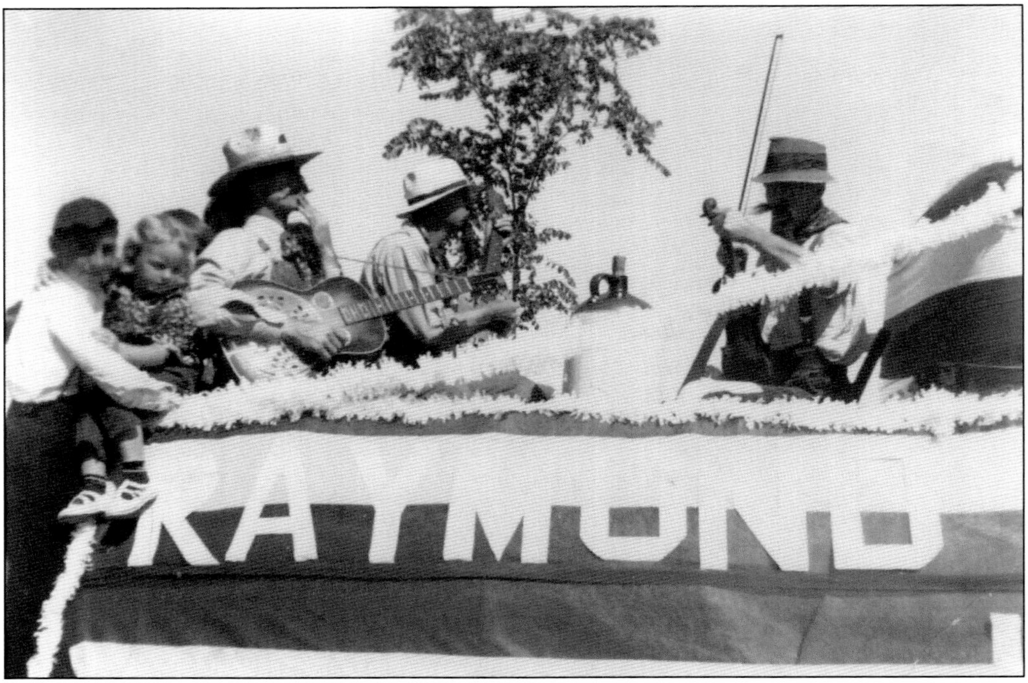

On the Raymond Hardware float on July 4, 1938, are, from left to right, Louis Capps, Jean Buchanan, Cleatus Buchanan, Mr. Thornton, and Mr. Hartley. Raymond Hardware was located on Gratiot Avenue near Martin Road and owned by Maxwell Raymond. Many of the local businesses sponsored and decorated floats for this popular family event.

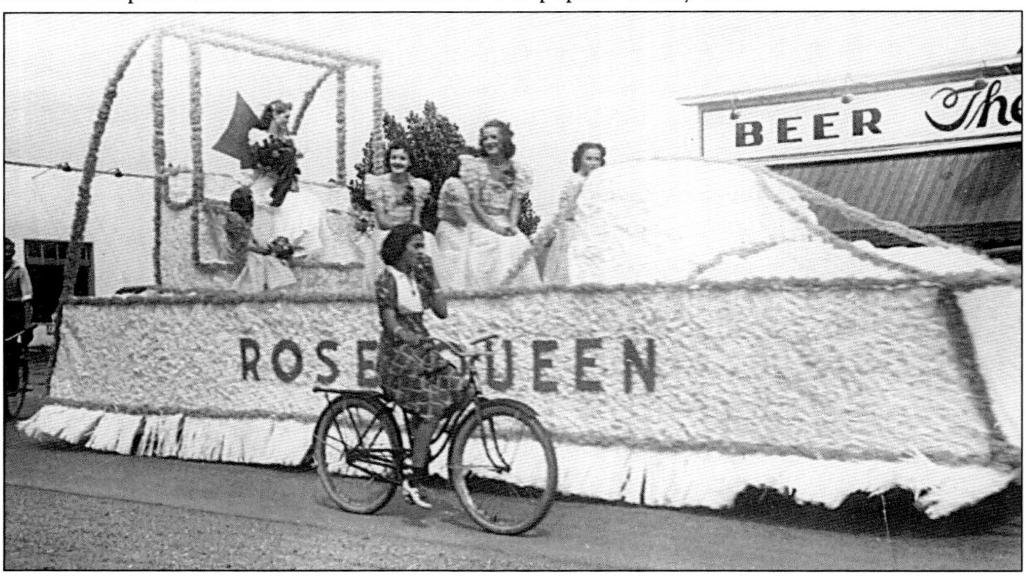

An unidentified bicyclist overtakes the 1940 Rose Queen and her court on their float passing by the Stein Beer Garden and Liquor Store owned by Norman Brohl. The beer garden was located south of Roseville's municipal building on Gratiot Avenue near Brohl Street. The parade floats were often quite elaborate, and this display was no exception. The queen, of course, was presented with a huge spray of roses.

Joan Hasenauer took the Miss Roseville honors in 1949 and was crowned Rose Queen. The origin of the city's name becomes somewhat blurred during this time, as the use of the flower as a symbol of the city became quite popular. The queen's throne on this float is that of a rose.

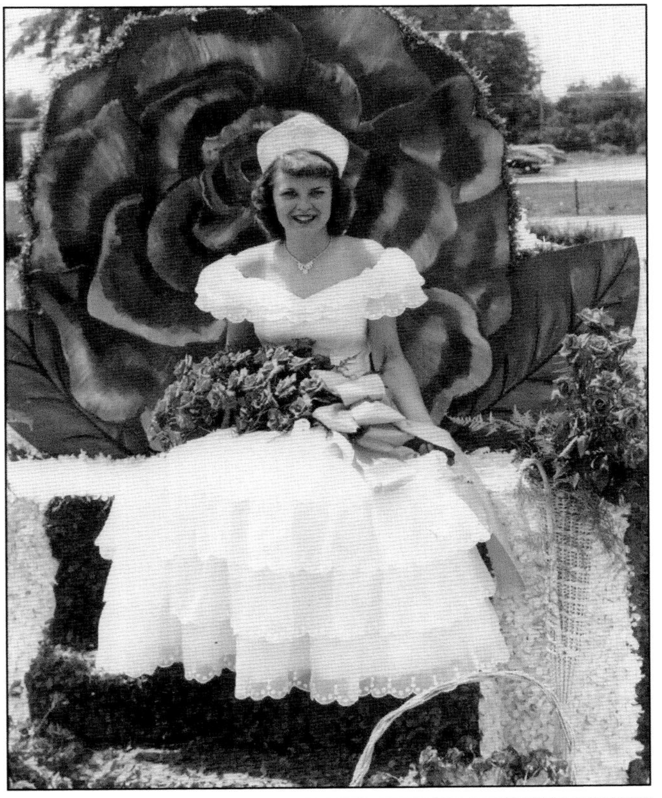

The Twin Pines float was pulled by the ever-popular Twin Pines milk truck in the 1949 Rose Parade. The trucks were quite the site throughout the 1950s and 1960s, when milk and other staples were home-delivered by the milkman. Most new homes built during this era were equipped with a milk chute with a door on the outside of the house and another inside. (Courtesy of Doreen Tavernier-Evans Baughn.)

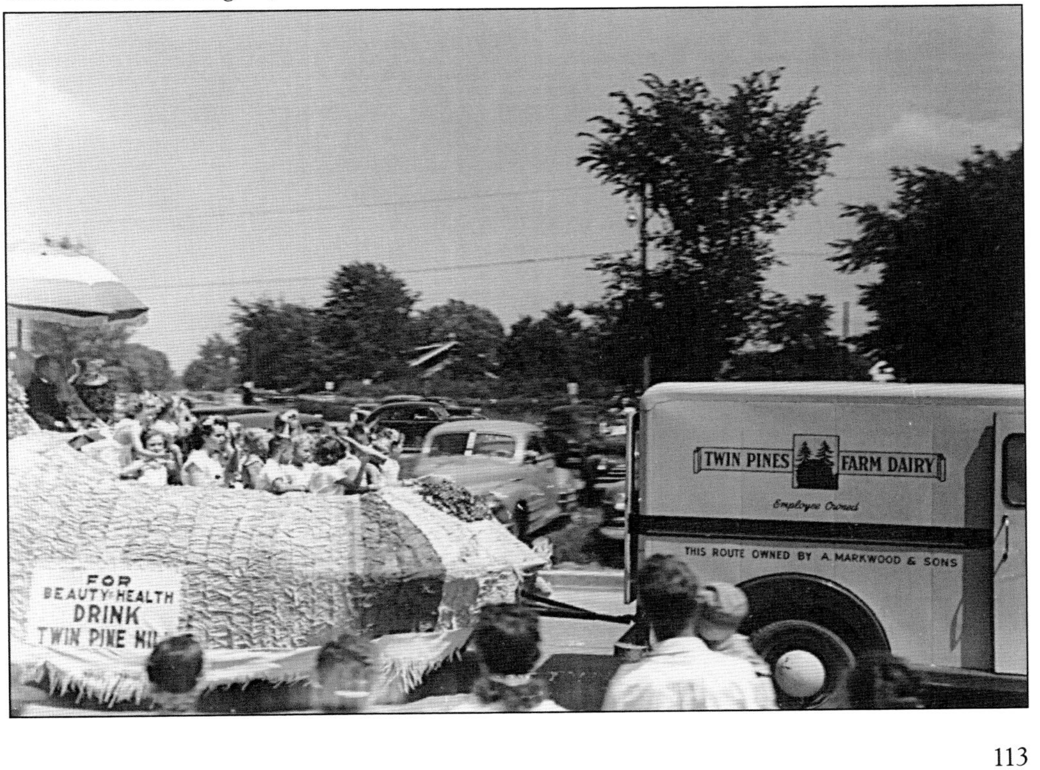

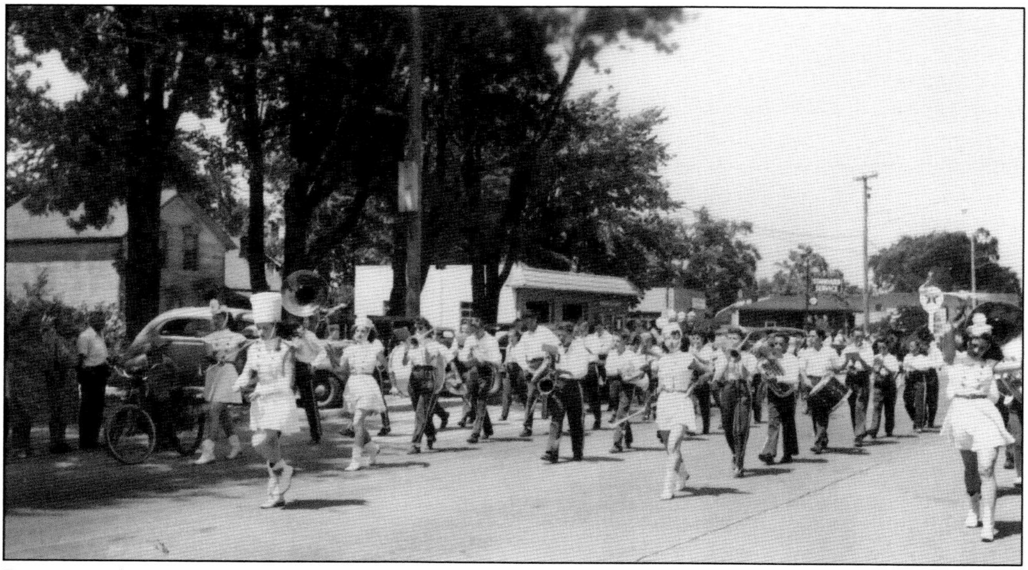

Baton-twirling majorettes and a marching band lead the 1956 Rose Parade. The businesses on the left and gas stations in background indicate this photograph was taken on Gratiot Avenue, just south of Martin Road. The Rose Parade always drew a large crowd of spectators, and families arrived early to get the perfect spot.

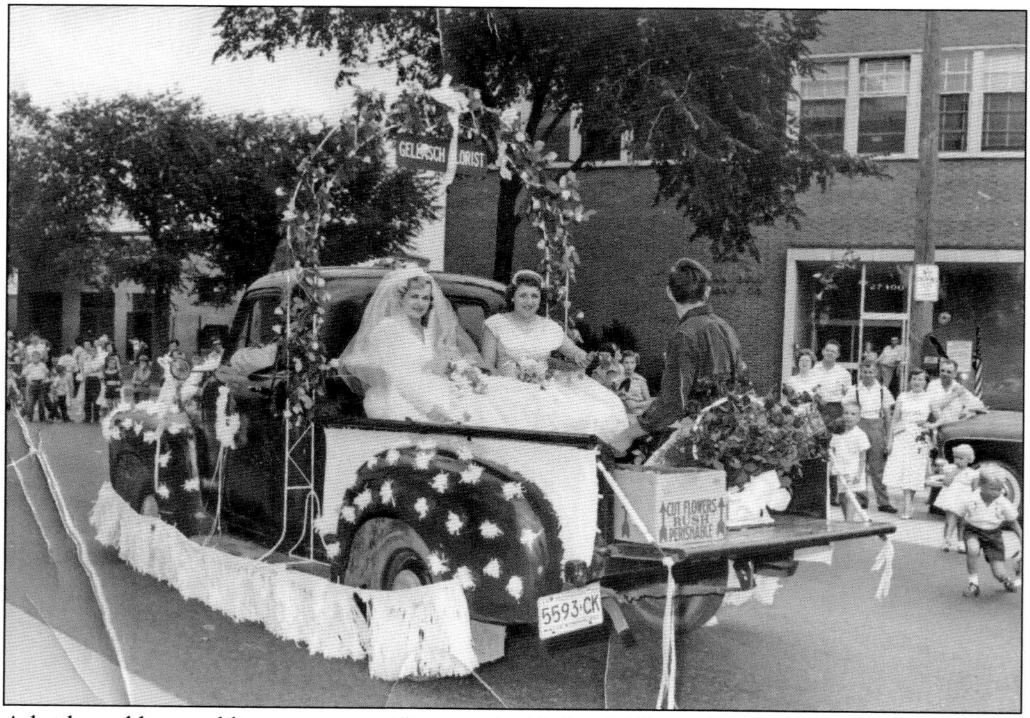

A bride and her wedding party are riding on the Gellasch Florist float in the Rose Parade. The "1956 Water Wonderland" license plate gives away the date of this photograph. The children watching the parade were always ready to scramble into the street to retrieve candy being thrown from the passing floats.

Marilyn Choma Waldmeir, daughter of Joe and Florence Choma, was a majorette at Roseville High School and may well have marched in the Rose Parade. After graduating from Roseville High in 1963, Choma worked at Warren Woods Public Schools for 13 years as a secretary to the assistant superintendent before marrying *Detroit News* columnist Pete Waldmeir. They had two children together: a daughter, Lindsey, and a son, Christopher. The Waldmeirs live in Grosse Pointe Woods.

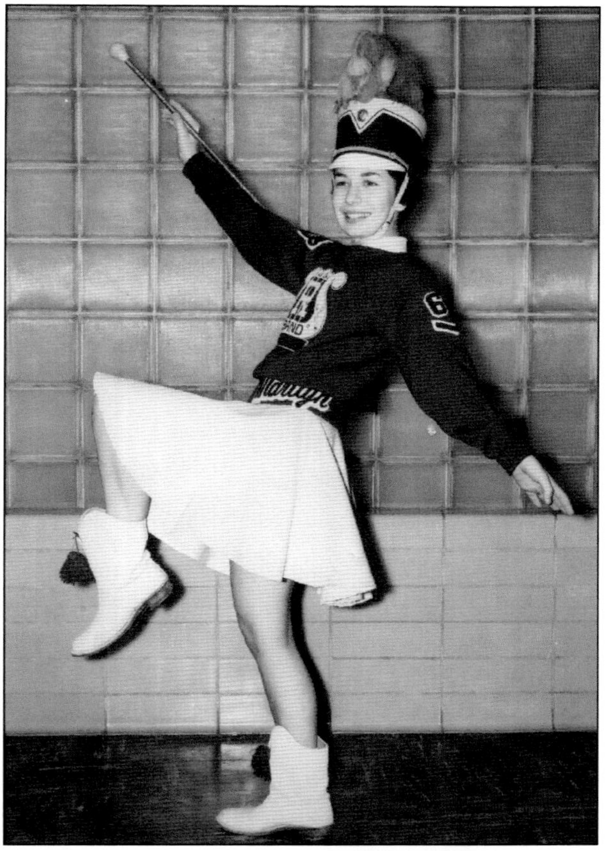

Mike Clancy, 1960 state rodeo driving champion, rides in the Rose Parade with his sister Karen (left) and girlfriend Harriett. The Pfeiffer beer distributor building (now Joe Randazzo's Fruit & Vegetables) can be seen in the background. Nino's Pizzeria, also shown, was previously Powser's Restaurant. (Courtesy Karen Clancy-Williams.)

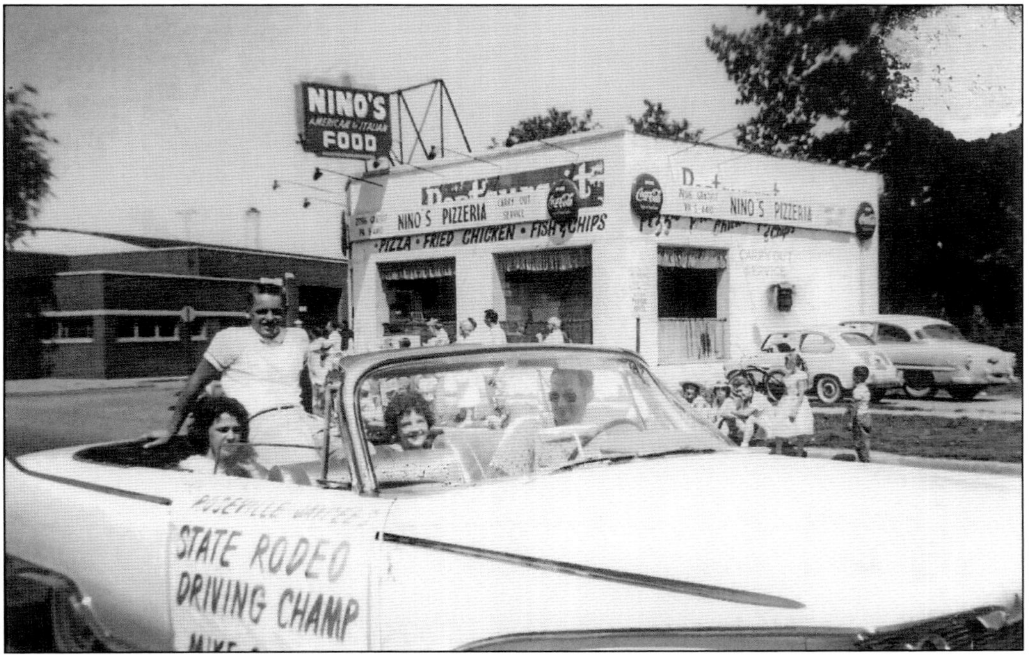

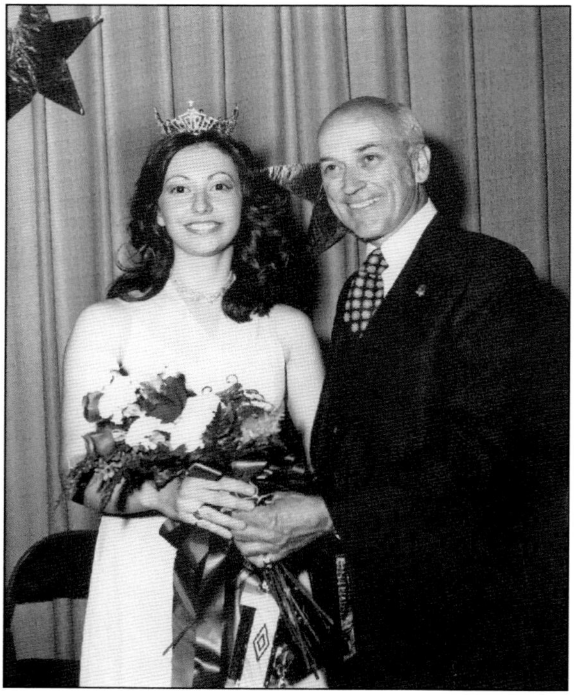

In his first year as mayor, Leonard Haggerty (at left) had the pleasure of congratulating 1975 Rose Queen Brenda Smith in the last year a Rose Queen was named. Peggy Buell (below) had the honor of holding the title of Rose Queen and Peach Queen in 1969. While 1975 marked the end of an era for the Rose Queens, it began the modern era for the city of Roseville in that it was the year the city opened its new civic center complex at Howard Street and Gratiot Avenue, one block south of Common Road. The complex was built with help of federal revenue-sharing funds and remains the site of the municipal offices, police and fire departments, court, and library.

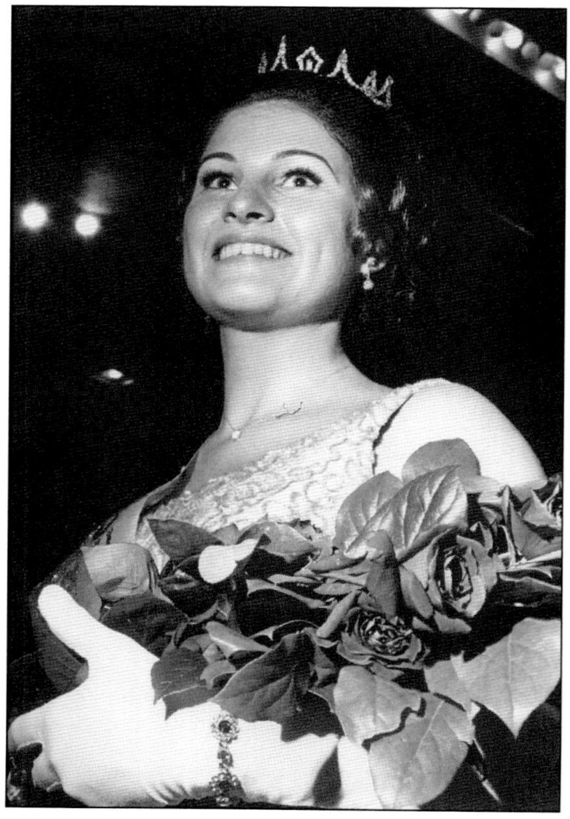

Nine

Roseville Walk of Fame

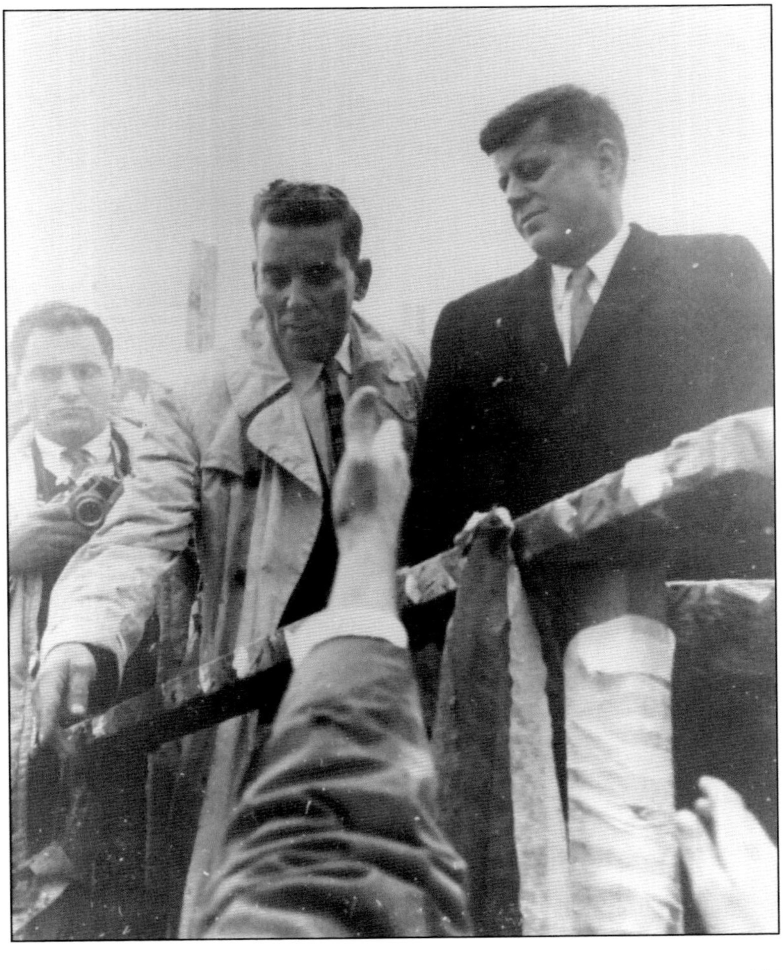

On October 26, 1960, presidential candidate Sen. John F. Kennedy (right) spoke at the Eastgate Shopping Center in Roseville. With Kennedy on the makeshift dais is Roseville mayor Arthur Waterman (center). Other dignitaries present included Gov. G. Mennen "Soapy" Williams, Lt. Gov. John Swainson, and Congressman James O'Hara. Undaunted by the rain, Kennedy spoke of the importance of a good education for all children.

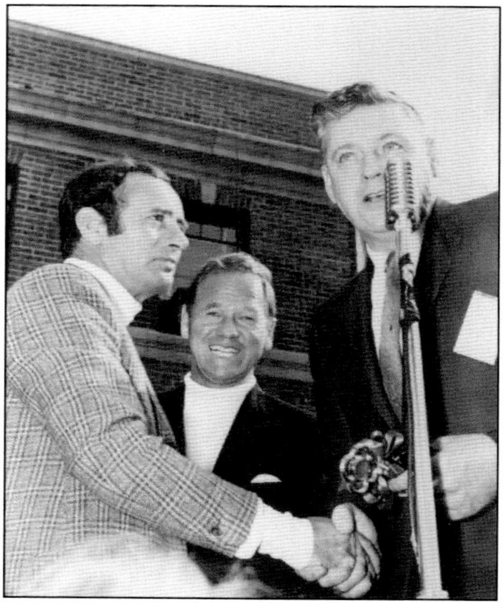

On the steps of the old municipal building, Mayor Arthur Waterman (right) and Councilman Glen Alsip (center) are on hand to welcome celebrity Joey Bishop to Roseville. Waterman and Alsip both served as village presidents prior to Roseville becoming a city. Bishop was likely in Roseville for presidential candidate John F. Kennedy's appearance at the Eastgate Shopping Center in 1960. Bishop would later serve as master of ceremonies at Kennedy's inaugural ball.

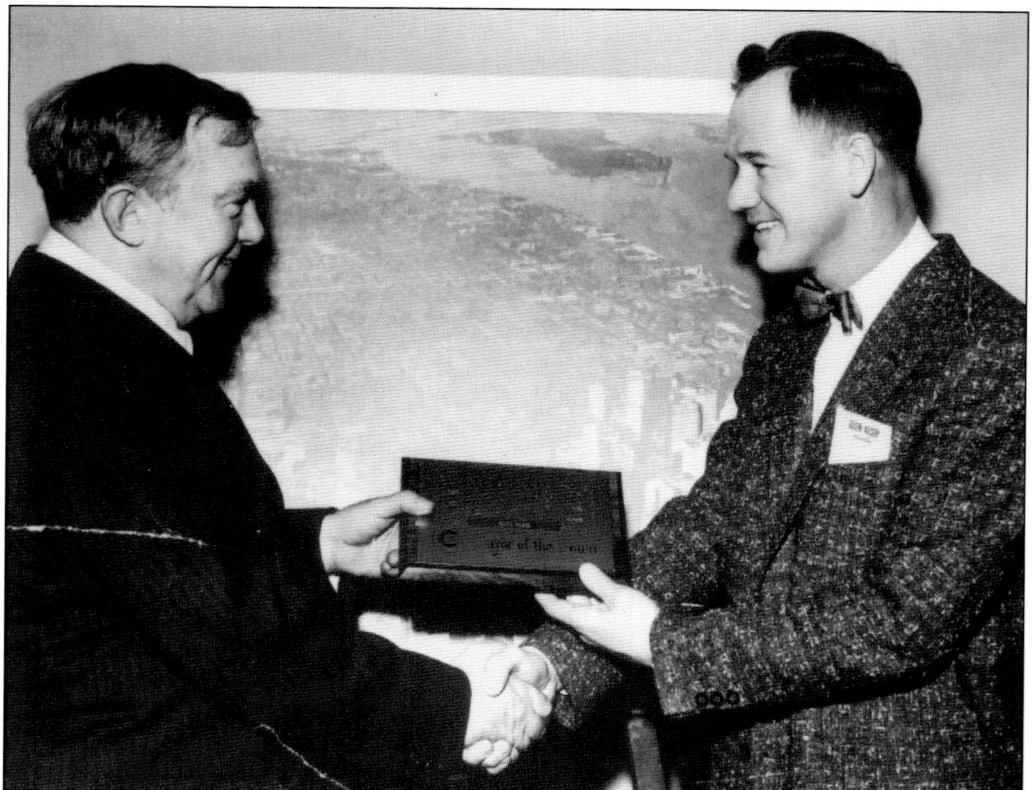

Glen Alsip (right), who served as a village president and city councilman, receives a plaque from actor Thomas Mitchell, who was the first person to win an Oscar, an Emmy, and a Tony Award. He had roles in *Lost Horizon* (1937), *Stagecoach* (1939), *The Hunchback of Notre Dame* (1939), *Mr. Smith Goes to Washington* (1939), *Gone with the Wind* (1939), *It's a Wonderful Life* (1946), and *High Noon* (1952).

Roseville mayor Arthur Waterman (right) and Councilman Leonard Haggerty (left) ride with Michigan governor G. Mennen "Soapy" Williams on the back of a convertible in a Rose Parade while Michigan's first lady, Agnes Williams (left), and Councilwoman Nellie Paver ride in front. Waterman was Roseville's first mayor, serving from 1959 to 1963 and again from 1965 to 1967. He also served as village president.

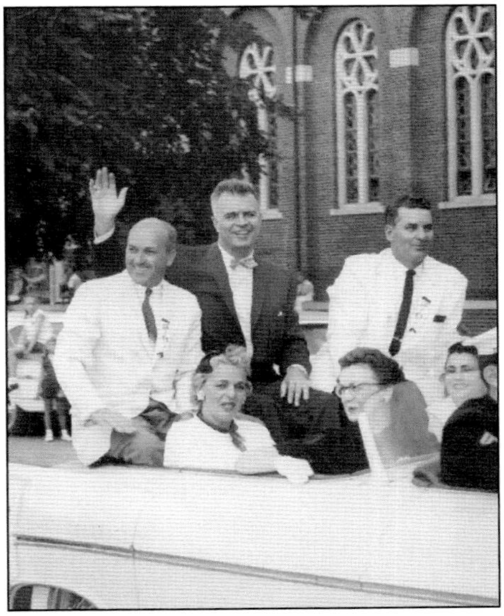

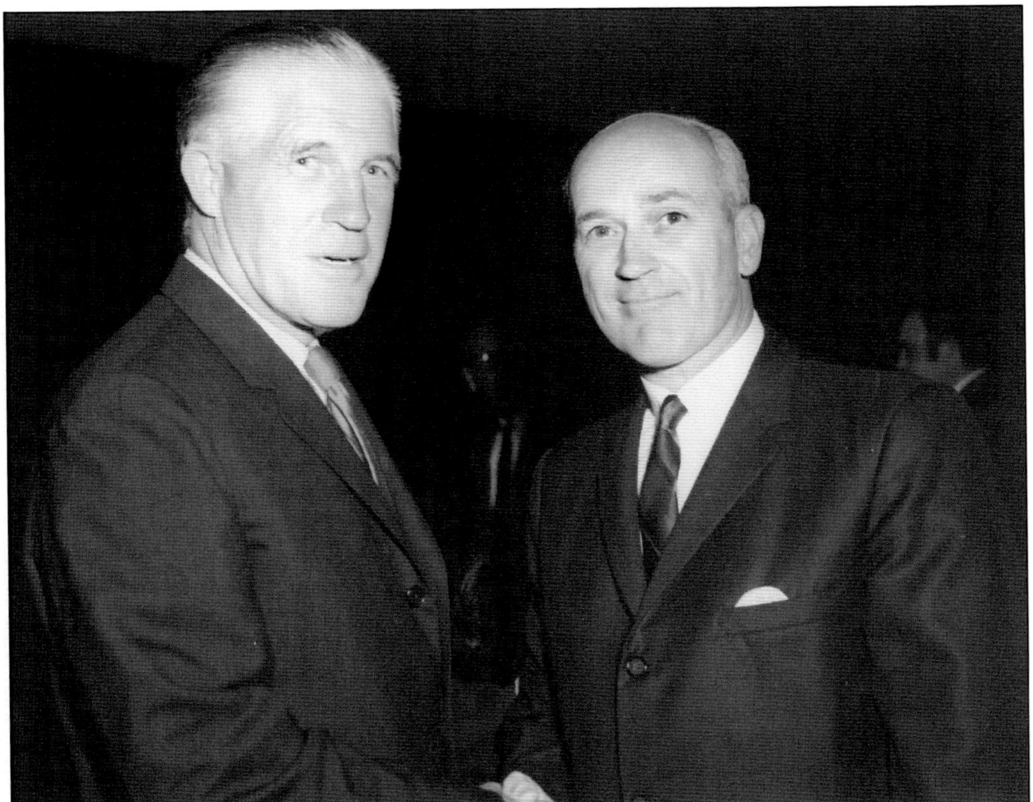

Michigan governor George Romney converses with Councilman Leonard Haggerty. Romney served as Michigan's governor from 1963 to 1969. He went on to serve as the US Secretary of Housing and Urban Development from 1969 to 1973. Romney served as spokesman for the American Automobile Manufacturers Association through World War II, and in 1948 he joined Nash-Kelvinator. He became chief executive of American Motors Corporation in 1954. (Courtesy of Jan Haggerty.)

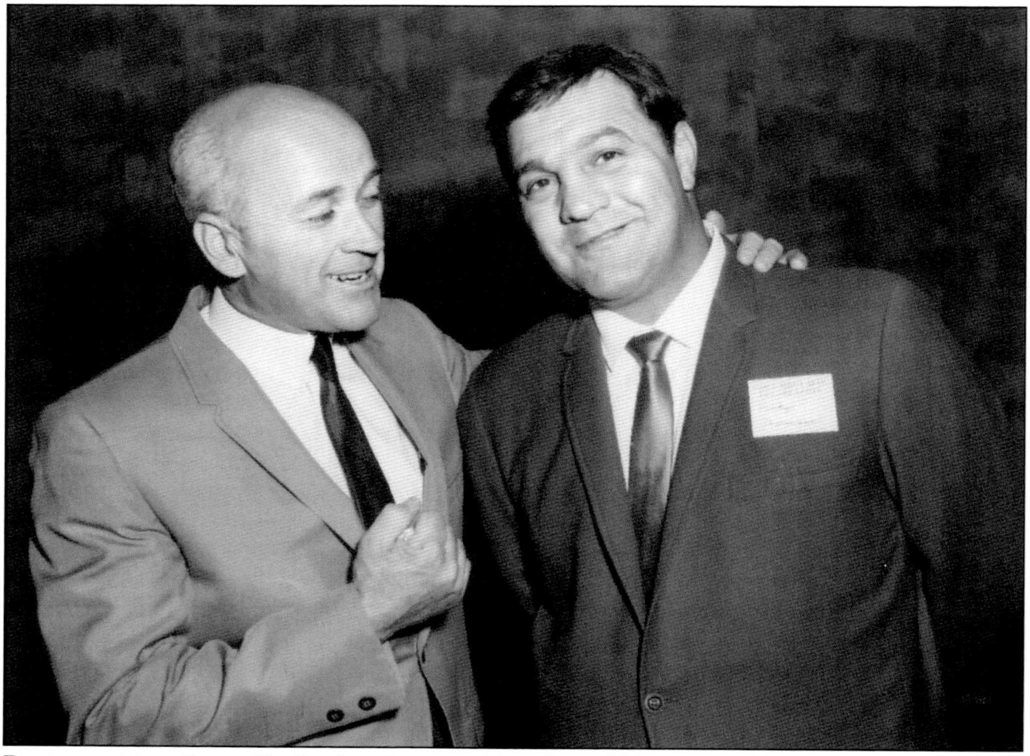

During a visit to Roseville, Rocky Marciano (above), world heavyweight champion from 1952 to 1956, keeps an eye on Leonard Haggerty's right punch. Also pictured with Leonard is Joey Bishop (below), who hosted *The Joey Bishop Show* for four seasons, beginning in 1961, and was the last surviving member of the Rat Pack. He died in 2007 at the age of 89. As a young man, Haggerty could evidently take care of himself. During World War II, he spent time as a personal bodyguard for Gen. George S. Patton. As an Army infantryman, Haggerty earned two Battle Stars in the European Theater, participated in intense fighting at the Battle of the Bulge, and served with a detachment that liberated the Nazi death camp in Dachau. (Both courtesy of Jan Haggerty.)

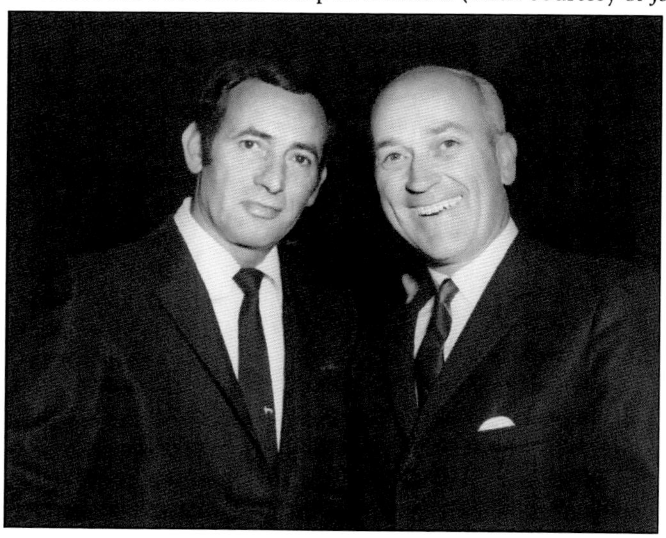

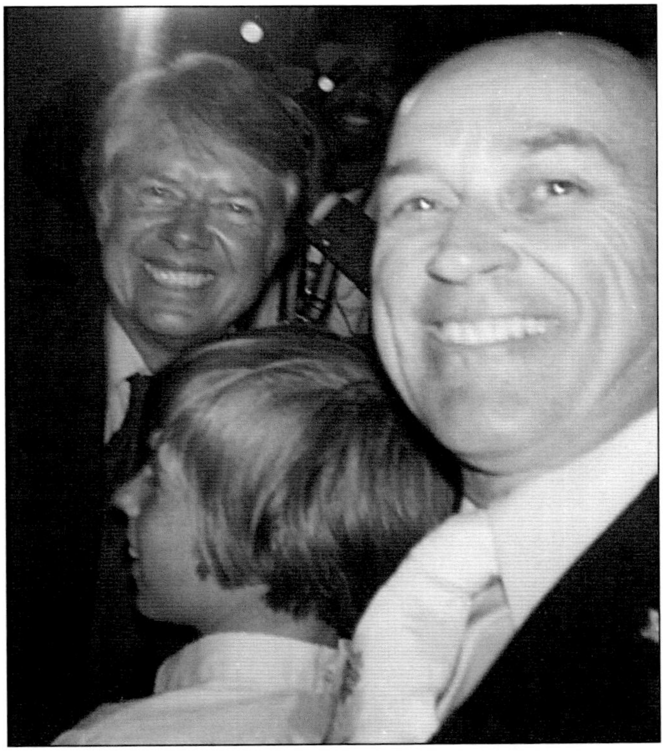

Leonard Haggerty is pictured at right with Pres. Jimmy Carter and below with Pres. Bill Clinton. President Clinton addressed a group of invited attendees at the Roseville Recreation Center in 1999. His message, with the Kosovo War (1998–1999) as a backdrop, was that fighting for the dignity and integrity of all people and a system of democracy and cooperation gives American children a better tomorrow. For humanitarian reasons, the United States, as a member of NATO, intervened in the uprising in then Yugoslavia when all diplomatic attempts failed. Carter was elected the 39th US president of the United States in 1976. He served one term. Clinton was elected the 42nd US president in 1992 and served two terms. (Both courtesy of Jan Haggerty.)

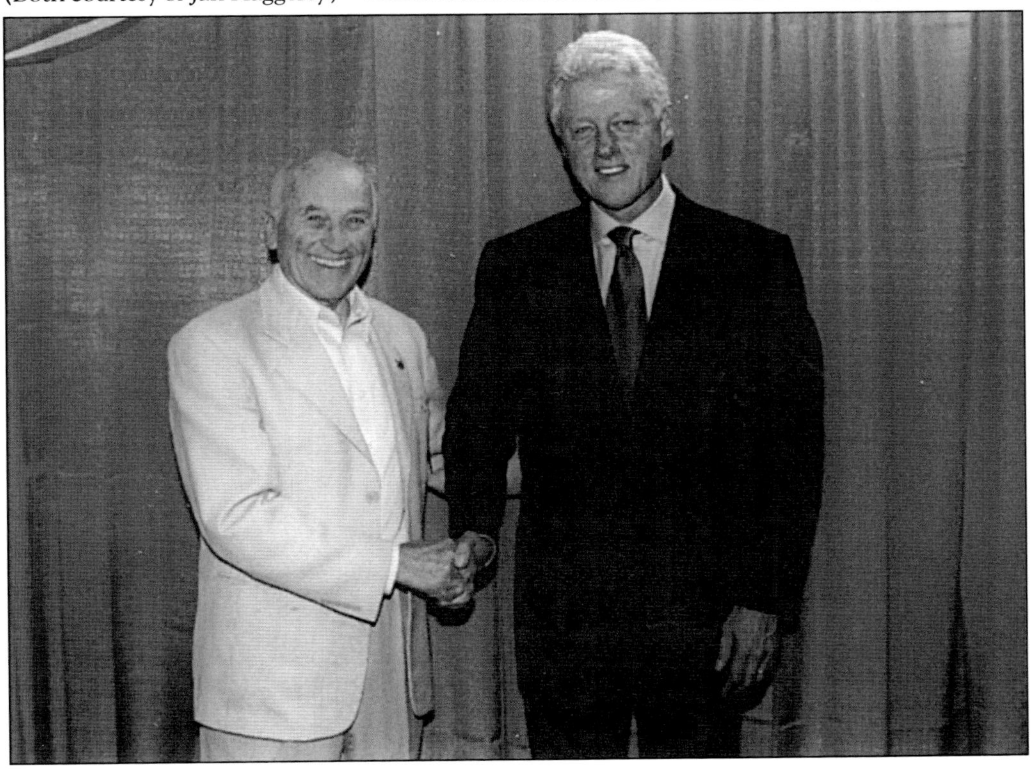

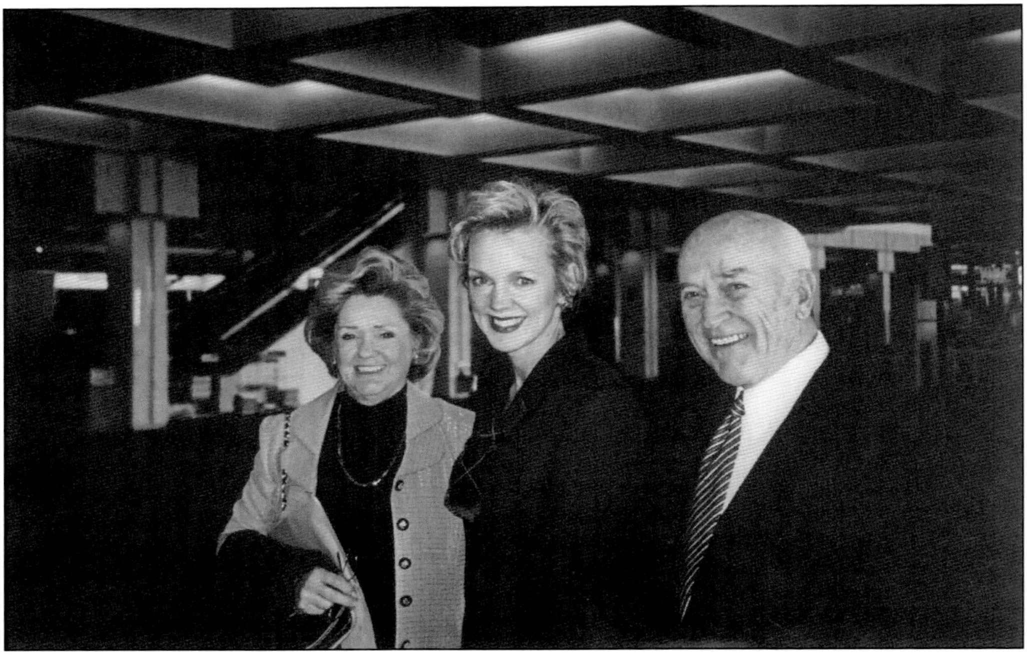

Jan and Leonard Haggerty are joined by Gov. Jennifer Granholm (center). Jan is a current member of the Roseville City Council; her late husband, Leonard, served 25 years on the Roseville City Council and six years as mayor. In 1998, at age 78, he ran for county commissioner and won. After a long bout with leukemia, Leonard Haggerty died on October 26, 2009. He was 89 years old. (Courtesy of Jan Haggerty.)

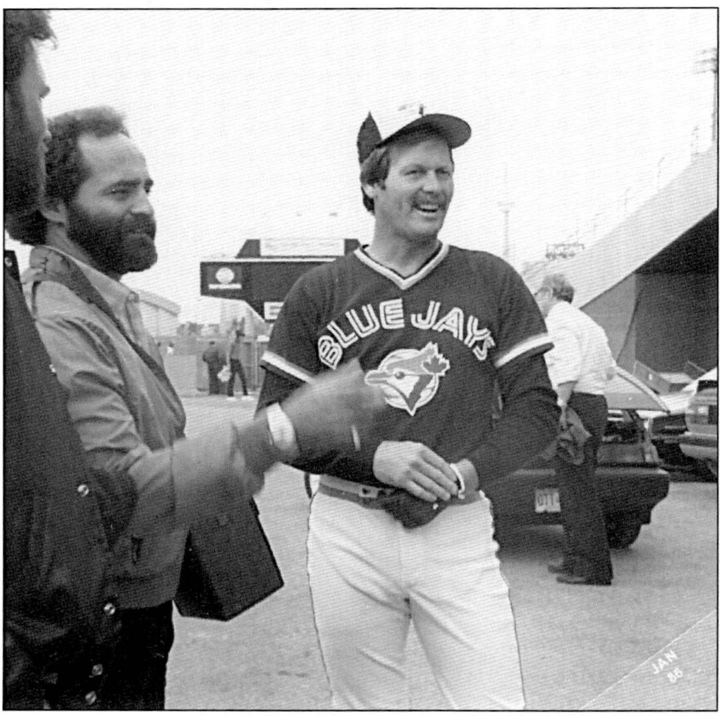

Leo Ernest "Ernie" Whitt graduated from Roseville's Carl Brablec High School in 1970. Whitt was picked in the 1972 amateur draft by the Boston Red Sox. He made his major-league debut on September 12, 1976, by pinch-hitting for Carlton Fisk (he grounded out). The Toronto Blue Jays All-Star is pictured here in 1986 with former youth baseball teammate and classmate Joe Bartalino. (Courtesy of Joseph Bartalino.)

Ten

Roseville Today

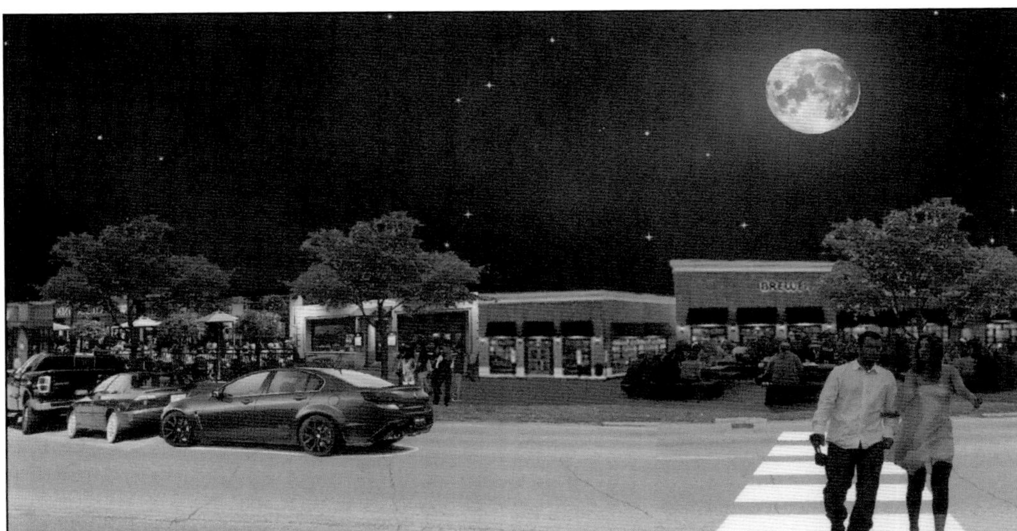

This artist's rendering by Peter Allen & Associates hints at the nightlife and navigability of Roseville's proposed new downtown area at Utica Junction, where Utica Road meets southbound Gratiot Avenue. On May 13, 2014, the Roseville City Council voted unanimously to create a Town Center Overlay District, harking back to the 1940s. The multiphase plans call for new streetscapes, storefronts, and commercial and residential buildings. (Courtesy of the City of Roseville.)

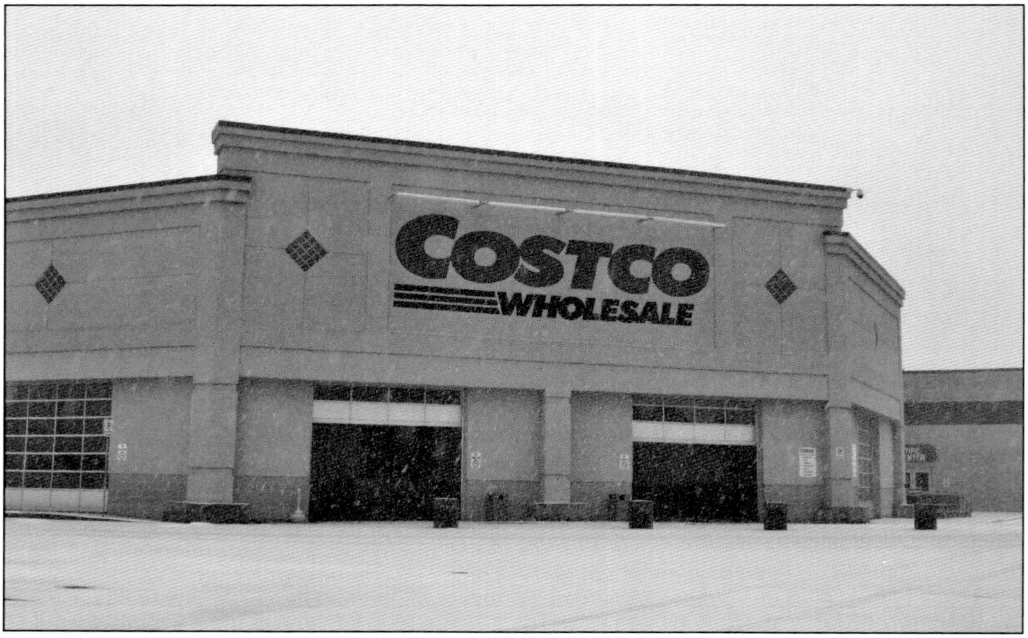

Costco and Sam's Club have long called Roseville their home. Costco, located at I-696 (11 Mile Road) and Gratiot Avenue, opened in 1998. Costco is headquartered in Issaquah, Washington, and was founded as Price Club in 1976 in San Diego, California. The first warehouse under the Costco name opened in Seattle, Washington, in 1983. Sam's Club is located on Gratiot Avenue near Masonic Boulevard, catty-corner from Macomb Mall. Sam's is named for Walmart founder Sam Walton, was founded in 1983, and opened its Roseville location in 2002. Both membership warehouse stores are regional attractions for shoppers to Roseville. (Both photographs by John Minnis.)

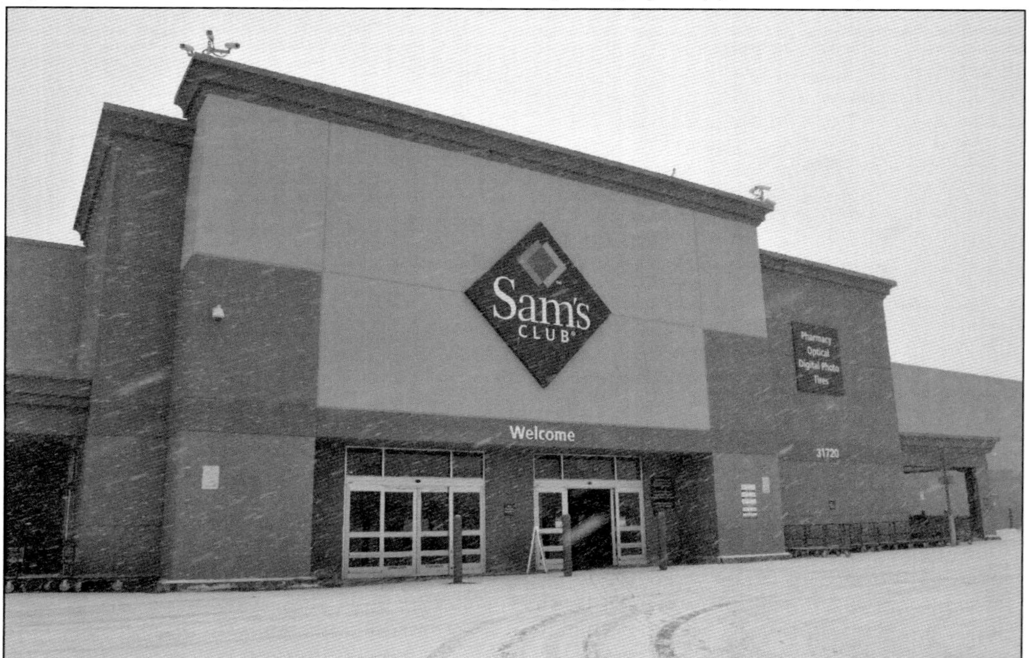

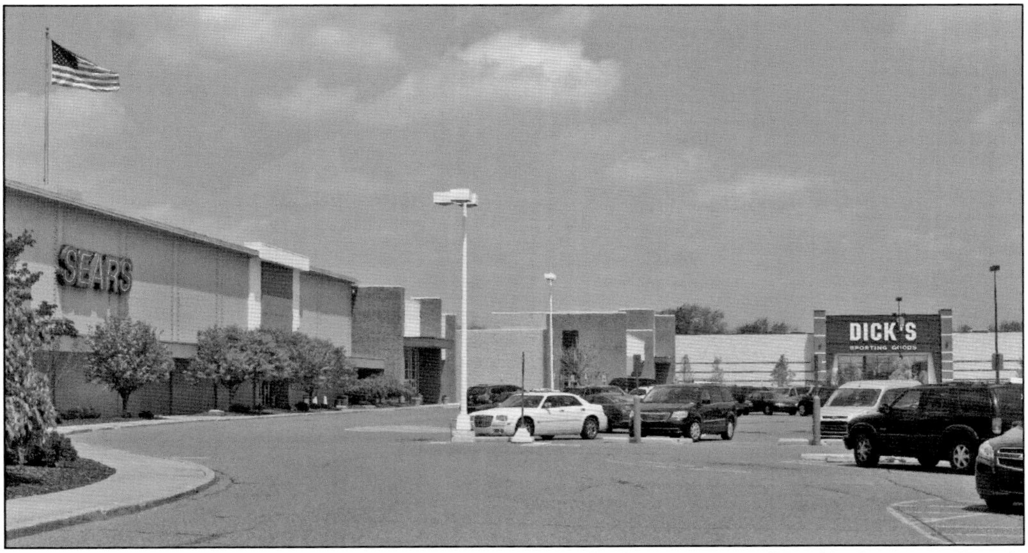

Macomb Mall celebrated its 50th birthday in 2014 with the opening of Dick's Sporting Goods where the former Crowley's was located. Sears, of course, still is a big anchor at the mall. Lormax Stern Development acquired the mall in 2013. Ulta, Shoe Carnival, and H&M have all announced openings scheduled for 2015. Currently, Macomb Mall is undergoing extensive modernization, which bodes well for the future of Roseville. (Photograph by John Minnis.)

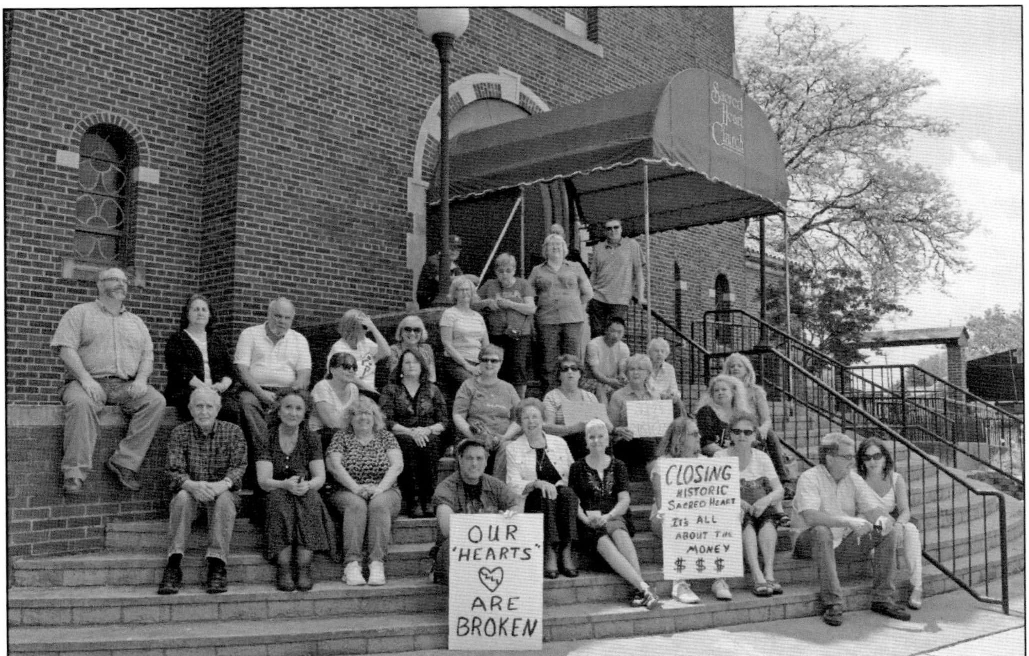

In May 2015, the Archdiocese of Detroit announced it will close the former Sacred Heart Catholic Church after 154 years at Utica Road and Gratiot Avenue. Pat Chownyk (center, in white blazer) leads a protest on the steps of the church. Chownyk, president of the Roseville Historical and Genealogical Society, is a lifetime parishioner, attended school there, and sent her children there until the school closed in 1971. (Photograph by John Minnis.)

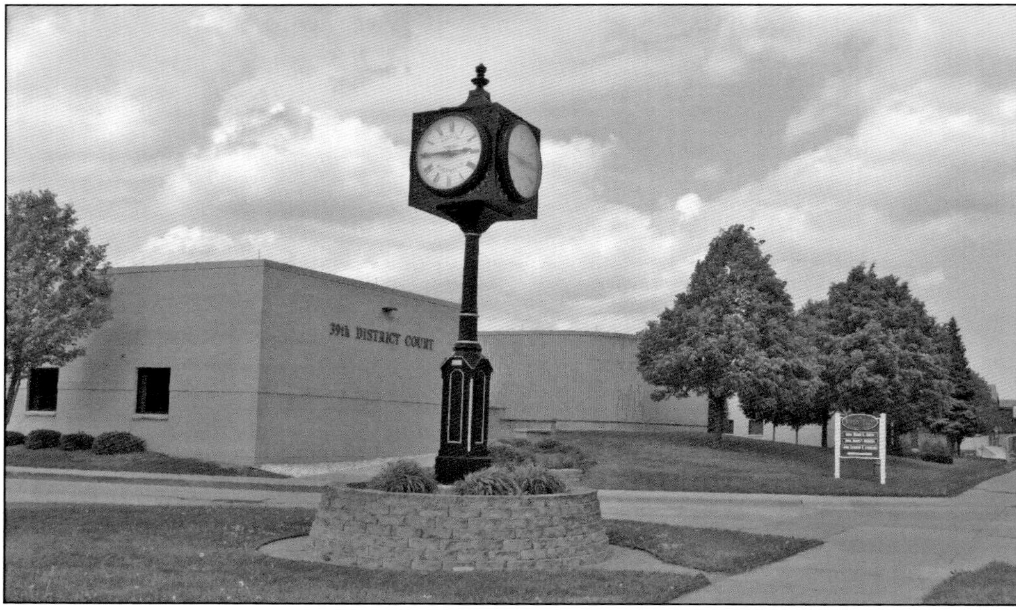

Roseville's *Vintage Clock* was purchased—along with the *Rosebuds*, *Once Upon Time*, and Doug Roberts sculptures—by Project Art in Roseville through fundraising activities and federal grants. The 39th District Court and Roseville Police Department were modernized in 2001. The Roseville Civic Center plaza, built in 1975, was expanded and improved in 1998 and in 2001 when the *Rosebuds* was acquired. (Photograph by John Minnis.)

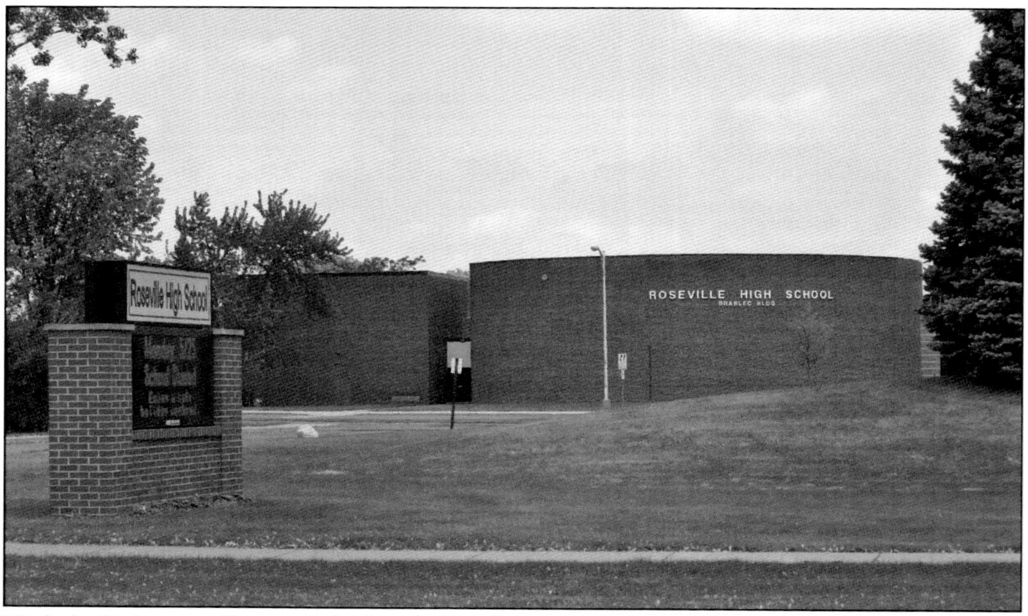

With declining enrollment in the late 1980s, the decision was made to consolidate the two high schools. In 1989, Roseville High School on Martin Road became Roseville Junior High, and Carl Brablec High School became Roseville High School. Guest Junior High was closed that same year, and the building became a community center. The Brablec building was expanded to accommodate grades 9 to 12. (Photograph by John Minnis.)

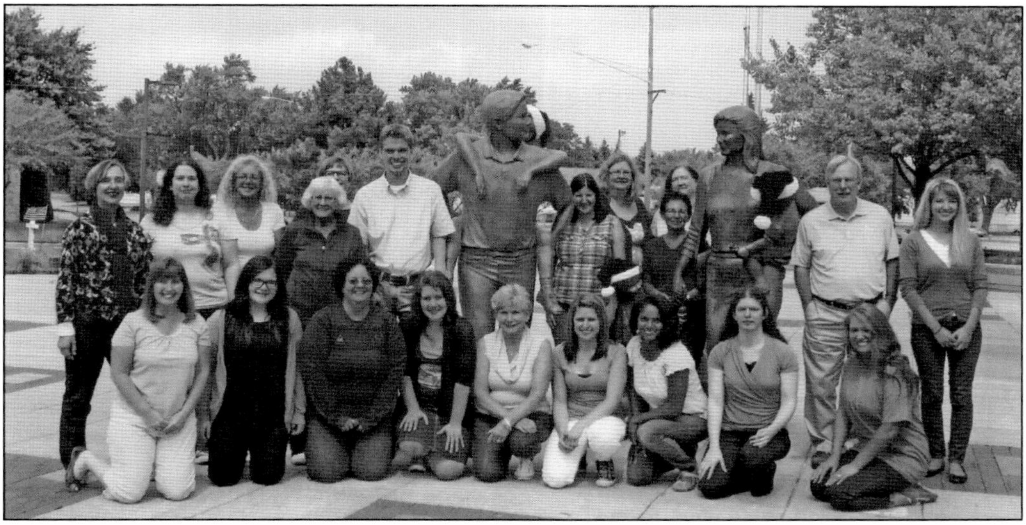

This photograph was taken on August 22, 2014, for use in that year's Roseville Public Library holiday postcard; note the Santa hats on the *Rosebuds* children. From left to right are (first row, kneeling) Theresa Gehrke, Jessica Gilley, Sarah Nagelbush, Christa Mitchell, Beverley Ortman, Jackie Larsh, Monique Jones, Sarah Marsack, and Sara Simich; (second row) Annamarie Lindstrom, Julianne Novetsky, Deborah Greene, Mary Pellerito, Sam Mitchell, Tracy Wilson, Rebecca Patterson, Bill Holleran, and Amy Pavlichek; (third row) Jackie Harvey, Kristen Valyi-Hax, and Pat Eick.

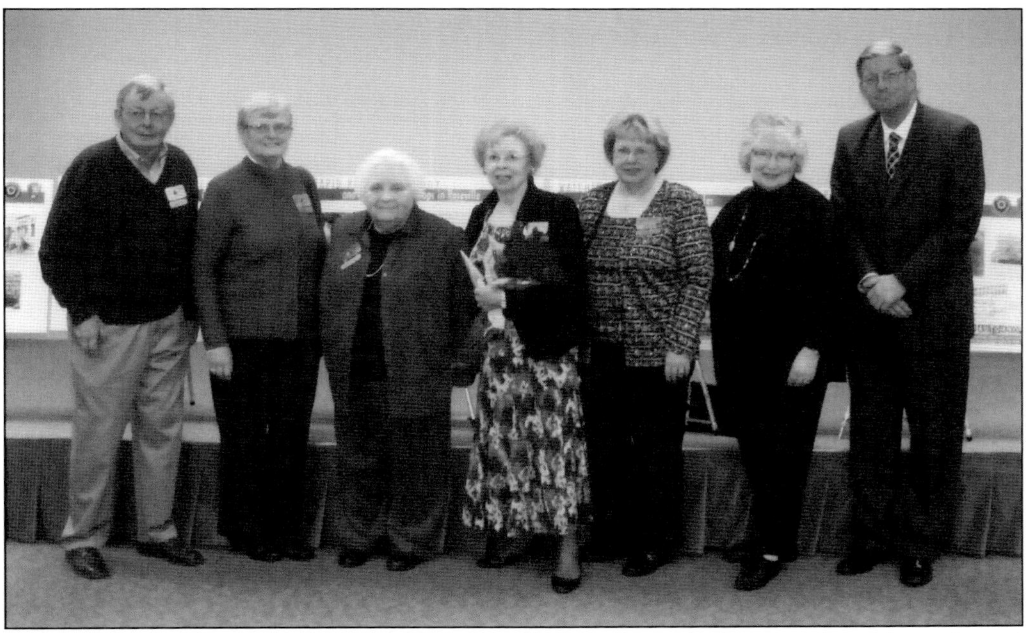

The 2014–2015 directors and officers of the board of the Roseville Historical and Genealogical Society are, from left to right, John Schober, Gail Elliott (recording secretary), Jane May (vice president), Pat Chownyk (president), Janice Carter (treasurer), Ann Spybrook, and Kenneth Schramm; not present is Barb Kushnar (membership director). (Courtesy of William Holleran.)

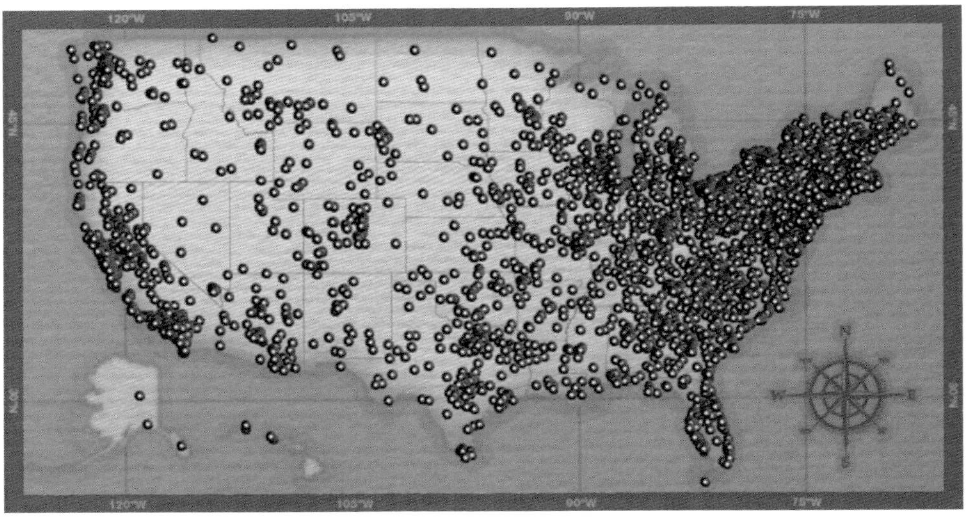